☆☆★ LINDSAY'S CAMPAIGN

LINDSAY'S CAMPAIGN

A Behind-the-Scenes Diary

by Oliver Pilat

BEACON PRESS   BOSTON

All photographs are from the following sources:

Roslyn Bramms: 36, 37, 55, 56, 77, 92, 102, 108, 111, 122, 134, 146, 158, 164, 169, 199, 247

F. Roy Kemp: 29

Meyer Liebowitz — *The New York Times:* 191

Life Magazine: 97

Magnum Photos: 259

New York Herald Tribune: 180

Nick Samarge: ii

Katrina Thomas: 15, 21, 50, 51, 65, 114, 196, 200, 207, 208, 212, 218, 223, 254, 267, 270, 293, 335

United Press International: 4, 43, 54, 110, 125, 154, 326, 328

Wide World Photos: 5, 10, 19, 25, 59, 81, 83, 94, 139, 235, 244, 281, 286, 294, 300, 304, 317, 321, 330, 336

☆☆★ LINDSAY'S CAMPAIGN

To those
who traveled with me
and to the New Yorkers
we met on the campaign trail

☆☆★ *May*

Thursday, May 13, 1965 — John Lindsay began running today for president by way of New York's City Hall. Naturally he did not disclose his ultimate goal. His immediate prospects are dim enough without an unnecessary handicap. In this Democratic town, no Republican, even one as young (forty-three) and as lucent as Lindsay, is given any chance of being elected mayor. He has no machine, no troops.

Come to think of it, Hernando Cortez had no chance either when he took 553 soldiers (including 12 arquebusiers) and went off to conquer Mexico in the sixteenth century. Cortez, of course, possessed great charm and guile. The twentieth-century Lindsay dispenses charm in buckets and for guile he has Robert Price, his campaign manager.

On impulse in midafternoon, I sent a wire to Price offering my services for the duration of the campaign.

Friday, May 14 — Ever since the Fiorello H. LaGuardia–Jeremiah T. Mahoney contest for mayor in 1937, when I went out every evening as a reporter with one or the other candidate, I have dreamt of keeping a political diary. It would trace a campaign from start to finish. This would give it the kind of unity possessed by an ocean voyage. The keeper of such a journal would require a consistent and intimate observation post. He would jot down whatever interested him without regard for discretion. He would strive for diurnal candor while recognizing its difficulty.

According to Alberto Moravia all diaries are untruthful because the writer "is not the same man to whom the event recounted happened but a Judge." I'm no judge but I have a

. . . and for guile he has Robert Price, his campaign manager.

. . . troops, including the arquebusiers . . .

habit of tinkering with words which by Moravia's standard may be worse.

Sitting at my desk in the city room of the New York *Post* late yesterday afternoon, I decided that if I went to work for Representative Lindsay I would keep a diary. Though not assigned to cover the five-borough tour undertaken by the Congressman to dramatize the opening of his campaign for mayor, I had access to all the wire service and other copy on the tour. I made notes for possible later use.

The comparison to Cortez did not float into my mind until I was in the subway on the way home last night. After supper I dug out an old copy of William H. Prescott's *The Conquest of Mexico*. Its precise statement of troops, including the arquebusiers, was an irresistible substitute for the previously accumulated wire service material.

Now I begin to realize that I threw out some raisins with the dough. Lindsay wrote his opening speech around the theme that cities are "for people and for living" and that "under the present tired administration New York is no longer for people and for living." He promised to improve conditions.

"As a Republican," interrupted a reporter, "isn't your race hopeless?"

Lindsay smiled. "It *is* a little like climbing Niagara Falls," he confessed.

That's better than the Cortez comparison. To cap it you have to go back to the national election of 1948 when Howard McGrath, Harry Truman's campaign manager, heard that the President had finally surged ahead of Tom Dewey in the late returns. Jumping on top of a desk in the press room at headquarters, McGrath roared: "This is like hitting the moon with a marshmallow!"

Saturday, May 15 — Since the name of the game of politics is winning, Lindsay must expect to win or make a sufficiently good showing to enhance his reputation. Here is no dilettante, but an accomplished and courageous politician who has been oriented toward public service since boyhood.

At thirteen, Lindsay paid an admiring visit to Mayor La-Guardia in New York's City Hall. At nineteen, he worked as a page boy at the 1940 Republican National Convention. In college he was interested in religion. He displayed early ability as an athlete, an actor, and a writer. He learned responsibility as the gunnery officer of a destroyer in wartime. He drew compliments from Justice Felix Frankfurter as a trial lawyer before the U.S. Supreme Court. Eventually he found use in a public career for all his varied talents and skills.

On the basis of campaign work for Eisenhower among young voters in 1952, Lindsay became an assistant to Attorney General Herbert Brownell in Washington the following year.

He returned to New York to run, in 1958, as an insurgent for Congress in a mid-Manhattan district. In a campaign managed by Robert Price, then still in law school, he upset the county Republican machine for the first time in local memory and went on to win the general election.

In Congress, Lindsay took a tough go-it-alone line. Specializing in civil rights, civil liberties, and foreign affairs, he became a thorn in the side of the party managers. In 1963, they deprived him of a coveted seat on the House Foreign Affairs Committee as a penalty for voting with the Kennedy administration to lessen the power of the House Rules Committee where a conservative coalition had been bottling up bills.

His constituents liked what he was doing. A profile of their appreciation can be drawn as follows:

1958: He won by 7,800 votes.

1960: He carried the district by 26,000 votes taking 59.8 percent of the ballots.

1962: He won by 53,000 votes.

1964: He carried the district by 91,000 votes taking 71 percent of the ballots as an anti-Barry Goldwater Republican. This was a higher proportion of the vote than virtually any other major Republican candidate in the country received last year.

How can Lindsay top that as a Congressman? Obviously, he cannot. He must find new territory or face a decline in popularity. If, on occasion, he looks toward the White House, it is not surprising in view of the chanting of his admirers. Michael Harrington, the Socialist discoverer of poverty in affluent modern America, hails him as "eminently President-able" and Professor Robert Hirschfield of Hunter College, a local pundit, discerns a "presidential style" in the way he reaches over the heads of leaders of voting blocs to individual citizens.

Mind you, there is nothing inherently disgraceful in aspiring to the presidency. The trouble is that we are unconsciously influenced by a Revolutionary tradition that the chief business of the country is business and that even the highest public office is a part-time chore, an accident, a sacrifice like responding to jury duty. Since presidential aspiration must be as furtive as possible, no disclaimer of it can be considered credible. That's a shame, because a man may change his mind.

There is something in politics—as in other kinds of competitive activity—called momentum. Unless a public official continues to move ahead, or to give the stir and bustle of impending movement, he risks slipping back. One small excuse can therefore be advanced for Lindsay's present recklessness. Running for mayor of New York, the second highest administrative post in the country, is a form of momentum.

Sunday, May 16 — In a recently published book entitled *The Future of the Republican Party*, Robert J. Donovan, the Washington correspondent, refers to Lindsay as "the least tarnished of the Republican presidential possibilities" and adds: "Lindsay's immediate problem is how to break out of the obscurity of the House. It would take years for him to become a national leader from his present post.

"Two avenues are open to him," continues Donovan. "If Rockefeller decides not to run for Governor in 1966 and Senator Javits does not run, Lindsay would be the strongest gubernatorial candidate the Republicans could present. The other possible avenue of advancement would be for Lindsay to try for Javits' senate seat if for any reason the Senator were not to run again in 1968."

A third road to the White House exists. Lindsay's familiarity with its topography became apparent a year and a half ago at a luncheon meeting sponsored by John H. (Jock) Whitney, publisher, and Walter Thayer, president of the New York *Herald Tribune*. Nothing has appeared in print about this meeting but I know about it from a friend who was one of the lesser figures in attendance. The crucial dialogue began when one of the Tribune editorial writers wondered out loud which road Lindsay would take to national prominence.

"How about Senator?" he said.

"We have two of them," replied Lindsay, meaning that two Republicans, Jacob K. Javits and Kenneth Keating, held New York's U.S. senate seats and showed no disposition to retire.

"How about Governor?"

"We've got one," said Lindsay, referring to Nelson Rockefeller, who also showed no disposition to step aside.

The conversation lagged until the Congressman said: "You left out something—the mayor of New York."

The ten faces around the table glazed and fell. City Hall was traditionally a dead end. Mayors of New York never went anywhere politically afterward—everybody knew that.

Lindsay gave them another nudge. The big cities were becoming more important in national politics, he noted mildly.

Indeed they were. A wave of redistricting had been set in motion by the 1962 U.S. Supreme Court decision that federal courts could rule on the way state legislative seats were apportioned. The likely result would be lessening of the influence of the conservative small town and rural population and strengthening of the metropolitan areas, where 75 percent of the country's population now lived. If the problems were greatest in the big cities, so were the political opportunities.

"A case could be made for running for mayor," exclaimed Barrett McGurn, one of the reporters present. "This city is dying of dry rot!"

The conversation took fire as others chimed in pro and con around the table. Gradually the idea emerged that a mayor of New York who qualified legitimately as "Mr. City" and who did not alienate the fast-growing suburbs around the center cities might go all the way to the White House if he were handled, say, by somebody like Robert Price.

(By the way, where is Price? Why hasn't he answered the wire I sent him three days ago?)

Monday, May 17 — To run for mayor, Lindsay had to outmaneuver Rockefeller and Javits. With Price's help he did this

. . . Javits' persistent favorite was Javits . . . Rocky preferred neither Javits nor Lindsay . . .

smoothly. Only a few insiders realized that Javits' persistent favorite was Javits and that Rocky preferred neither Javits nor Lindsay, but a tall, amiable Brooklynite named Gilhooley.

Javits subscribed to the belief that no self-respecting Republican of any prominence ever volunteered to run for mayor. He had to be drafted. As the party's best vote-getter in the state—demonstrated by his one-million-vote reelection plurality in 1962—he felt particularly entitled to help from the Governor. Rockefeller, however, had no desire to push a strong liberal who might create a GOP power base in New York City to rival his own in Albany.

On December 8, 1964, Javits made a public appeal for a citizens' movement of independents, liberals, and Republicans to oust the Democrats from control of the city in the 1965 elections. Though he paid passing tribute to Lindsay and other prospects, he had himself in mind as the leader of this crusade.

On December 13, Lindsay said Javits would be the strongest Republican nominee for mayor. With that and other encouragement Javits began to put pressure on the Governor for a party decision by January 1.

Early in January, Rockefeller wrote Javits that the city campaign should not start for several months. The state legislature already in Albany session might not adjourn until May or June. The Democratic legislators would give trouble enough over his tax program, he said, without stirring up premature partisanship in the city. Somehow the Rockefeller letter leaked to the press and reporters began to write avidly about a budding "feud" between the two men.

Javits now set a new deadline. March. When this also passed he withdrew as a possibility for mayor. Reporters turned to Lindsay as the next best hope for excitement in an election which would otherwise be dull. Lindsay stood on his earlier statement that he was not a candidate. Both he and Javits had their fingers crossed.

Early in March a Draft-Lindsay-for-Mayor committee materialized in the Bronx. The leaders were relatively unknown though some GOP stalwarts associated with Rockefeller or Price could be discerned in the background. Lindsay disowned the draft movement. Nevertheless the committee continued in existence for several more weeks, sending pro-Lindsay letters to the newspapers, financing pro-Lindsay ads, and even releasing a poll supposedly showing Lindsay as a prime fusion favorite for mayor who might win.

Suppressed irritation between Rockefeller and Javits erupted in Washington on Thursday, March 25. En route from Albany, Rockefeller remarked to reporters that Javits' deadline bore "no relevance to reality." This was relayed to Javits. At a breakfast meeting next morning with New York State GOP congressmen, Rockefeller and Javits were separated by a wide expanse of tablecloth. Toward the end of the meal Rockefeller boomed out: "How's for running for mayor of New York, Jack?"

According to Dick Aurelio, the Senator's administrative assistant, Javits had been trying for weeks to arrange a conference with the Governor on this topic. Almost apoplectic over what he considered to be a deliberate affront Javits roared back: HOW ABOUT RUNNING FOR MAYOR OF SALAMANCA, NELSON?

Unless there was some hidden meaning in the reference to Salamanca, a tiny place in upstate New York, this did not seem much of an insult, but the faces of Rockefeller and Javits indicated a rupture of diplomatic relations.

To reporters excited by rumors of an "ungentlemanly colloquy" at the closed meeting, Rockefeller said merely that Javits or Lindsay could settle the mayoral situation with a simple declaration of candidacy. Interviewed in his turn Javits said he would be sixty-one in two months. He felt his age. "For years I have almost killed myself," he said, referring to his intense and unremitting activity as a Senator. He was no longer tempted, he added, to risk his health in a struggle with his own party over who should run for mayor. This time he meant it.

Lindsay went into seclusion to prepare a new statement of withdrawal in his own behalf. Before releasing it he read it over the telephone to the Governor. Rockefeller had an opportunity to exclaim: "Don't do it, John. Please stay in the race." When Rockefeller made no such suggestion, Lindsay knew he had to go it alone.

About this time of year four years ago, Linsay paid an unpublicized visit to the Eagle's Nest, the top floor of Governor Rockefeller's triplex apartment in Manhattan, to suggest that with a little friendly encouragement he might run for mayor. Rockefeller said "Louis" deserved a chance to run. He meant Attorney General Louis Lefkowitz, a Manhattan resident who had been citywide campaign manager in Rockefeller's 1960 gubernatorial campaign. Lindsay subsided. He made no further effort to get the nomination that year.

This year things have been different. After the final Rockefeller rebuff, Price began to operate behind the scenes to see if he could obtain a million-and-a-half-dollar campaign kitty, a free hand for himself in running the campaign, and a free hand for Lindsay in picking running mates and lesser candidates in the city.

Meanwhile, new names were being brought forward as mayoral prospects: Congressmen Paul Fino, the Bronx County GOP leader; Congressman Seymour Halpern of Queens; former U.S. Attorney Arthur Christy; Manhattan Councilman-at-Large Richard Aldrich, a cousin of the Governor; and John W. Gilhooley, who had run fairly well for City Controller in 1961 on the Lefkowitz ticket and who was now a Transit Commissioner by appointment of Rockefeller. Gilhooley was vacationing in Italy. As soon as he returned, according to the Albany pipeline, a Rockefeller-sponsored draft would start.

Late Tuesday afternoon, May 11, with Gilhooley still in Milan and the state legislature still in session, Price leaked a story that Lindsay was "reconsidering" his decision not to run. The reaction was wildly enthusiastic. Partly, I think, because Americans were parched for some development which might restore two-party politics after the Goldwater debacle, the news aroused national attention. Adjectives like lithe, vibrant, articulate, handsome, and energetic rained down on Lindsay's head. Somebody said he was the best tonic for the elephant since Ike. Somebody else said he might change the national image of the Republicans. So effectively had Price done his secret missionary work that no local GOP opposition appeared.

A *New York Times* reporter tried unsuccessfully on the evening of May 11 to reach Rockefeller for comment. He did reach Javits. "It is very interesting," said the Senator in measured tones. "I have the highest regard for John Lindsay and I hope the story is true." Javits and Rockefeller received official word the next day. The story was true.

Tuesday, May 18 — Price phoned this morning. My wire offering to serve in the campaign went to his law office and was not delivered to campaign headquarters at the Hotel Roosevelt until today. Price wanted me to visit him immediately but I could not get free. I will visit him Thursday for a more detailed talk.

I now know where the troops will come from. Price says he will recruit volunteers, particularly young volunteers. They will operate out of nonpartisan storefront headquarters in each of the city's 76 assembly districts. I reminded Price that Richard Nixon opened 100 storefronts in New York City during his 1960 presidential campaign without arousing any particular interest or gaining any votes. Price said he has been using volunteers successfully in Lindsay's congressional campaigns. "Besides, Lindsay is not Nixon." He may have a point there.

Any serious Republican candidate in New York must supplement or bypass the feeble regular organization. The Democrats have a captain—often an assistant captain as well—in each of the city's 4,851 election districts, which are subdivisions of the assembly districts. The Republicans don't have captains in half their election districts. The local Democratic clubs can usually provide manpower for their captains in an emergency; not so the Republicans. Some GOP clubs exist on crumbs of patronage from the Democratic table. They are secret allies rather than opponents of the Democrats. Others are out of step with their constituents for economic or ethnic reasons and are ineffective. Only in a few areas are the Republicans really organized for campaigning.

I first sought out Price several years ago as a man who could provide reliable information on Lindsay's plans and opinions. Other local political reporters did so for the same reason, I am sure. In my book he gradually became a news source comparable to George Donahue, Mayor Wagner's confidential adviser; Dan Mahoney of the Conservative party; and Alex Rose, the Liberal party tactician. I found that Price often possesses information about Republican politics unrelated to Lindsay which he will discuss off the record. He is also a

. . . a prophet in the tradition of James A. Farley.

prophet in the tradition of James A. Farley. A few days before
New Yorkers went to the polls last autumn to decide between
Senator Keating and the eminent emigré from Boston, Bobby
Kennedy, I encountered Price at the Roosevelt.

"How do you think Keating will do?" he inquired.

"I think he will lose by 300,000 to 400,000 votes."

"Worse," said Price, gloomily. "It will be 600,000 or
700,000."

Keating's losing margin actually exceeded 700,000.

Price is only thirty-four but somehow ageless: a large, balding, moonfaced fellow with shadowed eyes and an afternoon
beard as black as Nixon's. He started out poor, the son of a
Bronx grocery worker. He became a GOP captain at the age of
seventeen. At nineteen he applied for membership in the New
York Young Republican Club and was excluded as too young
until he appealed to the club president, John Lindsay. Within
the club he became a Lindsay follower and later, adviser.

Price has a flair for business as well as politics. Some years ago he bought four deficit-ridden radio stations outside the metropolitan area. By now three of those stations are in the black and the fourth is breaking even. He leaves his law practice and business interests periodically to manage campaigns as a hobby without pay. There are those who consider him a political genius. In this field he is practical, intuitive, endlessly energetic, and very audacious. I believe he will try anything— almost anything—at least once.

John A. Wells, who managed Rockefeller's 1964 campaign for the GOP presidential nomination, persuaded Price to handle Rockefeller's bid for convention delegates last year in Oregon. Rockefeller won there, but he lost the next state primary in California and with it his last chance for the nomination. Conceivably he might have captured California if Price had remained on the West Coast after Oregon instead of returning east to start Lindsay's congressional campaign. Price's basic loyalty has always been to Lindsay.

Since Price had become a national figure, I wrote a close-up, or personality sketch, of him for the *Post* after he got back to New York. Among other things, I suggested that if a serious fusion effort for mayor were mounted in New York in 1965, he would manage it. The prediction amused him.

In January of this year, Price asked about the disappearance of a weekend political column which I had been writing for years. I explained that I had been taken off politics by the *Post* and assigned to feature writing. Ever since the Democratic National Convention in Atlantic City last summer, I had been periodically in hot water at the office. My chief fault was an inability to enthuse over Bobby Kennedy. While the decisive discussion with my boss did not involve anything written about the Senator, it did turn on an issue raised by his political followers.

Since I was president of the New York Newspaper Guild— a conspicuous but not powerful, unpaid post—the change in my status disturbed unionists at the *Post*. There was talk of a sit-down strike, which I squelched with the argument that the paper had a right to move me around so long as it did not cut my salary. As an alternative gesture of support, the Guild arranged a party for me in February. I mentioned this party in the course of my talk with Price.

Lindsay showed up unexpectedly at the party. With glass in hand the Congressman moved from one admiring group to another in the Heywood Broun room at Guild headquarters, asserting loud enough for me to hear that Ollie Pilat was the best political reporter in town and that he was there to say so.

It was a generous gesture on Lindsay's part. Assuming that his tentative plan of running for mayor worked out, Lindsay would soon need the editorial backing of the *Post*. The *Post's* endorsement could not possibly turn on such a trivial incident, yet an ordinary politician would have found a pretext to avoid a small affair for a former political reporter currently ensconced in the newspaper's most commodious doghouse.

Wednesday, May 19 — Leslie Slote, Wagner's press secretary, tells reporters at City Hall that the Mayor's initial reaction to Lindsay's candidacy was: "Sure I can beat him. Who ever heard of a Republican winning in New York City?" Slote adds that Wagner will make no quick announcement of his intentions and may not campaign for months. The press secretary compares Lindsay to Willkie, the attractive but vulnerable presidential choice of the Republicans in 1940. FDR waited until October of that year to declare: "I'm an old campaigner and I love a good fight," and then proceeded to tear Willkie to shreds.

Julius Caius Caesar Edelstein, Wagner's speech writer and brain-truster, informs friends that Wagner's reelection theme will probably be: A GREAT CITY IN A GREAT SOCIETY. In other words, Wagner hopes to run on the Johnson administration record as well as his own. Wagner's failure to speak for himself suggests that he is following the course of inaction recommended by his father, the late great New Deal Senator, in a difficult situation. That is stall, pretend the problem isn't there, on the theory that it may go away. Unfortunately for the Mayor, Lindsay will not go away.

Robert Ferdinand Wagner, Jr., grew up in his father's shadow. He was an only child of eight when his mother died. Inasmuch as his father did not remarry and was often preoccupied with public affairs, Young Bob learned a lot about loneliness in boyhood. As he grew older, he was permitted to listen to conversations between his father and such giants as Ed Flynn, Jimmy Walker, Al Smith, and Herbert Lehman. Since these men invariably talked shop, Wagner acquired a feeling for politics long before he became involved.

Senator Wagner, who liked the *Post* because it invariably praised his pioneering efforts in social security, tipped off that paper in 1937 that his boy was about to embark on a political career. I was assigned to the story. As a reward for graduating from Yale Law School, the Senator's son was being given the Democratic nomination for Assemblyman in the heavily Democratic Yorkville district where he lived. It was Young Bob's first newspaper interview. He stood at the window in his father's law office, Wagner, Quillinan & Tennant, looking out over the city, and spoke bravely of the reforms in housing, civil rights, and social security which he would espouse in Albany. In appearance and program he was his father's carbon copy.

Young Wagner performed conscientiously in the Assembly. After military service during the war he held appointive municipal posts: Tax Commissioner, Planning Commissioner, Housing Commissioner. In 1949 he was elected Manhattan borough president. Four years later he became mayor. He ran once for U.S. Senator, losing to Javits, and he has been mentioned on other occasions for senator, governor, and president, but he has not managed to escape from City Hall. If he wins another term, the walls of his political prison will loom higher than ever.

As Mayor, Wagner cultivated the Establishment, which in

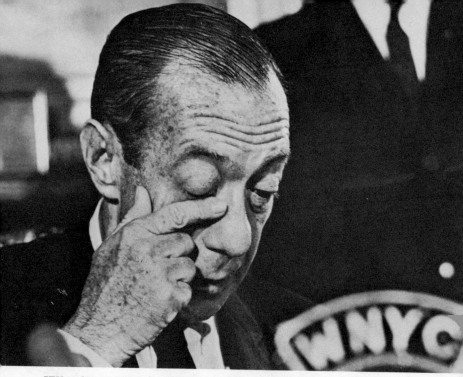

Why does he seem so used up at the age of 55?

New York ranges from labor unions and social workers to businessmen and philanthropists. He convinced the ordinary citizen of his interest in humdrum matters. He avoided the scandals which plagued his Democratic predecessors. He coped valiantly with the vast and growing difficulties of the metropolis. In view of his achievements, why has Wagner's bumpy countenance acquired such a discouraged look during the last two years? Why does he seem so used up at the age of fifty-five?

The grinding nature of his job may be partly responsible. A mayor of New York is more exposed than a president of the United States. Every citizen and his group feel entitled to present their grievances and needs. The ceremonial functions of the office alone are overwhelming.

During twelve years as Mayor, Wagner has been accumulating enemies. He is currently at odds with the Democratic

State Chairman. He lacks control of the Democratic machines in Brooklyn and the Bronx, two of the most populous of the city's five boroughs. Working out a city slate to avoid a Democratic primary contest this year will be difficult, particularly with Bobby Kennedy in the background.

Wagner has undergone a great deal of personal deprivation and grief. His wife Susan, with whom he was very close, died on March 2, 1964, of lung cancer, after having been ill for a year. Since she did not realize the seriousness of her condition, the Mayor persuaded the newspapers not to print the information they possessed. He carried his secret domestic burden on top of all the nagging concerns of his office. It was during this period that his once chubby face began to look gaunt and drawn.

After Susan's death, Wagner could not endure Gracie Mansion, the lovely reconverted Colonial home for mayors in the center of a park on the water's edge in Yorkville, so he moved into a hotel. For months he would burst into tears at any mention of Susan's name. He worried openly over the motherless status of his sons, Duncan, eighteen, a student at Kent Hill School in Maine, and Bobby, twenty-one, a Harvard senior who will go to England after graduation to study history on a Marshall fellowship. On the basis of his own experience, Wagner felt that his boys needed more paternal companionship than he could provide.

On at least six occasions during the past year Wagner has taken time off from City Hall to nurse minor ailments. On one occasion he had a checkup on the condition of his neck, from the right side of which a parathyroid gland tumor was removed in 1961. The doctor pronounced him physically fit.

Thursday, May 20 — Elizabeth Barnett (Barnie) Patterson, a bright thoughtful girl who was Lindsay's secretary in Washington and who has been active in previous campaigns, ushered me into Price's spacious fourth-floor corner room at the Roosevelt. Behind a walnut desk fit for signing State Department

The scene resembled a Charlie Chaplin satire on big business.

treaties, Lindsay's campaign manager was using two telephones at once, interrupting the callers on either hand to fling instructions at assistants hurrying in and out. The scene resembled a Charlie Chaplin satire on big business. With a feeling that it was all too much, I sneaked a pitying glance at Barnie. To my surprise, she indicated undiluted respect by blowing a kiss at the back of the great man's head.

A row of calendars for each month from May through November hung on the wall in back of Price. The side walls were covered with large maps of the five boroughs of the city with assembly districts outlined in red. Cutting me into the activity, Price explained he was working on Lindsay's first formal stand in the campaign, a formula for a police review board. A year ago, I remember, he fussed similarly over a formula on school busing for purposes of integration. That formula looked like a straddle at the time, but public opinion seems to have shifted toward Lindsay's position since then.

There is already a review board within the Police Department consisting of three Deputy Commissioners, all civilians. Price wants to add four civilian outsiders without taking final authority away from the Commissioner. He mentioned a last-minute inspiration: a requirement that one of the three police representatives be a patrolman. The present high-ranking officials often dismiss a charge of brutality against a cop, then penalize him for some minor infraction of the rules. Having somebody speak for the rank and file may soften police resistance to the whole idea of a civilian review board.

Price has already read the text of the statement over the phone to civil rights leaders. Their reaction so far is mixed, but they seem pleased at being consulted and they cannot deny that the proposal goes farther in the direction of protecting minorities against police brutality than anything else on the table.

Having disposed of the review board, Price relaxed a little. He spoke again about his plans for recruiting volunteers. Richard A. Lewisohn, a businessman who was formerly the Republican leader in Lindsay's home assembly district, is scouting locations for storefronts. Constantine Sidamon-Eristoff, Lindsay's former administrative assistant in Washington, is helping Price to select managers, or coordinators, of the storefronts.

Lindsay will make extensive walking tours starting at once. He will visit every neighborhood—New York City being a collection of neighborhoods—at least twice by the end of the summer. He wants everybody in town to recognize his face. He will concentrate on the Negro and Puerto Rican sections which normally go heavily Democratic. He will fight for the support of labor, civil service, and other groups to which Republican candidates as a rule make only perfunctory appeals.

Price exhibited some drafts of campaign literature. The Republican name and symbol are conspicuously absent. "That's not new," said Price. "Rockefeller and Nixon did the same thing in their campaigns. It's just as John F. Kennedy said: 'I'm a Catholic, but don't hold it against me.' In this case it's: 'I'm Republican, but don't hold it against me.'"

He is worried over Rockefeller and Javits. "They're so jealous of each other," Price said. "Each suspects the other of knowing about John's plans in advance. Actually neither one knew." Then he returned to the basic political situation:

"After all, the city has only 700,000 registered Republicans to 2,400,000 registered Democrats. At least 700,000, maybe 800,000, of the Democrats are the Pavlovian kind. They are hereditary partisans who would vote Row B (the Democratic line on the state ballot) if Lehman and Wagner were running on Row A (the Republican line). We hope to have at least one Democrat running citywide with John. Also, it's my hope that some of the Pavlovians will be open to the argument that it's legitimate once in five or twenty years to vote Republican if it is not in opposition to their fundamental beliefs."

Did I have any campaign ideas? I had one. I remembered a national poll in 1953 which established that most non-Republicans who voted for Eisenhower the previous fall did so because the Democrats had been in power nationally for twenty years and it was time for a change. The Democrats have been in power in New York City for twenty years, I pointed out. The time-for-a-change gambit has already occurred to Price. It is embodied in tentative campaign literature and may be given greater stress.

Almost absentmindedly Price and I completed the business between us. I will go to work for Lindsay as soon as I can pull away from the *Post,* where I have worked for twenty-nine years. Price suggested that tomorrow might be a good day to start but I am inclined to think that it will be Monday before I can batten down my hatches for the voyage.

Friday, May 21 — City Controller Abraham D. Beame, a small frog in a large pond in Brooklyn, intends to run independently for reelection. Beame confided to friends last night at the Kings County Democratic Committee dinner at the Hotel St. George that he had asked Wagner a month ago for a conference on the new city ticket. He received no answer until last week. Then the word came: "It's too early to talk politics. Tell Abe I'll talk to him at the appropriate time."

This sounded ominous to Beame in view of his own experience. Four years ago Wagner reshuffled the Democratic slate at the last minute, picking Beame, then Budget Director, for Controller in place of Controller Lawrence E. Gerosa, and Paul R. Screvane, Deputy Mayor and former Sanitation Commissioner, for Council President in place of Council President Abe Stark. Inasmuch as he and Wagner are no longer compatible politically, Beame cannot help wondering whether divorce papers are being prepared at City Hall.

Beame's news conference today was a puzzling affair because the Controller avoided any public mention of his rebuffed plea to the Mayor. His talk about running again "as an Independent and a Democrat" sounded contradictory. Reporters interpreted it as a warning that he might line up with an anti-Wagner slate in the primary. They wanted to know

His career has exhibited all the tropism for the top of an Alger hero.

whether he would go so far as to run on a fusion ticket with Lindsay. Beame gave evasive answers.

It is easy to underestimate Abe because of his size (five feet two), his Runyonesque manner, and his lack of sophistication. I heard him say once that the books which most influenced him were the novels of Horatio Alger. His career has exhibited all the tropism for the top of an Alger hero.

Beame was brought to New York from London by his immigrant parents at the age of three months. He struggled for an education. After winning a bachelor's degree at City College which has no tuition for city residents, he went on to become a certified public accountant, teaching during the day and attending classes at night. As soon as he could find the time he became an active member and a captain of the Madison Club, the largest and most influential of the old-line Democratic organizations in Brooklyn. In 1946 the club placed him as Deputy Budget Director under Mayor O'Dwyer and in 1952 as Budget Director under Mayor Impellitteri.

Four years ago, Beame was willing to settle for the machine designation for Brooklyn borough president until Wagner offered him something better on an anti-machine ticket. Soon after his election as Controller, Beame rejoined the machine by coming to the support of his club leader, Assemblyman, and old friend, Stanley Steingut, whom the Mayor wanted to remove as county boss. Beame has made a habit since then of criticizing Wagner's fiscal policies.

Reporters closed in on Lindsay this afternoon to find out how he felt about Beame as a possible running mate.

"I'd be deeply flattered," replied Lindsay.

Was this an invitation to Beame to join the Lindsay ticket?

"No," said Lindsay. "When I see a good man, I say so."

I doubt Beame is that good a man. His machine background, if nothing else, would make him an uncomfortable companion on a reform slate. I suppose Lindsay is just trying to encourage dissension among the Democrats.

Saturday, May 22 — Without assignment or function I dropped around to the New York Hilton last night to watch Lindsay unveil his police review board plan before the New York County Lawyers Association. He faced an audience fully aware of the proportions of crime in the city. Despite a police force of 26,000—more cops per capita than any other American urban center—New York has two murders and four rapes a day, rain or shine, with other felonies and misdemeanors in proportion. Half the crimes are committed by drug addicts, now 60,000 in number and increasing at the rate of 10,000 a year. Seven out of ten serious offenses are committed by youths under twenty-one as the rising tide of violence washes into the streets and the subways.

Middle-class residents of New York, for whom many of the lawyers work, are concerned chiefly over their personal safety.

They are not particularly impressed by the vast population shift which has aggravated the city's crime problem. Since 1950 the city has lost to the suburbs 800,000 middle-class people, productive and stable young couples with children, most of them whites but including some Negroes. During the same period there has been an equal influx of poor Negroes (mostly from the South) and poor Spanish-speaking migrants (mostly from Puerto Rico but also from elsewhere in the Caribbean and from Latin America). Many of the newcomers are semi-skilled or unskilled, uneducated or with language difficulties, hence prone in a more and more mechanized society to unemployment, discouragement, and lawlessness. It is from sections where these unhappy transplants congregate that the most persistent complaints about police brutality come.

"A police department, no matter how large or well-managed," said Lindsay, sticking pretty much to text, "cannot succeed if it does not have all law-abiding citizens on its side.

"Part of the failure to deal successfully with crime in New York City is due to the breakdown in the relationship between the police and a substantial part of the people—and again I am talking about those who respect the law and want to live within it. It is time for a change in this sensitive area of human relationships. New York must rediscover procedures which conform to traditional notions of due process. The appearance of justice is just as important as justice . . ."

One new detail in Lindsay's plan for an enlarged civilian-dominated board was that the four outsiders would be picked from a list of names compiled by the Presiding Justices of the Appellate Division and the Chancellor of the City University.

"Our city must deal with crime by developing a program that goes to the root of the problem as well as to its manifestations," Lindsay continued. "So long as large numbers of our population believe society cares nothing for them we cannot hope to be successful. These individuals must have better opportunities for jobs, better living conditions—in short, a better chance to find a purpose and a place in this busy and often indifferent city. While we share the problems of other cities, our city is unique. New York is the first city of America. It is our duty to show the way."

Was there a whiff here of a new urban populism with Lindsay as its prophet speaking for all the crime-ridden cities of America? No matter; the immediate reception was good. Some 400 members and guests of the County Lawyers Association listened without interruption for twenty minutes and applauded warmly at the end.

Since Price sent advance copies of the text to newspapers, radio, and TV stations on a hold-for-delivery basis, reporters reached Wagner for comment before the speech was actually delivered. The kind of answer he gave indicates the Mayor is upset over the prospect of being outflanked on the left at the very start of the campaign.

Wagner says he sees "some merit" in a recent proposal that the City Council set up a committee to review the actions of the present police review board. The trouble with this idea is that it possesses no merit at all. Placing a political review board over a nonpolitical review board with the prospect that Council members might not be able to resist reviewing their own review committee would be weird and unworkable.

The first round goes to Lindsay.

Sunday, May 23 — Starting tomorrow I will be the Number 2 man in the Lindsay press department assisting Harry O'Donnell, a burly, sometimes grumpy, ex-baseball writer out of Elmira, who later covered politics in Albany for the Associated Press. Harry claims he knows more about baseball than politics but he has handled publicity for every Republican state campaign since the days of Tom Dewey. The little man on the birthday cake, as they used to call Dewey, remains his idol but he gets along with Rockefeller.

Harry has taken a leave from his regular duties as public relations man for the Republican State Committee. Since his home is in Albany, he will live at the Roosevelt for the

. . . I will be the Number 2 man in the Lindsay press department . . .

duration of the campaign. That's nice for Harry if he gets any time off, because he has rights to a fine railside box opposite first base at Yankee Stadium. I've gone to more than one ball game with Harry. He has an endearing memory system based on the national pastime. He remembers the address of WABC radio, 1926 Broadway, for example, because "1926 was the World Series when the Cardinals beat the Yankees, 4–3. That was the first World Series of the Cardinals. . . ." He resembles the man who remembered his wedding anniversary because that was the day Man o' War won the Wood Memorial. Harry also has a hobby of collecting photographs of twentieth-century transatlantic steamships. The sense of open horizons this gives may compensate for the fact that his considerable weight, against which he diets unsuccessfully, and his periodic sciatic back pains tend to restrict his movements.

As a reporter I became an admirer of Harry because of his

genius in providing "overnights." These are releases, predictions, or tips which can be picked up a day in advance by an afternoon newspaperman and written in confidence that they will not explode meanwhile in some morning paper. Harry has the reputation of being unflappable in the most trying circumstances. He is a pro and I expect no undue difficulty in working with him.

Monday, May 24 — Lindsay visited the press office in midmorning. "I hear you are joining us," said the former gunnery officer of the destroyer *Swanson*, extending an appraising glance with his hand as if I were a stranger. "Welcome aboard!" Each additional recruit reporting for duty during the day received an identical "Welcome aboard!" No word wasted.

During the afternoon Lindsay remarked to a friend of mine that he now has a Rockefeller press agent (O'Donnell), a Price press agent (Pilat), and all he needs is a Lindsay press agent. The witticism recalls a comment I heard recently from a Democrat that Lindsay is "tall, pretty, and plays a good game of badminton." The candidate is tall and definitely handsome but I cannot vouch as yet for his prowess at badminton.

Tuesday, May 25 — Yesterday was confusing and exhausting. I worked from 8 A.M. to midnight by the clock and the minutes left a longer track than that in my mind. Even after I got to bed around 2:30, fragments of unresolved emergencies broke through my sleep. Today is quieter; the Congressman is in Washington to vote for the administration's three-and-a-half-billion-dollar foreign aid program and he will probably remain there tomorrow to argue for a stricter copyright law in the House Judiciary Committee, of which he is a member. I'm still sleepy and the skin twitches under my right eye but yesterday's irritability with everybody, including the candidate, seems to have subsided.

My small office on the fourth floor of the Roosevelt adjoins a slightly larger office occupied by O'Donnell. There is a joint entrance to the two offices from the campaign corridor, with a file card pasted up over the door marked PRESS. Harry's secretary is Hope Ritchie, the widow of George Ritchie, a rollicking City Hall reporter on the old New York *Sun*. Since the memory of George remains the central aspect of Hope's life and I remember George, Hope and I get along, but a secretary of my own would be helpful.

At the request of O'Donnell, who prefers the indoor life, I accompanied Lindsay on two campaign swings yesterday. These were uneventful except for a comment by the candidate to a *Post* reporter that he disagreed with Rockefeller's denunciation of a state direct-primary bill. Lindsay may see some political advantage at the moment in standing apart from the Governor.

Last night, in their first confrontation since the campaign began, Wagner and Lindsay addressed the 100th anniversary dinner of the Printing Industries of Greater New York, Inc.

Lindsay arrived first. More than 1,000 men and women in evening clothes were already eating in the Waldorf-Astoria grand ballroom when he came through the doorway for celebrities at the right of the dais. Heads turned, fingers pointed, and there was scattered applause as he strode toward his seat. When the toastmaster verified his name the applause deepened into an ovation.

A few minutes later Wagner emerged in a knot of bustling officials. "It's the Mayor!" shouted the toastmaster. To his horror and mine sudden boos overrode the applause. One red-faced fellow rose unsteadily at a central table to shake his fist at the Mayor. Others jeered. I was standing within a few feet of Wagner and the impact of the reception on his sad face— first surprise and then dejection—was shocking. He rallied quickly. Before he sat down he shook hands carefully with everybody in reaching distance. As an afterthought he got up and walked over to shake hands with Lindsay.

Both speakers had to cope with the unpalatable truth that

the printing industry, second in size in the city to the garment industry, is in trouble. Its need for horizontal space, its slowness in accepting technological advances, the pressures of traffic, the unions in the city, and the lower pay scales in the hinterlands have combined to put the trade under severe competitive pressure. Some printers have moved out of the city, others want to move. Those who remain are not necessarily grateful for past favors. Frequently their attitude is: What has City Hall done for me lately?

Lindsay was brought on with the dessert. He looked fine, if somewhat collegiate. He spoke earnestly, but his remarks about keeping business in New York by improving the climate for industry were painfully general. The applause when he finished did not equal his initial ovation.

Wagner followed the coffee. Speaking from a prepared text, he singled out leaders of the printers by name and glance, warmly and with great naturalness. He cited various obstacles overcome (with his help) in the past and fresh difficulties created by plans for a new civic center which could be alleviated (with his help) in the future.

"A hundred years is a long time," he said. "Sometimes I think I've been Mayor a long time, too."

The audience laughed.

"I want to work with you, help in any relocation that is necessary and not dislocate anybody unless it is necessary. We have so many strikes. When I read the editorials I sometimes wonder why I work so hard to settle them. Anyway I hope to be around for your 200th anniversary . . ."

Ben Franklin could have done no better. When Wagner finished the applause eclipsed Lindsay's best—and there were no boos. Wagner may be more unpopular than anybody realizes but Lindsay will not have much chance against him unless he does his homework.

Wednesday, May 26 — Price stormed into the press room. "I could tear his tongue out by the roots," he exclaimed.

Harry O'Donnell, Hope Ritchie, and I looked at each other in astonishment. Whose tongue?

"John's, of course. Don't you know what he said in Washington?"

We didn't know. For a variety of reasons including some lack of support from Price we have been unable to obtain a news ticker for the press room.

Apparently Lindsay let it be known at a news conference in Washington that he does not want any help from people like former President Eisenhower and Republican National Chairman Ray Bliss. Untrue rumors that he received promises of help from Bliss before he declared his candidacy are hurting his chances, he said. He is not using party labels on his literature and he is not campaigning primarily as a Republican. Asked about Rockefeller, he said he does not necessarily exclude the Governor from the campaign "since he is a New Yorker," but "I don't need officialdom to hold me up. "I'm sure New Yorkers will not vote for me on the basis of what some important persons and officials say about me."

Later in the day I encountered Price in the green-carpeted campaign corridor. "John is like that," he said. "He can't measure it out. If a thing has to be said he says it and he sleeps well at night as a result. I've already received phone calls from important Democrats in Riverdale and elsewhere. It removes their last doubts, they say, and they will work for John for Mayor!"

Not for a moment do I believe that Lindsay blurted anything in Washington which was not rehearsed with Price.

Meanwhile a sharpshooter was taking aim from City Hall. "I'm running as a Democrat with Democratic party support and the support of a lot of Republicans," said Wagner. "I am a Democrat and not ashamed of it. It seems peculiar that Lindsay suddenly does not want to be a Republican and yet he has the support of the Republican National Chairman. He must be afraid of being Blisskrieged."

Thursday, May 27 — The fact that public figures of world importance are as susceptible to small slights as the rest of us is a continual surprise to me. Eisenhower became upset over Lindsay's lack of interest in his campaign help. He mentioned his distress to General Lucius Clay, an old comrade who classes as a member of the Eastern Establishment on the basis of his present eminence in Wall Street. Clay tipped off Lindsay, who told Eisenhower at length over the phone why he thought municipal elections must be on a nonpartisan basis. The General accepted Lindsay's implied apology but could not refrain from a last minute dig. He wanted the Republican candidate for mayor of New York to know that he considered his plan for a police review board a mistake.

Today Lindsay had an unpublicized breakfast with Rockefeller, Price, Javits, and George Hinman, GOP National Committeeman for New York. The purpose was to iron out the conflicts among the state's leading Republicans. It was agreed that the Senator will serve as campaign chairman (a largely honorary post which will not interfere with Price's control as campaign manager) and that the Governor will do what he can, financially and otherwise, without being conspicuous.

As if one miracle in a day were not enough, Lindsay is now seated in the driver's seat of the city Republican machine. Even LaGuardia could not accomplish that; for two out of his three terms as Mayor, he operated from a self-created American Labor Party because he could not trust the local GOP. Bronx boss Fino, who wants to be mayor himself and who is as offended as Ike by the police review board plan, has been muttering rebellion but he has no support.

Lindsay called a news conference today to deny reports that Fino and others resent his disdain of the party label and may oppose him at a citywide nominating convention this evening at the Hotel St. George.

"I expect no opposition," Lindsay said calmly.

What would he do if the meeting did not designate him for Mayor?

"I'll run in the primary!"

That swept away the fog. Nobody now available in the party would have a chance against him in a primary fight. While he was at it Lindsay brushed some additional Republican burrs from his trousers.

"Will you use Nixon in your campaign?" a reporter asked.

"Who's Nixon?" said Lindsay, looking surprised at the laughter.

Somebody else wanted to know if Robert Moses, an elderly reactionary Republican who once held a half-dozen important state and city posts simultaneously but who has now been reduced to a million dollar job as head of the New York World's Fair, was being considered for a spot on the fusion ticket.

Lindsay looked at the ceiling before replying. "What we need in New York," he said, "is a World's Fair."

Friday, May 28 — The candidate took a bath in people up to his neck for three hours today in the Grand Concourse-East 170th Street shopping section of the Bronx. Most of the people were children. The affair was billed as the first of the daily sidewalk-and-street-corner tours Lindsay will make all summer. Actually it was not the first. There was a trial stroll last Saturday in Staten Island which drew small crowds. This time our press release attracted radio and TV as well as newspaper coverage and that in turn increased the crowds. A bullhorn was working and a few Lindsay-for-Mayor posters without party identification were visible. Our schedule took the candidate past a large public school just as its doors opened for the noon recess, thus providing a desired mob scene.

Lindsay has advantages for this kind of campaigning. His height keeps his All-American-Boy profile and bright blue eyes above the crowd. He is conscious of this and I have the impression that those of us in his entourage who exceed six feet in height might as well stay a little distance from him. He wears thin dark trousers and an ordinary white shirt open

He seemed to enjoy the mauling . . .

His height keeps his All-American-Boy profile and bright blue eyes above the crowd.

at the neck. He has tousled hair, broader shoulders than Bobby Kennedy, a quick smile, and a metallic, though not unpleasant, laugh.

When Lindsay shakes a hand he looks at its owner, which is something former Governor Harriman never did learn. He is less bouncy in his approach than Javits, who invented street campaigning, but if an adult asks a sensible question he pauses, listens, and answers quietly and to the point. On two occasions I found myself getting overprotective, once during the schoolboy crush and again when an aggressive TV interviewer insisted on shoving a microphone between him and his sandwich in a luncheonette. In neither case did Lindsay get upset. He seemed to enjoy the mauling he received.

Fino did not take part in today's Bronx tour. When a reporter reached him by phone the Bronx boss explained that he was staying home "because John Lindsay wants it to be nonpolitical." He may have been asked to stay away or he may be sulking in his tent. The difference is not crucial since he went along with the other four county leaders last night at the city-wide Republican meeting. In fact he seconded the nomination on the ground that Lindsay "will lead us out of slime and decay." Except for Fino's odd phrase the meeting was routine. It lasted only fifty minutes. Manhattan boss Albano nominated Lindsay. After seconding speeches, Brooklyn boss Crews, as host and presiding officer, obtained a chorus of ayes on the nomination without bothering to ask for negative votes.

Lindsay accepted the nomination with an undistinguished ten-minute speech from notes before hurrying off to attend a small testimonial dinner in Queens County. The important part of the evening was an earlier closed dinner for Lindsay and the five county bosses in the Patio Room at the St. George from which everybody, even Fino, emerged smiling. Nobody would disclose what was discussed but I suppose Lindsay mentioned that the storefronts for volunteers will remain in reliable hands, that he will endorse and give financial help to local Republican candidates, and that he will not exclude the party from patronage if he wins.

Saturday, May 29 — In an unexpected announcement which upsets everybody's campaign applecart Wagner says he may not run again. He will require a couple of weeks of consultation with friends and members of his family before he makes up his mind. "I find I can't spend as much time as a father should with his boys," he says, noting that he has been a widower for fourteen months. "I feel I must be both a father and a mother to them." He adds: "When I take on a job I want to be certain I can do it. This will be four more years and I am wondering how much it will tax my energy."

Headquarters was already buzzing with the news, carried in the morning *Times*, when I arrived at 9 o'clock. A conference soon convened in Price's office. Those present included Lindsay; his elder brother George, who handles campaign research; John Deardourff, a Rockefeller speechwriter freshly loaned to Lindsay; Price and me. Conflicting views were advanced as to the kind of statement to be made, with Price insisting on sympathy for Wagner.

Since O'Donnell is in Albany this weekend on a visit to his family, I had to leave the meeting to deal with converging waves of reporters and photographers. As eventually agreed upon, Lindsay's statement went as follows: "The Mayor has stated he is running for reelection and I must assume he is running until informed otherwise. I will continue to conduct an independent positive fusion campaign and I will carry it to the people of all five boroughs. If Mayor Wagner faces family or personal problems which force him to reconsider his decision to run, he has, of course, my deepest personal sympathy."

Price asked me to tell everybody that Lindsay would make no additional comment. I tried to do so.

The radio-TV people wanted the statement live. They set up opposite the elevators, the only place on the fourth floor of the hotel ample enough for them. I promised Lindsay would read it if they agreed to ask no questions. Unfortunately, Gabriel Pressman, NBC-TV's young elder statesman, arrived late, as usual, while I was placating an insistent reporter from a women's magazine.

As a result, when Lindsay finished reading the statement, Pressman opened up with questions. Suddenly furious, I lunged forward, hitting Pressman on the chest with both hands and knocking him back about a foot. "That's enough," I shouted. "You made an agreement and you broke it."

Gabe jumped up and down like an Apache Indian in a sun dance. He made no agreement, he yelled. He had interviewed Wagner in the men's room at City Hall and other unlikely places, he said, and he would interview Lindsay in the same fashion.

When the TV cameras swerved to catch the action, Price immobilized them by pulling their joint plug from the wall.

Immediately Mary Pengalos of CBS-TV and others swarmed over Price. Taking advantage of this distraction I grasped Lindsay's biceps with one hand, the arm of the insistent women's magazine reporter with the other, and led them both around back of the passenger elevators to a freight elevator. This carried us to the roof where the magazines' photographer was waiting by previous appointment. The picture-taking required about ten minutes. When the four of us returned to the fourth floor we found the TV-Price debate still raging.

"Gabe, are you all right?" inquired Lindsay as heads turned in our direction.

Pressman brushed back his hair like a movie actor. Everybody laughed. The argument resumed at a lower pitch.

"I don't mind answering a few questions," Lindsay volunteered.

Back went the plug into the wall. Did he take the Mayor's statement at face value?

"I take at face value anything any man says in political life because it's a strenuous life."

Would his campaign be in trouble without Wagner as a target?

"No," said Lindsay. "My campaign is waged against an administration that has been in power for many years. I hope people will vote for me in the hope of a change, in hope of a better city."

As questions ran out, Price apologized for pulling the plug. Everybody was smiling. The TV reporters promised not to use anything on the shoving match. I doubt they had anything to use, Price acted so quickly. Lindsay was as bland as custard pudding. "I'd like to leave now if I may," he said to Pressman before leaving on a walking tour in Harlem.

Sunday, May 30 — "The Liberal party regards Mayor Wagner as a good-government candidate. Should Mayor Wagner be out of the race, the Liberal party will give serious consideration to fusion. The Liberal party sees no other Democrat who equals Mayor Wagner, therefore a fusion possibility will be wide open."

This statement issued by Alex Rose, head of the Liberal party in New York, seems to hint, almost predict, that Wagner will drop out of the race and that the Liberals will join hands with Lindsay. It may be the start of a process of conditioning Liberal party members to fusion. On the other hand, it may be an attempt to bludgeon the restive Democratic factions into a united front behind Wagner. Everything depends on interpretation.

Rose has a huge stake in Wagner: in political patronage, according to reports. He and Wagner are old friends. Finally, Rose is genuinely interested in good government. This lanky, scholarly looking official of the United Hat, Cap and Millinery Workers Union is a complex man. He emerged on the political scene in the mid-thirties as executive director of the newly formed American Labor Party. When the right wing of the ALP split off in 1944 to form the Liberal party, he took over guidance of the Liberals. It is a measure of his capacity that the Liberals survive despite the disappearance of the ALP as an organized party in 1950. Considering that the Liberal registration is a miniscule 60,000 in the city, Rose's influence is amazing.

According to associates, Rose learned of Wagner's indecision Friday evening. He stayed up most of the night mulling over its implications. On Saturday he consulted only Dr. Timothy W. Costello, state chairman, and Ben Davidson, party factotum, on his statement. They approved it.

Several members of the Liberal party policy committee, which is supposed to make all decisions, are disgruntled because they were not consulted. The first they knew about the new tack taken by the party was when they read about it in the newspapers. The thing may be relatively simple. Rose has a flair for making practical decisions on high-sounding grounds of principle. He may simply wish to reassert in the city the old Liberal balance of power which has dwindled during the Wagner alliance.

Wagner seems to have acted impulsively. Since he was running, whatever triggered his uncertainty must be a development in the direction of not running. On the personal side, that development may be anything from sheer weariness to cancer. It may be the prospect of remarriage to Deputy Mayor Edward Cavanagh's sister, Barbara Cavanagh, with whom the mayor has been seen frequently in recent weeks. On the political side, it may be the implicit rivalry of Bobby Kennedy or the new friendliness between Democratic National Committeeman Edwin Weisl, Sr., President Johnson's personal representative in New York, and Brooklyn boss Steingut, Wagner's chief local enemy. It may even be the poll taken by Steingut showing 38 percent of the straws for Lindsay to 34 percent for Wagner, with the rest undecided.

Wagner's impulsiveness and Rose's lack of composure indicate that the Mayor's quandary is genuine and not the staging for a draft. A genuine quandary cannot easily be resolved in two weeks. Without further information or analysis, I'd bet a dime—ten cents being the top of my political bets—that Wagner will not run again.

Monday, May 31 — O'Donnell, back from Albany, is unhappy over the incident which is going down in history as the pulling of the plug. He must have read some condensed or inadequate wire service report over the weekend because he blames Price. I explained that Price's quick thinking saved us from a real mess but Harry persists in what may be a courteous effort to avoid putting the blame on me. Though I feel uncomfortable enough about my incapacity as a political public relations man, neither Lindsay nor Price has complained.

Harry believes a candidate or his press representative must apologize promptly in any row with a reporter. This applies particularly when the reporter is in the wrong. In such case the

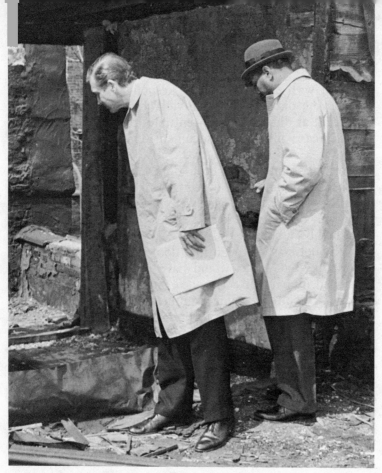

. . . a visit today to a city-owned tenement . . .

candidate or his press man takes satisfaction in the knowledge
that the apology has fooled the reporter. Harry calls it "one-
upmanship." While one-upmanship is expedient, it rubs
against my grain and it may rub Lindsay the wrong way, too.

My impulsiveness appeared in a different form during a
visit today to a city-owned tenement in the Negro-Puerto Rican ghetto in Brooklyn known as Bedford-Stuyvesant. On the
way over, Lindsay read carefully a twelve-page briefing on the
five-story building we were about to inspect. Upon arrival, he
went from one to another of the fifteen apartments. In con-

versation with each tenant who responded to his knock on
the door he discussed housing violations, repairs made, and
rents paid at different times—entirely from memory. He did
not even carry his briefing document. It was quite a performance.

Somebody must have been tipped off in advance to our
visit because ammonia had been sprinkled in the hallways to
cover the smell of urine. Men were installing a safety rail on a
shamefully unprotected roof. A rickety red door leading to the
cellar had been bolted.

Why not crash through that door to see what was hidden
downstairs? LaGuardia would have done it but Lindsay, it
developed, did not like the idea. Since the city owned the
building, I pointed out, any denunciation or talk of arrest for
destroying property could be interpreted as an effort by Wagner to conceal the grim condition of the place. Lindsay still
said no.

Lindsay pointed out to the reporters paint-splattered and
torn linoleum at stairway landings, holes in apartment ceilings,
electrical appliances dangling by their wires, and a bathtub
propped up on bricks. "This building is a monument to inaction and indifference on the part of the administration,"
he said. "I intend to war on slums and on bureaucracy. This
city must make sure people live in dignity." I still wish he had
smashed down that rickety red cellar door.

☆☆★ *June*

Tuesday, June 1 — Wagner has emerged from seclusion, more enigmatic than ever. He spent a couple of days "resting and catching up with paper work" at the home of an old friend on Long Island, while reporters looked vainly for him. "Well, I feel all right," he said today. "I had some rest. Fundamentally I'm healthy enough." The stress of office bothers him at times but personal considerations will weigh more than political considerations in his eventual decision, he declared.

The Mayor seems determined to enjoy his dilemma. He twitted reporters about missing an earlier statement that he might not run. This was made on May 1 at a Queens political dinner. "Nobody paid much attention to my speech out there," he said with a smile. He declined to estimate how his possible withdrawal would affect Lindsay's chance. "I never bet on politics," he said.

The newspapers are printing segments of a supposedly secret 76-page report on a Kraft poll taken for Steingut, that pistol eternally pointed at Wagner's head. "Mayor Wagner is in very bad shape indeed," the report concludes. "His job rating (with the voters) is so bad that any reasonable candidate could oppose him successfully."

Wagner scoffs at the polls. Four years ago, before he ran successfully for reelection, "somebody took a poll showing 85 percent of the people against me," he noted. "Polls are not particularly useful at this stage of a campaign. The time for them is when you approach election day."

Lindsay takes a similar view. The polls that have come to his attention—I understand two were taken at different times by E. R. Reilly Company—show too high a percentage of undecided voters. All they indicate, he said, "is a spirited race."

Worse for Wagner than the polls is the neutrality of President Johnson and Bobby Kennedy. Bobby breakfasted at Gracie Mansion last Friday. He remained sphinxlike about his visit until today when he revealed that he did not urge the Mayor to run "because a decision of this kind is one that the Mayor should make alone." As for the President, he came to New York on May 22 for a closed meeting of the President's Club. This club, started by President Kennedy three years ago, consists of rich Donkeys who contribute at least $1,000 each to the party. Wagner reportedly annoyed the President by reminding him that the club siphons off local funds for national political use. Today President Johnson was asked at a White House news conference whether he thought Wagner should run again. "That is *not* a matter for the President to decide," he said. However, any draft of Wagner for another term might well start at the White House.

Except for his swift changes of mood Wagner was active enough today to be actually campaigning for reelection. He made a luncheon appearance before the Officers Club at Floyd Bennett Field. There he told a sad story about a man who was talking to himself as he walked along the street. "Things are awful . . . air pollution, water pollution, overcrowded schools, traffic is terrible. . . ." Somebody stopped the man and said, "You ought to talk to the Mayor." The man replied: "I am the Mayor."

This evening Wagner went to a Democratic affair on Staten Island. "If LaGuardia were here today," he said, speaking without notes, "he'd be horrified that a fellow from the silk-stocking Congressional district is trying to usurp his mantle. Every time I run for Mayor, it seems I'm always up against another LaGuardia. First it was Rudy Halley, then Bob Christenberry, then . . . er . . . Louis Lefkowitz. They were all LaGuardias. . . ."

Changing his tone abruptly, he began shouting. "Lindsay

is the captive of the five GOP county leaders! If he wins they will dictate the kind of government we have! If he wins we will have corrupt government in New York City!"

Those who have felt right along that Wagner's uncertainty is more political ploy than soul-searching are surer than ever that he will run. The *Journal-American* says flatly today that "most of the Lindsay brain-trusters, including U.S. Senator Jacob K. Javits, his newly announced campaign chairman, are certain the Mayor will be pitching for a fourth term." The usually acute syndicated Washington columnist Mary Mc-Grory writes: "Lindsay has come on like Saint George, lance at the ready for big-city corruption, but Wagner will continue to run like Ol' Man River."

I'm not convinced. He is planning to leave on an auto trip next weekend to visit his sons at their schools. His outburst can be interpreted as the cry of a desperately unhappy man, sick and tired of trying to cope with the nation's largest city and rehearsing political lines which he may never deliver.

Wednesday, June 2 — Later today, John and Mary Lindsay's four children will move into a third-floor corridor-end suite at the Roosevelt, directly below the fourth-floor corridor-end office of Price. Since an almost unnoticeable little stairway connects the two corridors the family will virtually live in headquarters and yet have privacy. The combination office-home has already proved valuable to Lindsay. It makes him easily available for breakfast conferences. When he returns to the Roosevelt at the end of the day he can almost roll into bed. During the day he can slip downstairs to shower, change his clothes, watch TV, listen to the radio, read, rest, or relax.

The intriguing domestic arrangements of the Lindsays will be given as little publicity as possible. They reflect Mary's effort to assure the children a fair share of parental care and attention. During Lindsay's first two terms in Congress, the family lived in a Manhattan apartment. He worked in Washington Monday through Friday, sleeping in a hotel. When he returned to New York on weekends he was so besieged by constituents, and so entangled in social and political affairs that he had little time for the children. One day in 1962, one of Lindsay's three daughters wailed: "Why is it when Daddy comes home, everyone sees him but us?"

That jarred things into perspective. Mary saw immediately to the purchase of a white-brick Colonial house on the side of a hill in Washington. Thereafter the conflict between public and private life took a new turn. On weekends the Congressman still kept in touch with the New York silk-stocking district which returns him to office every two years. The Washington residence was supposed to assure his companionship to the family during the week, but he often came home preoccupied with developments in the House.

"He has such tremendous power of concentration that sometimes even I have trouble getting through," says Mary. On one occasion, after repeatedly and in vain trying to capture her husband's ear for a discussion of family finances, she sent his office a formal request for an appointment. That did the trick.

One odd aspect of the present arrangements is that nowhere along the fourth-floor campaign corridor can you find a desk earmarked for John's use. He uses any available desk in any available office, including the press office. This is one of Price's inspirations. It enables the candidate to escape entrapment of various kinds and, in theory at least, keeps the staff on its toes.

Mary has a desk across the campaign corridor from me in the office of Harvey Rothenberg, a textile manufacturer who serves without pay as office manager. There she handles her mail, phones, and performs a variety of campaign chores. She has worked in all her husband's campaigns. "I work with John, without him, with others, or by myself, but I work," is how she puts it.

Since May 13, when they were in New York for Lindsay's opening tour of the city, the four children have been in

Washington under the care of a Peruvian housekeeper. Mary is bringing them to New York tonight to install them in the campaign nest. Tomorrow, at Price's request, I shall escort them on a tour of the World's Fair.

Thursday, June 3 — The first time I saw Lindsay I was reminded of the Henry James character who had "the air of a happy temperament fertilized by a high civilization." He has money, too. His father, George Lindsay, an international banker, died three years ago, leaving $700,000, plus valuable suburban acreage on Long Island, to be divided among four sons and a daughter. The money is important only as it ranks among other factors, like a solid family life in youth, natural intelligence, the right schools, and exceptional stamina, which qualify and free Lindsay to do what he wants to do.

Mary Harrison Lindsay, called Mare by intimates, possesses a comparable background. She grew up in a comfortable country home in Greenwich, Conn., from which her father, a banker, commuted to New York. She was a tomboy who excelled in ice skating and other outdoor sports. She went to the right schools (Miss Porter's and Vassar). She was still in college when she met John at the wedding of one of her girlhood chums and his former roommate at Yale. Considering John impolite on this occasion, she told him so. Thereafter they encountered each other on skiing weekends. Since he always appeared with a different girl she concluded he was wild and she told him that, too.

One day in June, 1948, they became informally engaged in the kitchen of her Greenwich home. The engagement seemed long to her—"John certainly wasn't anxious to become entangled and he still says he was too young," she told one interviewer—but they were married in June, 1949. The details are at my fingertips because Price asked me to prepare a new campaign biography of Lindsay in my spare time. If I had to describe Mary on my own account I would say she is a slender woman in her late thirties, not pretty in the Hollywood sense,

. . . direct, intelligent, and stimulating.

but direct, intelligent, and stimulating. She wears loose-fitting clothes, little jewelry, no particular makeup, no hat, and she impresses me, an Amherst man, as being more Mount Holyoke in type than Smith.

Mary contributed to John's plunge into public affairs. She was an unenthusiastic cook who found the social life of the wife of a young lawyer on the dull side. At parties the men would huddle in one corner for a discussion of fine legal points while the wives gathered in the other corner to trade recipes. When Lindsay in his own restlessness began to dabble in politics, she dabbled with him, though her only previous experience had been voting.

Mary is absolute in her loyalty to John and his campaign

. . . they walked in the park as usual . . .

effort. Asked recently about an unpleasant description of him in a newspaper article, she snapped: "That's not the man I sleep with!" She concentrates on guarding him from overstrain. Most evenings they dine together and hash over the day's events. Mary can almost invariably make John laugh; if she fails, she rips the next day's schedule apart to give him more rest.

On the way out to the World's Fair today by campaign car, I commented that the new domestic arrangements at headquarters seem ideally designed to give the youngsters more time with their father. Mary smiled. When John makes a date with one of them, she said, he keeps it regardless of difficulties. John Vliet Lindsay, Jr.—known as Johnny to avoid the tag of Junior—celebrated his fifth birthday this year on the day before John decided to run for Mayor. Since they customarily take a walk in the park on Johnny's birthday, they walked in the park as usual, while the phones in the family's temporary New York quarters never stopped ringing. Today is the twelfth birthday of Margie and there will be a birthday party for her around supper time.

Today's jaunt may be the last family excursion before the children separate for the summer. Kathy, a large dreamy girl of fourteen, will leave in July with a chaperoned group of girls for Europe. Margie and Anne, a thoughtful and chunky nine-year-old, will go to camp, and Johnny will "stay with Rod and Nancy in Syosset." There will be other boys at Rod's place and Johnny will benefit from a little more masculine companionship, Mary said.

I couldn't resist asking who was Rod. With a touch of surprise—was it hauteur?—that a campaign press agent should be ignorant of such a matter, Mrs. Lindsay explained that Rod was Robert Lindsay, John's younger brother. I know George, John's older brother, who is a lawyer and a bird-watcher as well as our headquarters research boss, and David, John's super-energetic fraternal twin who is helping to set up storefronts in Queens, but I have not yet encountered Rod, a banker, who is chiefly involved in campaign fund-raising.

My function at the Fair was to guard the family against harassment by the press. This proved easy to accomplish since the reporters and photographers were quite willing to leave after a few comments by Mary and a few pictures of the children. I could have gone back to headquarters, but I hung around because I was enjoying myself. Mary had planned the conquest of the Fair on a map. She wanted to see Churchill and Lincoln, the city and state pavilions, the African and Pepsi-Cola exhibits, and a few others and she stuck to her plan. We lunched at the Belgian Village. While the kids tried various games of chance nearby, Mary and I chatted in desultory fashion at a sun-drenched table on the edge of the cobblestoned square. She had her shoes off under the table.

During the afternoon I talked in turn with each of the children. The girls are clever and well-mannered. Except for Kathy, who is shy, they seem sure of themselves and each other.

Johnny is a particular delight. His legs must have ached from so much walking but he did not complain. Sometimes two of the girls would swing him between them by the hands as they walked. Other times he and I would sit outside an exhibit while the tireless ones finished their inspection inside. We all relaxed over soft drinks before traveling back to Manhattan by subway.

Friday, June 4 — I've been hearing thunder on the right for more than a week. Dan Mahoney tells me that his Conservative party will definitely run somebody against Lindsay. Last year, the Conservatives ran Kieran O'Doherty, their national affairs committee chairman, against Lindsay in the congressional election. O'Doherty kept barking that Lindsay was really a Democrat, while Mrs. Eleanor Clark French, the Democratic-Liberal nominee, tried in her ladylike way to prove that Lindsay was a conservative Republican. The crossfire seemed to cancel out. That might happen again. On the other hand, a more adroit candidate than O'Doherty might be troublesome.

William F. Buckley, Jr., editor of the *National Review*, a conservative news weekly, was honored last night at a meeting of Public Action Inc., a New York outfit which sends out right-wing information on a national scale. Since Mahoney tells me that Buckley is the most likely of five mayoral prospects already interviewed by the Conservatives, I've been keeping my eye on him. He is a snob with mob appeal, a rich man four years younger than Lindsay. He first attracted attention in college with his book, *God and Man at Yale*, and he has gradually gained a national following as a polemicist and proponent of reaction.

Buckley seems to have been well-received last night by an audience of 3,000. "It would certainly not be possible from Lindsay's voting record in Congress," he said urbanely, "to infer that he ever came near the Republican party." Lindsay's civilian review board, he said, is designed to "investigate the fancied fears of a neurotic population." He cited the fatal shooting last summer of a Negro boy by Police Lt. Thomas Gilligan which sparked riots in Harlem, saying: "The sympathy in some quarters is with the young thug who lunged at

"I have to point to people in the windows."

Gilligan with a knife, rather than with the policeman whose act of self-defense has come close to ruining his life." Somehow, Buckley sounds formidable.

Saturday, June 5 — Lindsay's street tours are catching fire. As he lopes urgently from block to block, borough to borough, recruits flood into our new citywide headquarters for volunteers near Grand Central Station in Manhattan. The 7–2, Democratic–Republican registration is always on Lindsay's mind. "I have to point to people in the windows," he says. "Knock on doors, shake hands. I've got to make people say, 'Oh yeah, Lindsay, I know him. He was on the block. How do I find this guy Lindsay on the ballot?' "

Adults vote, but it's the youngsters by whom political

. . . it's the youngsters by whom political popularity is gauged nowadays.

popularity is gauged nowadays. The kind of teenagers who rave over Bobby Kennedy turned out for Lindsay yesterday afternoon in the Flatbush section of Brooklyn. They swirled around him until his slow progress down the sidewalk resembled a lunatic conga line. "We all want to touch the next mayor," gasped one thirteen-year-old girl. "Isn't he cute?" A tall boy standing by in a blue polo shirt added: "I just wanna say I shook hands with the guy who's gonna be the next mayor." The most frequent juvenile comment encountered by reporters who go along on these tours is: "Wagner has been a good mayor but he is now tired. Lindsay being young and full of energy can do more for the city." Candidates have been elected on less than this.

Connie Eristoff, our hereditary Georgian Prince who han-

. . . we opened a storefront for volunteers . . .

dles storefronts, says we are merely implementing the advice Abraham Lincoln gave an Illinois campaign committee in 1840. It's framed on his office wall: "Divide your county into small districts and appoint in each a committee. Make a perfect list of the voters and ascertain with certainty for whom they will vote. Keep a constant watch on the doubtful voters and have them talked to by those in whom they have the most confidence. On election day see that every Whig be brought to the polls."

As the climax of a street tour in the Jackson Heights section of Queens, we opened a storefront for volunteers there this morning—our first in the entire city. John and Mary Lindsay, David Lindsay, Price, and other campaign officials present were encouraged by the large and enthusiastic turnout. David is one of three borough coordinators in Queens, the other two being Arnold G. Fraiman and Lawrence Fiedler, who are young Manhattan lawyers. David himself is a lawyer working in Manhattan and living in Nassau County. According to Price, the borough coordinators in the rest of the city will be: Robert Sweet and Woodward Kingman, Manhattan; Matthias L. Spiegel, Robert Blum, and Daniel Hoffman, Brooklyn; Franklin Weissberg, Charles Moerdler, Herbert B. Halberg, and Joel L. Tyler, the Bronx; and Holt Meyer, a member of Lindsay's former law firm, Staten Island. Most of these coordinators hail from the New York Young Republican Club or from GOP clubhouses in Lindsay's congressional district. In other words, the steel core of the volunteer operation will be not only Republican, but Lindsay Republican.

This afternoon we went street-walking in the Bushwick section of Brooklyn. The shopping areas we select for these excursions are very much alike, with stores on the pavement level and people in apartments on the second and third stories. At one intersection, Lindsay paused and looked up at two open third-story windows from which came feminine squealing and frantic waving. From one window leaned a man and a woman and from an adjoining one a tousled, delightful girl, flimsily dressed as if she had just awakened from a nap.

Across my mind flashed a vague recollection of a short story by a well-known French writer—was it de Maupassant?—about a Parisian cocotte plying her trade from a third-story window. Lindsay must also have sensed the implicit invitation up there because he said loudly: "I'll be right up!"

There was great laughter from the crowd and perhaps a touch of suspense before Lindsay waved his hand in farewell and crossed the street. It was a small incident but I am still chuckling over the expression on that girl's face.

Sunday, June 6 — After a clumsy start the Number 2 city official, Deputy Mayor Paul R. Screvane, is bulling his way into the limelight. When Wagner declared his uncertainty, Screvane felt obliged to say that he, too, was going through an agonizing reappraisal which might lead to retirement from public life. A wave of ridicule, based on the obvious fact that his problems are not the same as Wagner's, soon forced him to concede that he will run again for Council President on a Wagner slate or for mayor as Wagner's political heir.

Screvane is a stalwart man of fifty, somewhat under six feet in height, who worked his way up over a twenty-nine-year period from a thirty-dollar-a-week garbageman to his present post. He is the son of an Italian immigrant and an Irish girl, is married to an Irish girl, has three children, and lives in strategically important Queens County. He seems to have been an efficient Sanitation Commissioner. As Deputy Mayor he won Wagner's respect by reorganizing the slack City Hall staff along military lines. He is a colonel in the reserves. Screvane's heavy voice and commanding presence are assets, but he has an acquired taste for sunlamp tan, a long black enamel cigaret holder, and stagy, arrogant posturing which are not so attractive.

This afternoon Screvane bumped Lindsay out of a group photo of celebrities in the grandstand at the annual Puerto Rican Day Parade. I would not have believed it if I had not seen it from a few feet away. This went beyond the discreet elbowing and pushing for position which often occurs on such occasions. A few seconds earlier, I had watched with amusement as Rockefeller and his wife Happy closed shoulders in front of Beame so that only Abe's hair remained visible to the photographers.

Screvane made his move just as another wave of picture-taking began. He pretended he was shifting to kiss the cheek of the parade queen, a redhead wearing a white damask gown and a glittering tiara, but Lindsay is a large man. Force was needed to jolt him out of place. The impact of Screvane's well-muscled body did not look accidental to me. It did not seem accidental to Lindsay either, to judge from the restrained fury on his face. Screvane did not improve the climate by shouting to a friendly newspaperman that Lindsay has no

A few seconds earlier . . .

chance. "He's known in the silk-stocking district but not in Brownsville," he declared.

On TV in the morning, Screvane said Lindsay was campaigning "on a pretty boy kind of thing where it's all handsome Willie handshaking and that sort of thing." This sounded like one of those "you're a sissy" insults which start schoolboy fights. If Screvane hopes to establish himself as the big Democrat in town by goading Lindsay into a quarrel, it won't work. Price set policy a couple of days ago by permitting no comment from our headquarters on Wagner's charge of inevitable corruption under Lindsay as Mayor.

As of now, neither Wagner nor Screvane is a candidate and Lindsay gains nothing by tangling with them, Price says. Lindsay's insurgent battle for the 1958 Republican congressional nomination, which started in April, was really won in the first few weeks of uncontested campaigning while the incumbent tried to decide whether to run and then, after he withdrew, while the organization looked around for a substitute. Lindsay has a similar advantage now, Price says, which will not be yielded to oblige Screvane.

Monday, June 7 — Yesterday's 15 hours of campaigning wound up in Bedford-Stuyvesant. First we attended a holy-roller meeting in the Storey Auditorium. For an hour we endured loud preaching with chorused amens, hymn singing to the accompaniment of electric guitars, and repeated exhortations to file up front with confessions of faith and cash. I had nothing to confess, but as one of the handful of whites present I felt obliged to part with a dollar bill.

When Lindsay was introduced, he showed that he had been absorbing the atmosphere. "Sometimes we sing," he said, "because there is nothing else to do. It's good to sing, IS IT NOT?"

There were scattered amens.

"It's good to rejoice, IS IT NOT?"

More amens.

"Every human being has a little of the divine, DOES HE NOT?" The audience was beginning to rock back and forth with him in true evangelical style. "And that makes us dignified people who stand up straight, walk tall, and hold our heads high!"

When we got outside Lindsay steered me to the curb for a talk. He wanted to slip away from the press to go pub-crawling. Only two afternoon newspaper reporters were following us. Since they had signed up for the evening, I did not think they should be duped.

"But one of them is a girl," objected Lindsay. She was more reporter than girl, I said. He shrugged his shoulders but he was not really convinced. Before we hit the first of four or five night spots he explained in an aside that this kind of campaigning did well without publicity since news of it spread through the community by word of mouth.

The day before election in his congressional campaigns, Lindsay confided, he invariably made an unpublicized round of bars in his district after eating a large steak and drinking a quart of milk as precautionary measures against loss of control. By this time I was convinced of the need for privacy but it was too late; the reporters had been told.

The first place I remember quite well, a fancy joint called the Monterey Club. With a succession of partners, Lindsay danced the jerk, twist, cha-cha, and what he said was a little of the monkey to the rapid beat of a tune called "It's Not Unusual," as sung by Tom Jones. Several patrons promised to vote for him. At two less swanky spots in the Crown Heights section, bartenders turned down their jukeboxes to introduce "the next mayor of New York."

Lindsay seemed to be doing more glass-holding than drinking, but I was tired and in no mood to be antisocial. Sometimes the liquor was purchased by Gilbert Robinson, our field campaign director, but more often it was on the house. Things began to blur a little. A campaign car conveyed me safely to the Roosevelt, but from there I had difficulty getting home.

Tuesday, June 8 — Campaign humor tends to be nauseous, out of repetition, if for no other reason. Lindsay has several stories he tells again and again to explain why he is running for mayor. All of them imply he is crazy to want the job. The best one has him leaving Washington by train for New York to declare his candidacy. When he enters the car only one empty seat remains on the aisle in the midst of a group of men who have their arms folded and are looking straight ahead. He takes the seat.

After a while, a man in a white coat comes along who is not the conductor and he starts counting over the contingent bound for an institution. "One, two, three, four, five, six . . ." he says, stopped at Lindsay. "Who are you?"

"Candidate for mayor of New York City!" replies Lindsay.

The keeper resumes counting, with a tap on Lindsay's shoulder. "Seven, eight, nine, ten . . ."

Lindsay has a story on how he became a congressman. It

seems he was campaigning in a public square one evening when a heckler began to shout: "Lindsay smokes, he drinks, and he goes out with women."

"That's fine," rejoined another citizen. "Send him to Washington. They won't have to break him in."

Sometimes he explains his work in Washington in a light vein. "I work in a House which is not a home. You can't get in trouble there. It's run by a group of elderly gents who may have been torn between conscience and temptation at one time in their lives but who have long since lost both."

Finally, there is a story he uses with certain female audiences. It's too awful to give in full but the punch line, delivered with a knowing look, is: "There must be a recess in heaven with all of you angels down here."

Lindsay used that story tonight at a Republican card party for women up in the Bronx. The battle-scarred audience, hardly a one of them under forty years of age or two hundred pounds, made such a dovelike twittering that it would have drowned out the heavenly choir itself!

Wednesday, June 9 — Vice-President Hubert Humphrey today disclosed his choice and presumably that of President Johnson for Mayor of New York. Speaking before Alex Rose's Hatters Union here in town, Humphrey delivered a ten-minute panegyric about his favorite, concluding: "I have a feeling that in the days ahead New York will have as its mayor, Mayor Robert F. Wagner!"

During the last day and a half there have been some preliminary signs of a draft movement for Wagner, such as a unanimous resolution by the fifty-six Democratic district leaders in Queens County that he must run again and a milder statement from Bobby Kennedy that he will work for Wagner if Wagner does run. Even though the silence in other areas has been deafening, today's audience rocked with enthusiasm in the belief that they were watching the triumphant climax of a draft. On the dais, Wagner sat motionless for several seconds before he permitted himself a feeble smile. Then he arose to shake Humphrey's hand.

In a surprise gesture the Vice-President brought out his own hat for Wagner to throw into a symbolic ring right there on the platform—how the hatters' union members loved that gesture!—but Wagner put aside the crown with the explanation that his own lucky hat was outside in his car. Reporters checked later: there on the shelf of his 1962 Cadillac sat the brown fedora worn by Wagner through three previous campaigns.

Tomorrow Wagner gives his formal decision. Lindsay bet Price $100 today that the Mayor will run. O'Donnell had a ten-cent bet with me that the Mayor will run. O'Donnell tried to prod me into raising our bet to a quarter today, but I refused. My only concern is that Hope Ritchie may run off with the stakes.

Thursday, June 10 — In an emotional mob scene on the steps of City Hall around noon today Wagner eliminated himself as a candidate for reelection. Since his return Monday from a visit to his sons he had not opened his mind to anybody except two close advisers, so his secret was well-kept. Somehow Gabe Pressman got a half-hour scoop for NBC-TV and as a result I hear that his CBS rival, Mary Pengalos, has been suspended. Most of the press, radio, and TV reporters were taken wholly by surprise.

In recent months, Wagner revealed, the City Hall routine became drudgery. Then Lindsay entered the race. "I began to feel the old excitement of political combat. I knew I could take this candidate's measure . . . Later there came back to me the overriding factor—the most personal and yet the highest of considerations—my family, my two sons."

During the 1961 campaign, Wagner said, he promised his wife Susan—here he began to cry—that he would not run again in 1965. He paused to finger the moisture off his cheeks. With Susan gone, he felt obliged to give more time to his sons—they were standing on either side of him as he said this—"one on the very threshold of manhood, the other son approaching that state. They have a claim upon me for companionship which I must now grant."

With possible reference to Barbara Cavanagh, who recently issued a statement that she and the Mayor have no matrimonial plans at present, Wagner added: "I have some obligations to myself, too."

Not for some time to come, Wagner said, will he express any preference among the Democratic possibilities for Mayor. His own decision, he added, is final and irrevocable. As he finished, many of his faithful followers at the Hall were weeping with him.

The best quarters at the Roosevelt we could secure for Lindsay's comment on Wagner's withdrawal was a 15th-floor suite without air conditioning. I hurried there as soon as the situation became clear. Some reporters had been waiting since 11:30. It became terribly hot and overcrowded up there. One TV technician fainted and had to be carried to a couch in a nearby room. Lindsay did not appear until 1:30. I caught him at the elevator to suggest an apology to the press. He started the news conference by calling loudly to me that Harry and I had "goofed" in choosing such a miserable place—which was what I wanted, I guess. Mary Lindsay was present, looking cool and nice.

Wagner had said an odd thing, that it was "perhaps time for a change, for me as well as the city." Lindsay picked this up. "The people also feel that New York needs a change," he said. "They feel that the complaisant arteries of our city administration are badly in need of a transfusion. That is what I would like to do for our city with the help of all the people, irrespective of their political beliefs."

Lindsay concluded with praise for the past services of "Bob Wagner"—one of Price's soft touches, I suppose—and expressions of sympathy for the Mayor. On the way out, Mary had a comment on the hot room. "Men are silly to wear those heavy

Mary went with him all the way.

jackets on a day like this," she said distinctly. She brought her husband in to see the collapsed TV gent in the next room. It developed that he is feeling better.

Going down in a crowded elevator, one of the Raiders—as the young volunteers who help in campaign advance work are called—congratulated me on my successful ten-cent bet. (No interplanetary missile travels faster than gossip in a campaign headquarters.) What was my next bet? the Raider asked.

Exubérantly and without too much thought, I replied I'd bet a dime Lindsay would gain Liberal party support and go on to win the election. Ten minutes later Price plunged into my room. "What are you saying about John winning?" he demanded. I looked at him in amazement.

"Don't you understand we have 15,000 to 20,000 volunteers and we'd lose two-thirds of them overnight if they got any idea Lindsay is not an underdog?" he continued. "Please don't say anything like that again!" His tone eased. "What about the Liberal party? Is there something we should do now?"

As soon as he left I began working the phone to get material for a memo on the Liberal party. During the rest of the day Lindsay kept to his usual tight schedule—a parade in Queens, a rally in Brooklyn, and a couple of street tours. Mary went with him all the way. At 10:30 P.M. they emerged from the Hotel Picadilly after an appearance before the Affiliated Young Democrats, an organization which a wag once said is not affiliated or young and perhaps not even democratic.

Lindsay steered me to the curb. "Mary and I haven't had dinner," he said. "We want to go to Sardi's in some sort of privacy. Can you lose the press?" I nodded and got the reporters into a campaign car with me. As we left for the Roosevelt, I caught a fleeting glimpse of the Lindsays still standing on the sidewalk. Mary was nuzzling John's coat sleeve and laughing up at him like a young girl in love.

Friday, June 11 — Only two Republicans have used volunteers successfully in local elections: Dewey as a candidate for Manhattan District Attorney in 1937 and Willkie in his 1940 Presidential race. Willkie drew more volunteers than Dewey, perhaps as many as 6,000. Our outpouring may exceed the 15,000 to 20,000 mentioned by Price the other day, which is disturbing as well as phenomenal. Any person who gears himself up to free work in a political campaign wants quick recognition.

A neglected volunteer is like a loaded gun: he can turn against you overnight. According to Connie Eristoff, only seven storefronts have been opened in three of the city's five boroughs, though leases have been signed on thirty-one additional stores. Connie, who is as unflappable as Harry O'Donnell, says soothingly that everything will be all right, but I wish the program would speed up a little.

Our first big rally for volunteers was held this afternoon in the grand ballroom of the Roosevelt. The news release said "more than 4,000" had been invited. More than 4,000 showed up. On the face of it that is miraculous.

Campaign literature, beer, and soft drinks were provided in booths around the perimeter of the ballroom and in several small rooms which were opened up at the last moment. The booths were supposed to be rallying points for volunteers from particular localities but crowding soon made that impossible. Long after the scheduled 5 P.M. start of the rally, new arrivals

—all sizes, shapes, sexes, and social conditions, but mostly young—poured into the ballroom and its overflow rooms to join those already drinking, smoking and shouting to each other over the din.

Lindsay might easily have entered the west end of the ballroom where the platform is located. Instead he and Mary were routed through the jammed, suffocatingly hot anterooms at the east end. As soon as it caught a glimpse of the Lindsays, the crowd roared and shifted massively in that direction. Raiders and others of us from headquarters linked arms to move the candidate inch by inch along that long ballroom. Mary had disappeared from sight.

When Lindsay finally emerged on the platform the frenzy expanded. He waited until Mary was located and brought to the platform.

"This campaign will be fun," said Lindsay, mopping his face. "If a campaign is well-designed, it has to be fun. It's part of living to be in a campaign, part of the fabric of society, part of human experience. You should enter upon it with a feeling of exhilaration. You should have a lively time. You should make your influence felt in the district headquarters to which you are assigned. It's important that you take initiative. Be sure your initiative is respected. It's important that you bring more New Yorkers into the effort to make a new start for this city. I want to demonstrate that we can make New York a place to live in, particularly for young couples with children. Maybe the time will come when the young couples in the suburbs will be envious of those in the city . . .

"The campaign will be nonpartisan. Let's all forget party affiliations and simply do what is right for the city. It will be an uphill fight. I make only one promise and that is to put together a nonpartisan fusion slate of which you will be proud."

The applause was intoxicating. Lindsay was about to shift from a conversational tone to oratory when Mary mouthed: "TOO HOT!" He nodded and finished in thirty seconds.

"I want to apologize to everybody for what you put up

with to be here—and this heat and smoke," he said. "Mary and I would like to swing around and get to know you better, shake hands, and maybe dance a little. Thank you for coming." He and Mary did go around shaking hands and saying hello to volunteers for another half-hour before leaving. There was no room for dancing until long after they left.

Saturday, June 12 — The vacuum created by Wagner's withdrawal will probably be filled by a Democratic primary fight over the citywide elective offices—Mayor, Council President, and Controller—and perhaps over several of the five Borough Presidencies. There are now three basic groups in the local Democratic party: Wagnerians, anti-Wagnerians, and reformers. Even if Wagner had run again, reconciling these factions would have been difficult. Now an ordeal by ballot—September 14 is primary day—seems inevitable. If I am right, Lindsay will not have an official Democratic opponent for another three months.

Bill Ryan, Congressman from Manhattan's West Side, held a news conference today, slapped Wagner verbally— "We're finished with mediocrity in New York," he said— usurped a Lindsay campaign theme or two and dashed off to shake hands along Broadway as an avowed contender for Mayor. William Fitts Ryan is a tall, lean man of forty-three, Ivy League (Princeton and Columbia Law), with great energy, a flair for publicity, a politically hep wife ("Patricia is the best doorbell ringer on the West Side," he says), and four children. He got his start as an Assistant to District Attorney Frank S. Hogan. Emerging in the late fifties as a reform district leader in Columbia University section, he elbowed rivals aside for an insurgent nomination for Congress, upset the incumbent, and has been angling for promotion ever since.

Paul O'Dwyer, fifty-seven, the stocky, white-maned brother of former Mayor William O'Dwyer, will declare for Mayor tomorrow. He is an I.R.A. agent at heart, an instinctive radical, a sentimental orator. He makes his living as a labor lawyer, but his favorite kind of case is defending a blind newsdealer who is being ousted from his street corner site by a large downtown bank. Back in the days when Bill-O presided over City Hall, Paul-O tried for Congress in uptown Manhattan and lost. He took an early role in the Democratic reform movement and is now Manhattan Councilman-at-Large.

Since Ryan and O'Dwyer are both affiliated with the Committee for Democratic Voters (CDV), as the reform movement is known organizationally, they reduce each other's chances. Screvane, who is expected to declare Monday, will inherit considerable CDV strength from Wagner, thus further splintering the reform movement. New York City Controller Abraham Beame and Queens District Attorney Frank O'Connor, who are due to enter the scramble separately next week, are anti-Wagnerians, so the disunity extends into the ranks of the old-line or regular Democrats.

A poll being taken by the *Daily News* at the World's Fair rates Franklin D. Roosevelt, Jr., over all other Democratic mayoral prospects. He has 41 percent of the straws to 20 percent for Screvane, 13 for Beame, 10 for O'Connor and a scattering for dark horses like Manhattan District Attorney Hogan, who is known to be highly regarded by President Johnson; Stephen P. Smith, brother-in-law of Bobby Kennedy and manager of all the Senator's campaigns; and Theodore W. Kheel, the labor arbitrator.

FDR, Jr. is the Lindsay or Ryan of yesteryear. I remember him in 1949, rampaging up and down Manhattan's West Side in an insurgent campaign for Congress: six feet four, deep voiced and magnetic, with his father's heavy head and hearty laughter. After he was elected he turned against his liberal sponsors and slighted his duties for travel, money making, and diversion. In 1954, he lost to Javits for State Attorney General. He became the lawyer for Generalissimo Trujillo, the Dominican dictator. He sold Fiat cars out of a Washington office. He drew national attention in 1960 by campaigning for John F. Kennedy in West Virginia and since then he has held one appointive federal job or another. He possesses a magic name and a West Side Manhattan voting address, but he lacks a base in any of the local factions. His best hope is to gain Wagner's support as the head of a compromise city ticket including one Wagnerian and one anti-Wagnerian.

Where, by the way, is Wagner? The Mayor has kept out of sight since his farewell to the troops at City Hall. Last night he turned up unexpectedly with Barbara Cavanagh at Shea Stadium watching the Giants murder the Mets. "I thought it would be a good way to relax after a trying day," he explained.

Sunday, June 13 — Price is fuming over an attempt by Javits to deal singlehandedly with the Liberal party. I know how delicate the situation is because my friend Harry Uviller, a Lindsay supporter who is state treasurer of the Liberal party, suggested several days ago that a meeting be held between Lindsay and Liberal leaders. Though there is no man I respect more than Uviller, I felt obliged to check with Rose. To my surprise, he did not like the idea. Such a meeting might create an impression among party members that Lindsay was getting preferential treatment, the Liberal tactician declared. The policy committee will meet tomorrow evening to name a group to interview all mayoral prospects and Lindsay can take his turn among the others, Rose suggested. When I mentioned this to Price he said he had received similar advice from Ben Davidson, the executive director of the party.

Javits has a room down the campaign corridor at the Roosevelt with his name on the door as campaign chairman, but the door is usually locked and the room empty. So far as day-to-day operations are concerned, Javits and his co-chairman, LaGuardia's widow Marie, are more or less figureheads. In any event, Javits consulted nobody at headquarters before spending an hour this afternoon with David Dubinsky at Beth Israel Hospital, where the union leader is recovering from a minor operation, and another hour at Rose's apartment in Washington Heights.

O'Donnell and I were in the pressroom when Price arrived, in a state of indignation, with the "bulldog," or evening, edition of the *Times*. A front-page headline read: JAVITS TALKS WITH DUBINSKY AND ROSE. According to the story, the Senator was "encouraged about prospects that Mr. Lindsay could become the first Republican mayoral nominee to receive the Liberal endorsement since 1949. The Senator told friends his conversations had made him more optimisitic than he had been."

"It was done without my knowledge, consent, or approval," said Price. "It's not the first time Javits has done this! I've a good mind to issue a statement on it."

Without any expression in his face or voice O'Donnell asked: "Wouldn't that lead to stories about a split in the Lindsay camp?"

Price shrugged. Though he continued to denounce Javits, he dropped the idea of repudiating our campaign chairman. Before leaving, he suggested a press leak that Lindsay will take a Liberal for either Council President or Controller on the fusion slate. Our earlier position was that we wanted "at least one Democrat" on the slate. The shift is timely in that Dr. Costello said on TV this morning that "solid sentiment" for Lindsay is developing in the Liberal party. Costello himself is a possibility for the ticket.

Monday, June 14 — I got thinking today about campaign paranoia. I have time to think because Lindsay is in Washington to deliver a House speech on the civil rights martyrs, Michael Schwerner, Andrew Goodman, and James Chaney. What I think is that campaign paranoia seems more routine when you are involved in it than when you are an observer on the outside.

This particular malaise starts with the hasty assemblage of campaign staffs. Lines of authority being poorly defined, overlapping and duplication of effort soon develop. After a while almost everybody suspects almost everybody else of stealing his duties and privileges. From mutual suspicion to hatred is a short and ugly jump. The maneuvering and backbiting in some campaigns are shocking.

The degree of campaign paranoia in the Lindsay-for-Mayor operation varies considerably. There is a touch of it in the relationship between Price and Javits, both of whom exercise nominal control over the campaign. More exists among the borough coordinators inasmuch as there are twelve of them in only five boroughs. Points at issue range from who selects the local representative to walk alongside the candidate during walking tours to who arranges for telephones and buys stamps and other necessities for the storefronts for volunteers. In at least one borough the coordinators are not on speaking terms.

Connie Eristoff, the ringmaster of the coordinators, says things will settle down when each one has his exclusive group of five to eight or nine storefronts to administer. Meanwhile Price is planning regular weekly meetings of the coordinators to iron out disputes before they become too engrained. In a transparent effort to build morale, Price calls the coordinators his "twelve disciples," which implies in a humorous way that he is Jesus Christ and Lindsay is God. For the purposes of this campaign, the analogy is apt.

On campaign trips there are two major contenders for Lindsay's favor. Our field director, Gilbert Robinson, is a middle-aged, Rockefeller-oriented public relations man who once ran unsuccessfully for Congress in the Washington Heights section and who presided over the famous kitchen debate between Khrushchev and Nixon in 1960 when he was director of an American exhibit in Moscow. Robinson was also involved in the Draft-Lindsay-for-Mayor committee earlier this year. Our advance man in the campaign and head of the Raiders, is Sydney H. Davidoff, a twenty-six-year-old lawyer who was once heavyweight wrestling champion at City College. To the annoyance of Robinson, Davidoff often has ideas for picturesque behavior which Lindsay adopts. However, if a third party like me suggests breaking down a rickety red cellar door in a tenement, Davidoff and Robinson promptly close ranks in opposition to the idea.

Edith (known as Edie) Radley, the new secretary in my office, is a self-contained girl of twenty-six or twenty-seven from Greenwich, Connecticut. Because she works long hours, Edie has rented an East Side apartment for the duration of the campaign. She is a nice, competent, conscientious girl.

The question arises: should I be concerned over the fact that my secretary is not really my secretary? She was hired at the suggestion of O'Donnell for whom she worked previously, she takes instructions from him and she reports to him. When she answers the telephone she says: "Harry O'Donnell's wire," not my wire or the press office wire. A lot goes on in my own office of which I am ignorant but to which I can make no valid objection since I am often out with the candidate.

The press room is involved in a deeper rivalry between O'Donnell and Price. O'Donnell speaks scathingly of "that bellboy at the end of the hall," implying that Price is a mere flunkey of Lindsay. Price hints that O'Donnell may be disloyal to Lindsay because of his relationship with Rockefeller.

The trouble between these two men—which does not get out of hand because both are smooth operators—has historical roots. Four years ago the GOP mayoral campaign was run by a triumvirate: Louis Lefkowitz, the candidate; Fred Perrotta, the research man; and O'Donnell in public relations. The retiring nature of Louis and Fred gave O'Donnell a chance to demonstrate his theory that politics is 85 percent public relations. Since the 1961 campaign went well, with Lefkowitz losing to Wagner by only 400,000 votes, O'Donnell keeps trying to assert himself in this campaign only to find that Price has no intention of yielding an ounce of authority. The lack of rapport between them has become so glaring that I hesitate to say a friendly word about O'Donnell to Price and I cannot receive a visit from Price or talk to him by telephone without inspiring a black-Irish mood in O'Donnell.

Perhaps the time has come for a resolution:

I shall, if I can, keep out of the Price–Javits, Price–O'Donnell, Robinson–Davidoff rivalries, the struggles between coordinators, members of Lindsay's secretariat, and any others.

I shall, if I can, stay on good terms with all these ladies and gentlemen even at the risk of diminished personal efficiency in the campaign.

So be it.

Tuesday, June 15 — The Liberal party has named eight leading officials to interview mayoral prospects. Four are known to me to be pro-Lindsay: Uviller, Rose, Costello, and the Reverend Donald Harrington, a brilliant Unitarian minister who is state vice-chairman of the party. Two are probably anti-Lindsay: Louis Stulberg and Charles S. Zimmerman, both officials of the International Ladies Garment Workers Union. Two are reportedly undecided: Benjamin M. McLaurin of the Sleeping Car Porters Union and Dr. LeRoy Bowman, professor emeritus of sociology at Brooklyn College. All I really know about McLaurin is that he is a Negro trade unionist of distinction who hates Adam Clayton Powell. Bowman seems to be a freewheeling independent with a fixation on city finances. Without trying to predict the eventual stand of Bowman or McLaurin, I think Lindsay has a good chance with this political jury.

Time is riding with Lindsay. Assuming a Democratic primary fight, there can be no official Democratic candidate for mayor until mid-September. The Liberal party wants to make a quick decision. How can it—or Bobby Kennedy or President Johnson, for that matter—gamble on some Democratic contender who may be eliminated later? Three Democrats—Ryan, O'Dwyer, and Screvane—are already in the race and others may join them.

Price concentrated on the Liberal party today to the exclusion of everything else. First he issued a statement in Lindsay's name asking for an interview with the newly designated committee. Word reaching our headquarters unofficially is that the interview will be Saturday. Lindsay will discuss not only his candidacy but also his hopes for "the formation of a fusion ticket for a nonpartisan city administration." That comes close to saying publicly that he will accept a Liberal for Council President or Controller.

Later today we got out a release pledging Lindsay to the continuance of rent-control. This happens to be a shibboleth of the Liberals. For tomorrow we have a release supporting proportional representation as a way of electing members to the City Council. The Liberal party favors this idea because under it they would have a chance of electing a few councilmen. The sequence of releases seemed too apposite to be accidental. More out of mischief than anything else, I suggested to Price that somebody other than Javits must have conferred over the weekend with some important Liberal on the proper gestures to be made. Who conferred with whom?

Price grinned. "I'll tell you that when I tell the candidate," he said.

Wednesday, June 16 — Lindsay often behaves best when his back is up against a wall. He may be a Boy Scout, as some of his detractors at headquarters insist, but he can only be pushed so far. The idea occurred to me when I met him at LaGuardia Airport around supper time last night upon his return from Washington. My function was to prepare him for a busy evening schedule and to brief him on late news developments, one being a statement from the Committee on Racial Equality that it was "not near" endorsing anybody for mayor. My impression was that CORE had been quite near to endorsing Lindsay late last week.

During the ride to the hotel, Lindsay gave me the private reason for CORE's public statement. He held a final meeting with CORE officials Sunday night. "They hammered me quite a while," he said. "Then I hammered them a little, mentioning that they had been expelled from an organization of other civil rights groups. I asked whether I could count on them to act in a constructive way if I landed in City Hall. They called that intimidation and walked out."

This evening Lindsay made an appearance before the Metropolitan Council of the American Jewish Committee in a cathedral-like setting on East 84th Street near Central Park. He expected to deliver a short talk before this wealthy and social group before moving to the Bronx for a street tour. Upon arrival we found a great collection of radio, press, and TV reporters, drawn by a completely false report of a debate between Lindsay and Stanley Lowell, a former chairman of the Commission on Human Rights and former State head of Americans for Democratic Action whose forte in the past two years has been defending Wagner in radio and TV debates. Since Lindsay has been avoiding joint appearances with contenders for the Democratic mayoral nomination he was certainly not going to debate one of Wagner's axe-men without warning.

When I complained bitterly to Lowell and to Murray Gordon, the AJC chairman, they pleaded innocent, but argued that the reporters would be disappointed if there were no debate. Lindsay insisted on talking first and leaving. Gordon had to agree, but in his introduction he remarked waspishly that Lindsay could not remain to debate because he was going walking on University Avenue up in the Bronx. He congratulated Lindsay on wearing a yarmulka at a recent Jewish function.

"Some members of this group also wear yarmulkas on occasion," he said. "It will be good for the candidate to walk in a good Jewish area up in the Bronx. He will meet some good Jews up there."

Lindsay's face remained blank during Gordon's display of sarcasm. He assumed the microphone with a little extra politeness. He had made two previous appearances during the past week in the Bronx area he was about to visit, he said, so it would not be strange to him. Three visits to the Bronx, he added, looking pointedly at Gordon, were undoubtedly more

Three visits to the Bronx . . .

than the chairman had made in the entire time since he left there.

The bold allusion to the Bronx Jew who escapes to Manhattan's gold coast as soon as he becomes successful and is never again seen in the Bronx delighted the richly dressed matrons sitting with after-dinner drinks on trays in their laps. They applauded so extravagantly that Lindsay's rather stiff little talk proved anticlimactic.

Maybe I imagined it, but during his subsequent street tour Lindsay seemed more buoyant than usual. "When are you going to run for President, John?" one man asked. Lindsay laughed. "Just help me over this one first," he said.

Thursday, June 17 — Lindsay's search for running mates has gone through three distinct phases. At first it was assumed that a Republican might be chosen to run with him for either Council President or Controller. An extensive canvassing of GOP prospects occurred. Only recently I heard from William Passannante, the Greenwich Village Assemblyman, a Democrat who used to be a stooge for Tammany boss Carmine De-Sapio but who has become independent since DeSapio's eclipse, about a breakfast meeting at the Hotel Gotham several weeks ago at which the makeup of the Lindsay ticket was discussed.

Javits wrote on a piece of paper at one point in the meeting and passed it to Price, saying: "I'm very much interested in this name." Price glanced at the paper, crumbled it into a ball, and tossed it to the floor. The name on the paper, according to Passannante, was I. D. Robbins, president of the City Club, an independent Republican who flirted a while last Spring with the idea of sponsoring himself for mayor.

Republican prospects dropped out in favor of Democrats during the second phase of the search. With Wagner an apparent, though undeclared, candidate for reelection, dissatisfaction spread through the Democratic ranks. Various figures at our headquarters made preliminary contacts with prominent, unhappy, and ambitious Democratic politicians. The method was to phone somebody you knew well, ask how things were going and how he felt about Lindsay. The talk proceeded informally from there. Even I, with Price's permission, spoke with such Queens County Democratic mavericks as State Senator Jack Bronston and reform Councilmen Edward Sadowsky and Jack Katzman.

Wagner's withdrawal ushered in the latest phase. Lindsay became interested in a possible Liberal party running mate. Simultaneously the search for an ideal Democrat became more difficult.

Realizing that a primary contest was in prospect which would open up new avenues for advancement in their own party, many Democrats who had been viewing Lindsay with interest averted their eyes. Beame let it be known that he would not be available as a fusionist under any circumstances. Before he announced for mayor, Ryan stole some publicity by declaring that he had been sounded out on joining the Lindsay team but had recoiled virtuously from the suggestion. Jonathan Bingham, a Bronx reform Congressman, issued a similar statement of Democratic purity. Sadowsky won redesignation from the Democratic regulars and Katzman and Bronston decided to concentrate on their own primary fights for redesignation.

The flight of Democratic hopefuls from fusion has become so pronounced that Lindsay felt obliged today to call a news conference to announce that one hundred names have come under consideration for places on his citywide ticket but that no Democrat, not Beame, Bingham, Ryan, O'Dwyer, or anybody else, was ever actually invited to join his slate. This is undoubtedly true. What's more, I suspect that consideration of any Democrat will now be postponed until after the Liberal party makes up its mind.

Friday, June 18 — Theodore H. White, author of *The Making of a President*, is fascinated by the clash of individuals in politics. "The object of the exercise," he writes at one point, "is for one man to kill the other. You watch them clobber each other to death. They bleed, but they bleed internally." Though White may overstate the case a little for dramatic effect a kind of naked personal struggle does lie at the heart of politics. There is often a decisive confrontation between candidates in which one, by a superior exhibition of determination, intellectual capacity, or imagination, gains a subtle and far-reaching advantage. From that moment the winner has the Indian sign on his opponent so perceptibly that the public can sense the relationship and be affected by it.

This evening Lindsay and Screvane tested each other's mettle in a most unlikely setting, a dance at the Statler-Hilton

Hotel of the Hispanic Society of the Department of Sanitation. Since he used to be Commissioner of that department, this was Screvane's home territory. He arrived first, but he came alone. Lindsay, wearing a dinner jacket, brought along Mary in an orange evening dress. If she was grumpy, it was not out of any prejudice against the Spanish-speaking street cleaners of the city but because her husband had defaulted on a promise to take her to a Broadway play that evening.

As we filed in along the side of the dimly lit ballroom around 11 o'clock, Screvane grabbed both my hands in enthusiastic welcome. It took me a second to realize that he had concentrated on me because the Lindsays had looked right through him as they marched by. Earlier in the day, Screvane has issued what he called a "newsletter from City Hall" in which he blasted Lindsay once again as a handshaking Willie and Pretty Boy from the silk-stocking Congressional district who knew nothing of city problems. Lindsay had endured it in silence but he was not pleased and it may have led to his decision to visit the Hispanic Ball.

After asking about Bridie, who had not been able to come, and assuring Screvane that my own wife was in excellent health, I broke away from the Council President to join the Lindsays at a table. We ordered drinks and looked around. The Hispanic Society members were in evening clothes, as were their ladies. Some couples had grown children with them, nice, clean-looking, well-dressed girls and sturdy young fellows. They danced the modern dances to the music of an excellent band, gaily, but with no signs of disorder or drunkenness. During the past couple of weeks, we must have dropped in on a half-dozen similar dances of Negro and Puerto Rican groups. Folks who weep professionally over the plight of urban minorities should visit these functions. Some of the dancers may live in ghettoes, but for an evening at least they are kings and queens.

Screvane, I realized abruptly, had undertaken a handshaking tour. He was circling the ballroom, hitting every right

. . . a particular reason for celebrating . . .

hand at every table he reached. He was moving around back of us. I held my breath as he came closer. Would he touch those two stiff Lindsay backs or say hello? And if he did, what would happen? To my relief, Screvane came within a few inches of the Lindsays, then passed by quickly. He had half-finished his tour when the toastmaster called hm up for greetings. Screvane bounded across the cleared dance floor in a markedly masculine manner, throttled the loudspeaker, and barked that he didn't want to interrupt the dancing and had only a few words to say. The Spanish-speaking members of the department had made great strides under him and Wagner, he said, and they would make greater strides in the future.

He was glad to be there, God bless them all, and goodbye. He got a big hand and I realized with a sinking feeling that Lindsay would come next. How could he possibly equal such a performance?

When called upon Lindsay walked quietly to the loudspeaker. In precise, almost English tones, he said he appreciated the invitation to come to this lovely dance and he was glad to be there. His wife Mary was with him, he said, and he would like to introduce her. She stood up, smiled and waved, and was generously applauded.

What was Lindsay saying? "My wife and I have a particular reason for celebrating—it's our 16th wedding anniversary!"

Laughter and cumulative applause greeted this revelation.

"There is no other place Mary and I would rather be tonight to celebrate our wedding anniversary," Lindsay continued relentlessly, "than here with you fine people."

The utter insufferable impudence of it! Yet the audience was delighted.

Mary Lindsay put her head on her hands and grimaced sideways at me. "After that," she grated, "I've a good mind to get pregnant and sit the campaign out!"

During an earlier family visit to the World's Fair, she had mentioned that she always began to think of a new child when the youngest got out of the baby stage. Johnny was now five. Since Mary Lindsay's directness is contagious, I whispered: "Are you pregnant?"

"When," she demanded, "would I have time?"

That was that. They were still applauding when Lindsay returned to his seat. Screvane was leaving. He waved to two or three friends on the way out but he looked furtive and harried, almost as if he were running away.

Saturday, June 19 — All the political reporters knew in advance that the place selected by the Liberal party for its confidential 11 A.M. interview with Lindsay and its confidential 2:30 P.M. interview with Ryan was the Presidential

Liberal leaders Leroy Bowman, Donald Harrington, Alex Rose, and Louis Stulberg talk with Lindsay.

Suite, Room 672, at the Hotel Astor. Only one of them, Paul Weissman of the *Herald Tribune*, did anything about it. He checked into the next room in hope of hearing something interesting.

Politicians themselves are largely responsible for the journalistic traffic in confidential information. They exchange tidbits of fact and fancy among themselves and they often pass secrets to reporters on the theory that a friendly version of events in print is preferable to an unfriendly one. A reporter fed daily on leaks can perhaps be pardoned for doing a little eavesdropping.

Somebody mentioned to Rose during the noon recess that Weissman had been seen coming out of the room next to the conference room. Rose charged up upstairs and banged on Weissman's door. The door was opened by William G. Wing, a *Herald Tribune* reporter substituting for Weissman, who had by then returned to his office to start writing the Lindsay story.

Since he and Lindsay had given a noncommittal account of the interview to the press, Rose became more agitated than ever. He pushed his way into Weissman's room. Noticing a piece of jagged wire protruding from a wall he jumped to the conclusion that he had been bugged by an electronic device. He protested vehemently to the *Herald Tribune* over the telephone and issued an indignant statement calling Weissman's action "terribly immoral and terribly unethical." The scooped reporters duly phoned in the statement to their scooped newspapers.

An AP reporter who drifted into our headquarters later said he saw a connecting closet between the two rooms at the Astor with a perceptible crack in the wall. Weissman might therefore have listened to the Lindsay interview without any electronic device. In any case I saw no cause for concern. According to Price, Lindsay agreed to a suggestion by Uviller that, if elected, he should hold weekly cabinet meetings of his commissioners. He accepted a McLaurin suggestion that free tuition in the city colleges be mandated. He urged repeal of the anti-closed-shop Section 14B of the Taft-Hartley Act. He promised to try and hold the fifteen-cent subway fare. He balked at three Liberal proposals—raising the federal minimum wage to $1.50, setting up a police review board composed entirely of civilians, and imposing a city income tax— but even so it would be hard to imagine any Democrat squeezing closer to the Liberal position.

One side effect of Weissman's coup was the blanketing of Ryan's interview. In their excitement over the bugging incident of the morning, the newspapers, radio and TV ignored the afternoon interview. So far as I can discover, Ryan made no particular impression on the Liberals anyway. On Monday they will interview Screvane, who has just picked that renowned Wagnerian debater, Stanley Lowell, as his campaign manager. Later they will entertain O'Connor, who expects to be a candidate; FDR, Jr., whom Steingut now wants to run for mayor on a ticket including Beame for Controller; and perhaps others.

This evening we waited with trepidation for the bulldog edition of the *Herald Tribune*. Among quite a few accurate and exclusive facts, Weissman had one error, to the effect that Lindsay promised the Liberals to "get as far away from the Republicans as possible" if he became mayor.

A check with the stenographic record showed that Weissman caught only a portion of what was said. Lindsay was asked if he would use his position at City Hall to build up the Republican party. He replied he would give the city a nonpartisan administration, but he would reserve the right to endorse individual Republican candidates. Such endorsements, he said, would be "kept as far away from City Hall as possible." Under Price's instructions we issued a news release to clear up any misunderstanding.

Lindsay had the last word—or laugh. He came into the press room with a copy of an April 8 review he wrote of two books on civil liberties: *The Naked Society* by Vance Packard and *The Privacy Invaders* by Myron Brenton. "Frame this somehow," he said, "hang it on the wall and let Paul Weissman get a good look at it!"

The review had occupied the whole front page of the *Herald Tribune* Sunday book section. It was illustrated with the drawing of a gigantic ear into which a large ugly insect was crawling. The headline read: "They're Coming Through the Cracks in the Liberty Bell; QUIT BUGGING US."

Sunday, June 20 — Lindsay has to be tagged as a quiet religionist. He acquired Episcopal beliefs from his father George, a prominent member of the Church Club of New York, and he has never forgotten them. As a boy he sang in a church choir. His undergraduate thesis at Yale concerned "The Effect of Oliver Cromwell's Religion on Politics." He handles political associates with an even-handedness and compassion which are essentially spiritual. In speeches he refers openly and without apology to his conscience. His decisive adjectives on public issues are frequently "right" and "wrong," "good" and "bad." Recently he addressed a luncheon of a businessmen's prayer group at the Biltmore so eloquently that Bob Sykes, a hard-boiled AP reporter, said it was the best speech he ever heard.

Despite these indications of genuine religious feeling, I was flabbergasted today when our schedule called for Lindsay to deliver a sermon in a new and modern church in upper Harlem. During the 1961 campaign, I remember Wagner going to a small Negro church on Lenox Avenue. The preacher told his congregation he never mixed in politics but he wanted them to know two eyes would be fixed on them when they voted to be sure they voted for Wagner. One would be his eye, he said, and the other would be that of God!

Things were more decorous today. Lindsay handled virtually the entire service, reading a selection from the Bible, leading in the responses, giving out the hymns, singing and praying, in addition to delivering a sermon which he told me he wrote himself. The regular pastor was up there with him to lend comfort and support.

"It is a happy privilege for me to be invited by the men's club of Grace Congregational Church to participate in your service this morning," Lindsay said from the pulpit. "I come here to worship with you as a citizen of our city who is deeply committed to achievement of the rights of man—who wants to see New York develop into the best city in the world for people to live in peace and harmony with their neighbors.

"For a text," he continued, "I have selected some verses which have always impressed me because they say what we should remember most—and they say it with tremendous impact. They are from the First Epistle of St. John, chapter 4, verses 20-21: 'If a man say I love God and hateth his brother he is a liar. For he that loveth not his brother whom he hath seen how can he love God whom he hath not seen. And this

commandment have we from Him: that he who loveth God
love his brother also.' "

Lindsay then delivered what amounted to a civil rights
speech, starting with an analysis of Amendments 13, 14, and
15 to the Constitution and working up to the 1957 Civil
Rights law which, as executive assistant to the U.S. Attorney
General, he helped to write and the three later civil rights bills
in the deliberations on which he played a large role. The sermon went well. I glanced around at the racially mixed congregation which almost filled the church and, except for a UP
reporter slumped half-asleep in his pew, it seemed attentive.
As a backslid Protestant myself, I found the whole service,
particularly the rich and powerful singing, quite satisfying.

Monday, June 21 — Our headquarters had to absorb two overnight senatorial punches, one from Javits and one from Bobby
Kennedy. Appearing on TV, the GOP Senator said it would be
nice if the Liberals went along with Lindsay but that Lindsay
could win on the Republican line alone. No doubt Javits'
motives are pure, but his comment seems diabolically calculated to enrage those Liberals who pride themselves on being
the balance of power in New York and to alienate our own
underdog-loving volunteers.

With the transparent candor which is his trademark,
Bobby Kennedy remarked that Lindsay seems to be leading
in the race for City Hall. Lindsay felt uncomfortable enough
about this seemingly innocent remark to call a news conference before leaving for Washington to take part in House
debate on two important bills. With 15,000 volunteers already
signed up, he said, the campaign is moving along well, but
he has to rate himself an underdog in a city with a 7–2 Democratic registration. "It's still a tough fight and I have a long
way to go," he added. A Lindsay spokesman (O'Donnell)
added later that "it's a cold day in summer when a Republican
is ahead in New York City." Today, I believe, is the first day
of summer.

Friends at headquarters argue that my constant references to "Bobby" Kennedy imply disrespect or distaste. This may be so. I am aware that followers of the Senator who are allowed to carry spare shirts for him, since he perspires greatly in his intensity and requires several changes every day, refer to him as "Bob." I am admittedly no shirt-carrier. From where I sit Kennedy is an intelligent young man with a considerable capacity for inner growth. The trouble with Bobby is that the gothic means he employs often taint his objectives.

Tuesday, June 22 — Mary Lindsay delivered her first speech of the campaign today. Since the Women's National Republican Club is on the stuffy side anyway, and its members had expected Lindsay himself, the reception was somewhat reserved. Mary took it in stride. She wore a purple dress trimmed in white with a little white hat on the back of her head and shoes with three-inch heels. To the female newspaper feature writers covering the luncheon she explained that she always carried walking shoes in her shoe tote bag. "My basic colors in campaigning are black, white, and beige and I have shoes to match," she said in a matter-of-fact manner. "Our constant walking tours are good for me, I guess, since I have no time for tennis this summer. Usually John does all the speechmaking but he is in Washington today so I have to work for my lunch."

Having to some extent disarmed the press, Mary continued in the same frank vein when introduced. She enjoyed her job as the wife of a candidate, she said. "I like to meet people and I never think of the results of a campaign until the night of the election." Things had been hectic of late, what with commuting from Washington and preparing the children for the summer. By next week all four of them would be finished with their dental work. Since two of the girls were going to riding camp in Vermont she had been sewing on nameplates. "I never sewed so many in my life. Neither

Margie nor Ann ever had a dozen pair of underpants before this . . ."

To read her speech, Mary slipped on a pair of dark-rimmed glasses. Voter-registration figures in the city were overwhelmingly Democratic, she stressed. Lindsay needed and valued Republican support, but even if all the Republicans voted for him he would have no chance of winning unless he also won the attention and approval of Democrats, Liberals, independents, and "a great number of New Yorkers who do not categorize themselves politically." Lindsay was therefore carrying on "in the LaGuardia fusion tradition," she said.

The women applauded generously at the end of the speech. Mary's mother, Mrs. Randolph C. Harrison of Greenwich, Conn., who had been beaming throughout the proceedings, accepted congratulations on all sides. "She does well, doesn't she?" she kept saying. Somebody broke out a dozen huge shopping bags with "It's In the Bag for Lindsay" stencilled on the side for pictorial purposes. Then Mrs. Elizabeth S. Igelhart, the club president, read a statement undoubtedly prepared in advance endorsing John Lindsay as the regular Republican nominee for mayor.

Wednesday, June 23 — The fratricidal strife between New York Democrats is illustrated by Screvane and O'Connor, both of whom are now avowed contenders for their party's mayoral nomination. They are political neighbors in Queens, a rapidly growing borough second in population in the city only to Brooklyn. Each, in fact, controls approximately half of the Democratic machine in Queens. Moreover, Screvane has advanced to the Number 2 city post as a prime favorite of Wagner, whereas O'Connor challenged Wagner's hand-picked choice for Governor, U.S. Attorney Robert Morgenthau, at a riotous Democratic convention in Rochester three years ago, almost won, and has remained a leading anti-Wagnerian ever since.

In making his declaration Monday, Screvane reached for the best of two possible worlds by promising to carry on in areas where Wagner excelled, while working out new programs where Wagner failed. In his corresponding news conference today at the Queens District Attorney's office, O'Connor wrapped Screvane up with Wagner and then kicked the package.

"We have had enough vacillation at City Hall," O'Connor shouted. "We have had enough ineptness. City Hall needs strength. . . . The new charter gives the mayor unprecedented authority. I propose to use that authority to make our city progressive, alive, and dynamic." He added that anyone as closely associated with the Mayor's record as the Council President had no choice but to defend it.

O'Connor is fifty-five, a wiry, energetic, likable man of medium height with a devout Catholic wife named Mary, a brother who is a priest, and three sons. He went to sea in merchant ships as a youth, worked his way through law school partly as a lifeguard on the beach at Coney Island, and got his start in politics as a conservative worker in the Democratic machine.

After moving up from State Senator to boroughwide office, O'Connor tried to become flexible and social minded in order to appeal to a wider public. As a Democratic prospect for U.S. Senator in 1958 he took a more open-minded position about admitting China to the United Nations than any of his rivals, Catholic or non-Catholic. Asked why he went so far he explained: "There are two Catholic positions in the matter and I stand on the liberal Catholic or *Commonweal* position." His daring probably contributed to his loss of the nomination.

O'Connor took a similar leap today before the Liberal screening committee. He came out for a city income tax, a highly sensible idea for bringing urban revenues in line with runaway expenditures. The Liberals were pleased because no other candidate, including Lindsay, had been courageous enough to support this tax proposal of theirs. O'Connor had hardly returned to his newly opened headquarters, however, when a storm of inquiries and complaints forced him to backtrack. He will probably wind up by opposing all taxes.

Screvane exhibits a different kind of spontaneity. In appearing before the Liberal committee he attacked Lindsay at length as a "Republican fake." The highly opinionated Liberal leaders did not need his opinion on Lindsay and they were either amused or annoyed at this effort to guide their thinking. Screvane hedged on the police review board. He did not even know whether he wanted a Liberal on his citywide ticket. Asked about this by reporters on his way out of the presidential suite at the Astor, he said: "I haven't thought about it yet." Like a prizefighter glimpsing an opening, Price promptly leaked word to the press that Lindsay is prepared to take a prominent member of the Liberal party on his slate even if the Liberals do not endorse him for mayor.

Campaigning last night in Brooklyn, I hear that Screvane addressed the Flatbush Jewish Center as the East New York Yeshiva, a natural enough mistake since both were on his schedule. In correcting himself he said with hearty masculinity that one school was very much like the other and moved on with no apparent consciousness that he had left both feet firmly planted in the stew.

Thursday, June 24 — Though the local press seems bored with our routine, more and more reporters from abroad are observing us. The foreigners appear to be fascinated with every aspect of the campaign, from the way our press limousines are boarded up high with three-colored, Lindsay-for-Mayor signs to the commencement addresses the candidate is now delivering daily. They tag along uncomplainingly on street tours which usually end in the opening of another storefront. By this time we have twenty-six storefronts with another fifty to come by July 1. Lindsay has opened them all except for a few handled by Mary.

Today was United Nations day. Our foreign contingent

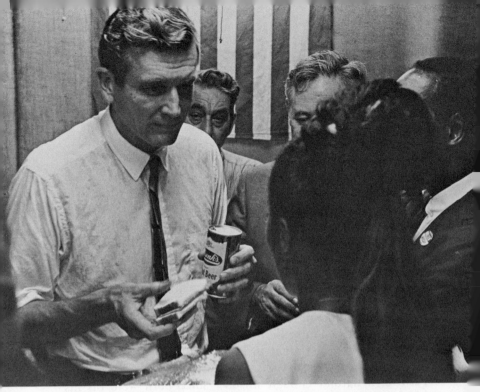

Over sandwiches and soft drinks in a Queens luncheonette . . .

included Knud Bro, twenty-seven, a member of the Danish parliament who writes for a Copenhagen weekly; Bruce Phillips of the *Ottawa Citizen;* Paul Fabre of *Le Monde* in Paris; and Wanjohi Waciuma, of Kenya, a graduate student in international relations at Harvard.

Over sandwiches and soft drinks in a Queens luncheonette Lindsay wanted to know why they bothered with an American municipal campaign. One of them said it was because Lindsay was a magnetic young WASP running for mayor of the most polyglot metropolis in the world.

"It should be ASP," said Lindsay. "All Anglo-Saxons are white. Why be redundant?"

My unexpressed theory is that the foreign reporters are looking for a messiah. They have been assigned to do a political color story but their editors have been attracted by some odd flavor of personality in Lindsay. Other meteors have flashed across the sky: FDR in his day and then briefly, FDR, Jr.; John F. Kennedy and now Bobby; George Romney, Ronald Reagan—make your own list. If more Americans get the quick inquisitorial global treatment than any other nationality it may be due as much to our national capacity to help or hurt other nations as to our public relations techniques.

During our street tour today Lindsay was asked twice what to do about the war in Vietnam. Once he replied: "Negotiate," and the other time: "Get out if we can." If he was brief I believe it was because of the sidewalk crowding and jostling. Generally he tries to answer anything which is asked in good faith.

In the luncheonette Lindsay said he was very much interested in the issues of war and peace because he lost his college roommate in the second world war. "Twenty-five percent of my high school class and almost 25 percent of my college class died in that war," he said. "One of my reasons for going into public life was the wreckage of war."

The foreign reporters pressed him in detail after he remarked that the Johnson administration was "myopic on foreign policy and particularly on Far Eastern foreign policy." He quoted warnings of Churchill, Eisenhower, and MacArthur against getting involved in a land war in Vietnam. Our position at present is worse than it was three months ago, he said, and it is likely to be worse in another three months. "The trouble with escalation in this part of the world is that you can never level off. Each time you try to do so you land in the position you were before escalation."

The discussion in the luncheonette soon took on the lively air of a graduate seminar. Lindsay made references to the 1954 peace-keeping operation in Vietnam, the possibilities of elections, and even of a new swap of populations. Our well-informed foreigners spoke without undue respect. I was delighted by the sharp and pertinent talk but I shall take care not to mention the session to Price. He has been warning John

All Tory hauteur laced with wit . . .

against discussing foreign affairs, on the ground that they are inappropriate in a municipal campaign and sure to lose more votes than they gain.

Friday, June 25 — All Tory hauteur laced with wit, William F. Buckley, Jr., met the press today at the Overseas Press Club to announce that he would run for mayor on the Conservative party line.

How many votes did he expect to get? he was asked.

"One," he said with the toothy smile of an alligator.

What would he do if he were elected?

"Demand a recount," he replied firmly. He will not engage in street campaigning, he specified, having neither time, money, nor inclination for such activity. The patrician twist he gave to "activity" made anybody else's effort in that field seem faintly sordid.

The right-wing editor lives in a large house in Stamford, Conn., with his wife Patricia and their ten-year-old son, but he also pays rent on a city apartment. "I've lived here as long as Bobby Kennedy had when he ran for the Senate last year," he said with a grin. He was on firm ground: in passing on residence requirements for public office the courts generally hold that a man lives where he says he lives if he takes certain precautions such as listing a phone in his name and paying bills there.

Lindsay, said Buckley, "having got hold of the Republican party now disdains the association and spends his days, instead, stressing his acceptability to the leftwardmost party in New York, the Liberal party." He accused both Lindsay and the Democrats of "coolly contriving their campaigns to avoid offending major voting blocs."

"Victims of oppression should be helped to advance by other means than undifferentiated infusions of politically employed cash," he said. "We cannot help the Negro by adjourning our standards as to what is and what is not the proper behavior of human beings." Was there an opaque highbrow appeal there to certain lowbrow prejudices? If so it was not the concern of the reporters. The only opinion perceptible in their stories is that the latest entry in the municipal sweepstakes is likely to prove colorful and intriguing.

Saturday, June 26 — For almost two weeks, not every day, but every second, third, or fourth day, Lindsay has been rudely received on the streets. I'm not sure how much farther it can go without touching off the violence which always lurks just below the surface of politics. I'm annoyed that the organized harassment is done in the name of the Conservative party whose candidate, Bill Buckley, professes disdain for street campaigning.

The same pickets hit us on two separate walking tours in Queens the other day. Apparently they knew our schedule. They had cars to convey them from one place to another. Except for a few older men and women to whom they referred occasionally they were mostly Irish lads in their teens, poorly dressed, ignorant, tough, and loud. A British reporter who was traveling with us referred to them as lumpenproletariat. They carried signs saying SUPPORT YOUR LOCAL POLICE and DOWN WITH SO-CALLED REVIEW BOARDS. When Lindsay was walking they tried to push their signs under his nose. When he climbed to the platform built over one of our Carey limousines, as he did periodically at intersections to deliver a brief talk, they tossed questions and insults up at him. Since he had a loudspeaker he overrode the noise fairly well at first.

After a while the hecklers began chanting: "Fake," "Traitor," and other epithets. Lindsay seemed cool enough but the rest of us showed strain. When one picket—a short boy no older than sixteen—began bawling "Commonist, Commonist," Lindsay's twin brother David rushed toward him with a murderous look. David is as large as John but there is something more elemental and volcanic about him. Since a killing right there on the street would have been bad publicity, however desirable from another point of view, I headed David off, promising to take care of the picket myself.

Leading the boy aside, I asked in a quiet tone what he meant. Lindsay and the other "Commonists" in Congress, he said, had tried to kill the House Un-American Activities Committee. I told him I was a former reporter and that I knew the facts. Lindsay was not a Communist but a strong believer in civil liberties. He and some other liberals in Congress did try to make HUAC a regular subcommittee of the House Judiciary Committee—so it would live up to more civilized procedures—instead of an independent committee. When the motion failed, however, Lindsay voted for the full HUAC appropriation.

By this time other pickets were listening.

"What proof you got, mister?" demanded the boy. "How do I know you're not lying? I got proof."

The boy meant something in writing, a campaign leaflet of some kind, but he did not have it with him and he did not

If a cop had not been watching . . .

know or wish to say who issued it. Since I did lack proof, I resolved to see to it that a Lindsay campaign leaflet was prepared quickly on the subject. The boy began repeating his
original charge, louder than ever. Fortunately, David seemed
to have gone. I let the boy alone then, but later I found myself
shouldering him out of the candidate's path. If a cop had not
been watching, I might have ridden that kid right into the
gutter.

More and more volunteers take part in our walking tours,
particularly when the objective is a storefront opening. These
volunteers tend to form a mobile protective shield around the
candidate, but strangers, particularly shopkeepers, seem puzzled by the clamor of the hostile pickets. One middle-aged
woman asked me seriously whether Lindsay was really against
the police. I said no without convincing her. How do you
make a convincing denial of a charge like that? Being against
the police is like being against God or motherhood.

Many of the pickets are boiling with hatred. I wondered for some time who was stirring them up. Then by accident I got a close look at a SUPPORT YOUR LOCAL POLICE sticker on one of their cars. In small type at the bottom was "Printed in Belmont, Mass."

That's the tipoff, I guess. Belmont, Massachusetts, is the home of the John Birch Society. From earlier journalistic research on the radical right I know that Robert Welch, the founder and leader of the society, prides himself on using Communist tactics in his anti-Communist crusade. Come to think of it some of these pickets resemble the young Communists who used to plague our labor unions in the thirties.

Sunday, June 27 — An increasingly partisan attitude by the police on the civilian review board issue is complicating our street campaign. John J. Cassesse, president of the Patrolmen's Benevolent Society, says he will throw 10,000 pickets into City Hall park tomorrow to protest any civilian review board. This may not greatly affect public sentiment but it will tend to fix opinion within a department which has 26,000 members, most of them married, with large families, many relatives, and friends.

Our schedule today consisted of four short walking tours in Brooklyn neighborhoods ranging from Park Slope to Bay Ridge and culminating in the opening of four more storefronts. In each section we were ambushed by teenagers who, by their behavior and picket signs, were Birchers. They were joined by other apparently non-Birch Conservatives, identifiable by oaktag placards denouncing compulsory school busing, high taxes, and relief payments. Stray signs like WHEN I GROW UP I'LL BE TRUE TO MY PARTY—this on a baby carriage—and COLOR HIM PINK BECAUSE HE'S A FINK may indicate individualists at work.

Walking along Seventh Avenue in Bay Ridge, Lindsay went into stores whenever he saw anybody to greet. He was entering a fur shop when a very fat woman howled from the sidewalk: "Watch out for that hand. It's got Goldwater blood on it!"

Mary Lindsay, who was traveling with us, looked jittery enough to faint for a second or two, but Lindsay cooly completed his handshake with Irving Zack, the proprietor, before turning to rake the fat woman with a glance. At the next corner when he climbed on top of a campaign car for a few words, the pickets worked out a new chant—"Lef–tee Lin–zee, Lef–tee Lin–zee"—which grated with particular unpleasantness on the ear.

Many of the police sympathize openly with the pickets. We have a different detail in each district. In one area I asked the Sergeant to keep the pickets at a distance on the ground that any candidate is entitled to access to the public. The Sergeant listened but did nothing; he seemed amused by the situation. One young Jewish fellow in his twenties, after walking along with us for a couple of blocks listening to the pickets, became furious and shouted at one of them so violently that a fight almost resulted. They sounded like Nazis to him, he said. I approved his show of spirit and gave him the address of our nearest storefront.

LaGuardia had a way of dealing with street harassment in his day. He organized a corps of Italian strongarms called Ghibbones to keep order. Even Javits, during his 1956 senatorial campaign, kept muscular young volunteers on hand to prevent hostile pickets on the Israel issue from disrupting his outdoor meetings. Our advance man, Sid Davidoff, has some husky Raiders. Why not give them some exercise? I suggested today. Davidoff hedged. The situation is not too bad, he said. If it gets worse, he promised, he will note the particular troublemakers and, after Lindsay has moved on, not before, he and his friends will take direct action. Assuming that the pickets hang around long enough to be dumped, this may improve matters, but I am not optimistic.

Monday, June 28 — Today was the day Lindsay won Liberal

endorsement. Our headquarters surged with excitement from early morning until the event actually occurred in the evening. During the day, with an air of deceptive calm, Lindsay delivered one commencement address at Stuyvesant High School and another at the Seth Low Junior High School, addressed a rally or two of volunteers, and opened six storefronts. Except for his periodic dashes to telephone booths to phone Price, nobody could have guessed that this was not an ordinary day.

When the Liberals opened their citywide convention tonight at the Astor, their leaders did not conceal the real reason for Wagner's withdrawal. "You know why Wagner is out?" shrieked Dubinsky. "He had an internal situation in his own party. They wanted him out. He didn't want to tear out his guts. He had enough." More delicately, alluding to last winter's alliance between Brooklyn boss Steingut, Bronx boss Charley Buckley and Bobby Kennedy against Wagner in the struggle over state legislative leadership, Rose said the Mayor stepped aside because of "the persistent and unrelenting obstructionism of his enemies."

The Liberal party policy committee reported 18–1 for Lindsay. The sole holdout was Professor Bowman from Brooklyn College. On the floor of the convention an associate of Luigi Antonini, ailing head of the Italian Dressmakers Union, read an appeal for Screvane, but nobody seemed to be listening. The final vote of the convention was approximately 800 for Lindsay to 50 opposed. The opposition came chiefly from oldtime Socialist unionists who distrust Republicans. "No sooner Lindsay gets elected, the Republican party will not let you forget the Republican party," said one of them. "Let's not build up Lindsay today to fight him tomorrow."

Meanwhile Beame declared for mayor. The amiable bookkeeper, as Javits calls him, read a short statement to reporters at his office in the Municipal Building, without family or friends in attendance. He pledged a regime of fiscal caution if elected. He will be content to end his career as mayor, he said. He made this promise: "I will absolutely not use City Hall as a stepping stone to higher office." During brief questioning by reporters the pint-sized candidate remarked humorously that he did "not see eye-to-eye with Lindsay, politically or physically." His good nature quickly evaporated when a tv interviewer asked if he were "the Steingut-Buckley machine candidate." "I'm sick and tired of that kind of characterization," he replied testily.

Despite his machine origin and machine connections, Beame has a reputation for honesty. In exposés over the years I have found him occasionally on the outskirts of messy situations but never close enough to be identified as conspirator or culprit. Beame also has two disadvantages which may prove advantageous. He fits the mold of mediocrity at City Hall to which regular organization Democrats have become accustomed—and he is a Jew. The large Jewish population in New York has always wanted one of its own for mayor, but with the possible exception of LaGuardia, who was half-Jewish, it has never had one.

Tuesday, June 29 — A 9 A.M. conference today between Lindsay, Price, and the Liberal leaders settled on Dr. Costello as our fusion choice for Council President. The way I heard it, Lindsay left the decision up to Dubinsky and Rose and they picked the good doctor.

Tim Costello is forty-nine, a professor of psychology at New York University, the kind of intellectual Irishman who affects a corncob pipe and waves away a proffered drink. He looks a little like O'Connor but he is both smarter and more idealistic than O'Connor. His father, a city fireman, died when Tim was two. His mother worked as a firehouse matron to support Tim and another child until they became big enough to earn their own money.

Tim set practical objectives for himself in education from which he did not deviate, but he always found time for causes, particularly for the civil rights movement and community mental health programs. Serving as state chairman of a mi-

". . . greater progress can and will be made through fusion government."

nority party like the Liberal party is in itself an idealistic exercise. Tim is the lay commentator for the 10 A.M. mass at his local church. He and his wife Genevieve, a school teacher and certified psychologist, have six lively children. As an Irish-Catholic, Costello adds balance to the ASPish Lindsay but his residence on tiny Staten Island, where he has run unsuccessfully for everything from Council to Congress, does nothing for the ticket geographically.

For lack of suspense, the second evening of the Liberal citywide convention drew a smaller crowd but it seemed exciting enough to me as Lindsay and Costello were approved by acclamation. To please the many Liberals who still love Wagner, Lindsay's speech included a parting pat on the back for the Mayor, to this effect: "I believe that, giving full credit to the present city administration for the contribution it has made to New York, far greater progress can and will be made through fusion government."

In a pleasant but hardly oratorical manner, Costello delivered a talk around the theme that cities consist of people rather than buildings. The fireworks were contributed by Liberal party veterans like Uviller, Rose, Harrington, and McLaurin. The Liberal leaders and the Lindsay contingent then adjourned for refreshments in Rose's sixth-floor suite at the hotel.

Besides the Lindsays, the Costellos, and Price, I noticed Victor Riesel, the blind columnist, picking out friends miraculously by the sound of their voices. Then I joined an admiring group around Dubinsky. He was telling how Javits visited him in hospital one Sunday afternoon not long ago. The two of them watched Costello on a TV-interview program, after which Javits commented: "There's an impressive man. He handles himself very well."

Squealing in triumph tonight at the recollection, Dubinsky said: "We didn't talk about fusion! We didn't need to talk about fusion! I knew what he was saying!" Apparently Dubinsky made up his mind on the nomination of Costello that Sunday afternoon.

Wednesday, June 30 — The time has come for the circulation of designating petitions. Each candidate for citywide office must file at least 5,000 valid signatures by August 10 to get on his party's ballot. When I returned home at 11:30 this evening after a grinding day, I found the living room packed with supporters of Bill Ryan. My wife Avice, a Ryan captain in Park West Village, our middle-income housing project, was preparing petitions with the help of a half-dozen other members of the Riverside Democratic Club. Avice prides herself on being politically independent of me.

"I didn't know you were a Republican, Ollie," remarked one of the visitors. Caught off guard, I replied that I never was a Republican and everybody knew it. Lindsay does better. When somebody refers to him as "the Republican candidate" on the stump he shakes an admonishing finger and says: "Not Republican, *fusion*, remember that."

"Look, I admire Ryan," I told the Ryan zealots. "Lindsay admires Ryan, too. They have a lot in common but I can't understand why you waste your time on a candidate who has no chance."

This annoyed my heckler, who answered that Ryan had a chance. "He's won against odds before this!"

I was willing to be diplomatic. "All right, assume he does his best and loses anyway. How many of you will vote for Lindsay?"

We took a poll. Three said they would ride with the winner of the Democratic primary election and three said they would switch to Lindsay if Ryan lost. Avice declined to commit herself. Even so it looks as if Lindsay will inherit a lot of Ryan Democratic reform support.

☆☆★ *July*

Thursday, July 1 — FDR, Jr., left in mid-air by Steingut's decision to back Beame for mayor, returned to earth today. He told a press conference in Washington that he had discussed his possible New York candidacy with President Johnson— "who said he could give me no specific advice"—and with Bobby Kennedy and Wagner, neither of whom urged him to run. Under the circumstances he saw no point "in being a sixth devisive force in an already divided party." He would not express a preference among the present Democratic candidates —Screvane, Beame, O'Connor, O'Dwyer, and Ryan—since the enrolled voters of the party would attend to the matter on primary day. "I am disheartened and unhappy that the Liberal party has endorsed a Republican," added FDR, Jr. "No matter how you slice it, Lindsay still comes out Republican with a capital R."

During the afternoon we opened 10, yes 10, storefronts in Queens. Toward the end of the interminable tour, word reached me by phone that Homer Bigart of the *Times* wanted a comment on Wagner's departure for Denmark with his sons on vacation while the city is in the grip of a turbulent taxi strike. Lindsay refused to make the expected critical statement. It would cause reporters to descend on Wagner in Denmark, he said, which would be unfair to the Mayor and unfavorable to U.S. prestige abroad.

This evening we held a private party for the Negro press at Frank's Restaurant in Harlem. Lionel Hampton, the musician, was the ostensible host but Harry O'Donnell picked up the $600 tab for the buffet and the drinks. Later we eluded the press and went pub-crawling through clubs on Lenox Avenue. Lindsay did his usual talking, handshaking, dancing, and glass-holding act. He couldn't have done much drinking because he seemed entirely sober when he left at 11:30 for a party in honor of Stephanie Fuchs, a college girl who is working as a volunteer with Mary Lindsay.

Friday, July 2 — Adam Clayton Powell has endorsed Beame. The Controller is squirming a little, but he cannot escape the Harlem Congressman's embrace. Earlier in the campaign Powell said kind words about Lindsay to Lindsay's embarrassment and before that he made tentative gestures in the direction of running for mayor himself.

It was in March, Lindsay mentioned today, that Powell came up to him on the House floor and said: "What are we going to do to get this fellow Wagner out of City Hall?"

To avoid the "we," Lindsay replied: "If you don't like Wagner, why don't you run against him?"

Powell promptly issued a press release that Lindsay had advised him to run for mayor.

A couple of weeks later, Lindsay was waiting for a cab at the Capitol, when Powell came by with an exotic girl. As a gentleman, Lindsay looked the other way while the Congressman and his girl climbed into a red Jaguar and roared off.

On the House floor next day Powell approached Lindsay. "You didn't speak to me last night," he said.

"I thought you wanted privacy," said Lindsay.

Powell laughed. "Not at all. She's Eurasian."

Not quite catching the word, Lindsay said: "What's that?"

"Her parents were Indian and English," explained Powell. He waved his thumb and forefinger in a gesture of ecstasy. "Isn't she wonderful? She's in the office right now. She's one of my secretaries. Come over now and meet her."

Lindsay evaded the invitation but the invitation stuck in his mind. Why did Powell act that way, he asked. I could have replied that Powell is a swinger and Lindsay something of a square, but that might have caused annoyance and it would not have been a real explanation. I guess, I said, that most Ne-

groes who succeed want to display all the white man's virtues.
Powell is different; as proof of his success he wants to exhibit
all the white man's vices.

Saturday, July 3 — A harsh masculine voice has phoned headquarters several times in the last few days to say: "John Lindsay must be killed. We have to kill him." Efforts to trace the
calls have been unsuccessful. Price delayed doing anything
about the threats until he heard reports of the rabid picketing
we encounter during street tours. Then he asked for police
protection.

When our campaign caravan left the hotel this morning
on the start of what was expected to be an exciting three-day
invasion of the city beaches, Detective Barney Allen in civilian
clothes sat in the lead car with John and Mary Lindsay and
Johnny. The reporters riding with me in the second car were
curious about the anonymous, neatly dressed, middle-aged
man with the candidate. I explained he was an old friend of
the family, a businessman who for personal reasons desired no
publicity. Reporters being what they are, the explanation did
not entirely satisfy them. One commented that the man did
not look particularly like a businessman.

Barney Allen's advent bothers me less because of possible
exposure of his role than because of my memory of New York
politics. John Purroy Mitchel, the last pre-LaGuardia fusion
mayor, was shot at by an unemployed dock worker in 1916.
The bullet missed its target and hit another official riding in
Mitchel's car. Before that Mayor William Gaynor was assas-
sinated, I believe by a disgruntled city employee on a ship in
mid-Atlantic. Going outside of New York, there's the assassination of President Kennedy and the attempted killing of
both President Roosevelts and President Truman. Cranks
were involved in the cases of the Roosevelts but the attempt
on Truman was made by Puerto Rican nationalists.

Today's goal was Orchard Beach. Despite cloudy, rather
chilly weather, John and Mary made a brave appearance. He

. . . warmed up by rock-and-roll . . .

was in shirtsleeves and she wore a beige blouse and black skirt and carried a blue plastic pail for Johnny to use in the sand. Our difficulties began with three scheduled preliminary stops in the North Bronx on the way to the beach.

Our news release about the campaign weekend had mentioned various entertainers, including Sammy Davis, Jr., and Liza Minnelli. Sammy is still in hospital recuperating from an unexpected kick in the stomach received from a dancer last Wednesday during a performance of *Golden Boy* and it was specified that his participation depended upon continued recovery. The release also noted that Judy Garland's daughter might not join us until Sunday or Monday. Since the newspapers did not stress these qualifications, the North Bronx crowds, warmed up by rock-and-roll outfits on our flatbed truck, began to ask for Sammy and Liza.

Conservative pickets were out in force. The Birchers among them went through their usual repertoire of annoyance. To some reporters, catching it for the first time, it seemed exciting. Over SUPPORT YOUR LOCAL POLICE signs, the Birchers shouted: "Vote for Lindsay for crime in the streets," and "Hey, John, why don't you debate Bill Buckley? Are you afraid to debate Bill Buckley?" Lindsay ignored them. I was busy scrutinizing the noisier hecklers for possible homicidal intent; it's amazing how many assassins you see if you start from a conception like that.

After the final North Bronx stop, Lindsay talked to the reporters. "I'll debate any candidate, even a nonresident," he said. Asked when such a debate might be held, he replied: "I'll wait and see if Mr. Buckley becomes a serious candidate." Wasn't Buckley a serious candidate yet? "No," said Lindsay, curtly.

A light rain began to fall. The pickets were getting noisier by the minute. John and Mary conferred. They saw no particular point in pulling an army of pickets with them to a deserted beach in the rain so our cars headed back for the hotel. Halfway there the rain stopped and the skies began to clear but by then nobody had the heart to change plans again. Johnny never did get a chance to use his fancy blue plastic sand pail.

Sunday, July 4 — As a candidate in a bathing suit Lindsay has certain undeniable assets. His shoulders, cut square, are as wide as you would expect in a man who once rowed stroke on the Yale freshman crew. He is reasonably well-muscled, with slim hips, tapering legs, and no midriff fat, so his body takes the classic shape of a long triangle pointed down. In swimming he uses a ragged Australian crawl. If there is a board handy he can do a slightly-too-stiff swan dive and a front jackknife which does not quite make his toes. His height keeps him visible above the swarm on the beach and the particular swarm at Rockaway where he plunged into the Atlantic today in his unending search for votes showed considerable enthusiasm.

A sample feminine comment was: "He's adorable. Besides

If there is a board handy . . .

he's got a good honest face." The men may have been envious of his looks and build but they generally liked his appearance. One young fellow with a skeptical jerk of his chin at the passing candidate said: "Is he for real?" I assured him Lindsay was for real.

One young girl, sleeping on her back on the beach, was awakened by the scattering of sand from stampeding feet. She scrambled angrily to her hands and knees only to succumb to blissfulness as she caught a glimpse of the candidate and heard the message of the bullhorn: "John Lindsay, YOUR candidate for mayor, is here to meet you. Step right up and shake hands with John Lindsay, YOUR candidate for mayor. He wants to meet and greet you. . . ."

A middle-aged dimwit at Curly's Baths, where Lindsay and a dozen staff members changed for swimming, boasted that he had shaken hands with the candidate outside the shower when they were both naked. Somebody joked that all men are equal in a shower room. His companion replied that Lindsay was an unusual politician in that he concealed nothing.

Some Conservative party pickets dogged our steps today but they were pretty well submerged in the mob. During a walk on the boardwalk one Bircher grazed Lindsay's cheek with the stick of a SUPPORT YOUR LOCAL POLICE sign. It was the sort of thing we had been worrying about. A swinging stick could catch a man's eye. Teddy Mastroianni, a powerful young Raider, took the picket in both hands, carried him like a parcel to the rail of the boardwalk and dropped him into a vacant pocket of sand eight feet below. Teddy then picked up the fallen sign, destroyed it and placed the pieces in a wastebasket while one of our three alternating police bodyguards, Detective Pat Vecchio, in civilian clothes, watched benevolently.

Show biz and the sun came out today in support of fusion. Up on our flatbed truck rigged with Lindsay panels Lionel Hampton's All Stars played to pull the crowds at several beachfront stops until Lindsay arrived with the comedians, Allen & Rossi, who had been provided by Hal Prince, head of our theatrical division, to add a little color to the campaigning.

"We came down from the mountains," said Marty Allen, "just for this beautiful looking guy who is going to be mayor of New York. Anybody who looks at him, oh boy . . . Marlon Brando is already wearing a black armband."

Steve Rossi then introduced Allen in various quick impersonations, as President Nasser, as Martin Luther King, as Governor Wallace, and finally as Traffic Commissioner Barnes, saying: "Want to solve New York's traffic problem? Make all the streets one-way streets heading West . . . then it will be Jersey's problem!"

Lindsay was introduced as "the star of the show." "Everybody happy?" he inquired like a master of ceremonies. Everybody was happy.

"Thank you for coming here. I hope you'll join with me in making New York a place where everyone wants to stay, not just to visit. I only wish my running mate, Tim Costello, was with me. He's a great liberal, you know."

There was heavy applause for the word "liberal," and Lindsay wound up that stop. Allen & Rossi had to return to town before the next stop leaving us bereft of theatrical celebrities. Youngsters began asking about Sammy Davis. Lindsay was pushing his way through the crowd toward the truck for a speech when I mentioned the restlessness of the crowd. He nodded.

At the outset this time Lindsay apologized for the absence of Sammy Davis. He had visited Sammy in the hospital that morning, he said. Sammy was feeling better and he would definitely be campaigning next weekend. He and Lindsay already had a routine. The candidate then played both parts.

"Sammy will ask me if I have a solution to the traffic problem and I'll say: 'Yes.' Sammy will say: 'What is it?' and I'll reply: 'Make all the streets one-way streets running West.' Sammy will look puzzled. 'How will that solve New York's problem?' he'll say, and I'll say: 'Oh then it will be New Jersey's problem.'"

Lindsay rendered the dialogue of the stolen Allen & Rossi joke so expertly that you almost had the illusion that Sammy Davis was with him. The crowd liked it fine.

If Mary Lindsay had been along, Johnny would not have gotten lost, but she was substituting for her husband at an "I Am an American Day" celebration in Central Park. Johnny was passed from one temporary custodian to another until somebody realized he was missing. Lindsay was getting dressed at Curly's Baths when a group of Raiders triumphantly produced Johnny. The boy's face was tear-stained. He was upset, it developed, not over getting lost but over missing a promised swim.

In a flash Lindsay changed from candidate to father. He began taking off his clothes again. He pulled on his wet green plaid trunks. Johnny donned his own blue and white trunks and they walked hand in hand underneath the boardwalk out on the beach.

Ten or fifteen minutes earlier the sight of Lindsay had excited thousands of bathers. Now nobody spared him and his

The high point was Liza Minnelli's singing . . .

son a second gaze. The pair of them might have been invisible for all the attention they created. It was a miracle. The only explanation I can think of is that New Yorkers do not look at each other unless they have a particular reason, like boy or girl watching, or are reminded to do so.

Monday, July 5 — Another long warm day of beach-and-surf campaigning. The high point was Liza Minnelli's singing of "Hello Dolly" on impromptu stages at several Brooklyn beach clubs as a way of drawing crowds to hear Lindsay. Since Liza had to return to Manhattan to prepare for her role in *Flora, The Red Menace,* the schedule was curtailed, John and Mary and Johnny Lindsay left for the Syosset residence of Rod Lindsay, and I arrived home earlier than expected.

The phone rang. Len Cortella of CBS-TV wanted to know if Lindsay had any comment on the *Newsweek* article giving Rockefeller credit for persuading Lindsay to run for mayor. I promised to call Len back, sent out for a copy of *Newsweek* and braced myself for more calls. Since O'Donnell was away in Albany for the long weekend, they came as expected. I told them all I'd call back when and if we had anything for publication.

The *Newsweek* article, entitled "Untold Tale," appears under the byline of columnist Emmet John Hughes, a former Rockefeller speechwriter. It claims that from the very first the Governor wanted Javits or Lindsay to run for mayor. Rocky explained to his aides that he "had to address his initial appeals to Javits rather than Lindsay" because "Javits is senior and until he says 'No,' I cannot go to John."

Newsweek continues:

> "For some two months, beginning in late 1964, the Governor kept pressing the Senator. One early February day in Washington, Rockefeller (and two of his aides) left a long, quiet lunch with Javits quite convinced that the Senator, at last, was persuaded to run. He was wrong: by Sunday, Feb. 28, Rockefeller learned that Javits had finally decided against the race, and on that day the Governor held his first long conference with Lindsay."

Elsewhere in the article, Hughes mentions Javits' "aspirations to be at least Governor or, more hopefully, the nation's first Jewish Vice-President." It was "almost refreshing," he writes, "to find a senior U.S. Senator calculating his own ambitions a bit unfastidiously, with some imprecision. . . ." Somehow that does not portray Javits as the kind of man a sensible Governor would boom for mayor of New York.

Hughes concedes what he can not deny: that Rockefeller publicly and privately opposed an early candidacy by either Javits or Lindsay. According to Hughes, this was in their interests. "The Governor doubted the wisdom of prematurely pushing a Republican nominee on stage—to be forced to take stands on all controversial legislation still being conducted in Albany."

In late March, the article continues, Price met William Pfeiffer, one of the Governor's advisers, to outline the conditions under which Lindsay might move back into contention for mayor. Far from being remote and ineffectual, Hughes asserts, Rockefeller played a decisive role. "He did what a party leader should; he led." How? By promising that he and his family would "guarantee the covering of $500,000 of campaign expenses."

With the details in alignment in my mind, I phoned Lindsay at his brother's home. He listened carefully as I read excerpts from the article. The statements about Rockefeller persuading him to run or promising a half-million dollars were untrue, he said sharply. "Hogwash, hogwash," he kept repeating.

I phoned Len Cortella who had alerted me to the article first with the denial which he used on his 11 o'clock show. I also called other reporters. Though that completed my official work for the evening, my mind turned to an extremely confidential source within Rockefeller's official family who had helped me in bygone days as a reporter. When I reached him, after considerable effort and some luck, this is what he said:

About two weeks ago, Emmet Hughes talked to George Hinman, the GOP National Committeeman for New York, and the politician closest to the Governor, then visited Rockefeller at his Pocantico Hills estate. (This indicates a deliberate Rockefeller leak.) Rockefeller's choice for mayor was neither Javits nor Lindsay, according to my friend, but Gilhooley. (This squares with what I had previously heard.) When Lindsay told the Governor on May 11 or 12 of his decision to run, my source added, Rockefeller was taken by surprise but had to go along.

Tuesday, July 6 — A man in Rockefeller's position cannot act idly. There must be a political purpose behind the Hughes column. The timing also requires explanation. If the column is directed at Lindsay, why was it published now rather than closer to election, when it would be more deadly? Price provided a clue in midmorning. "Rocky is trying to pressure us into supporting him in case Javits challenges him for state control of the party," he said, "and we won't do it." Later Price flashed into my room, moaned "Oh the terrible things that man is doing to us," and disappeared without identifying the culprit or the things being done.

According to Washington dispatches to the New York newspapers, Javits is being boomed secretly for Governor next year by State Senator John Hughes of Syracuse (no relation to Emmet John Hughes of *Newsweek*). Senator Hughes argues that Rockefeller is incurably unpopular because of his divorce and remarriage, his tax measures and other activities, and therefore should step aside in favor of Javits.

"A campaign in which the Governor runs for reelection will bring nothing but disaster," Senator Hughes wrote Javits on May 14 in a letter subsequently copied and sent surreptitiously to GOP leaders all over the state. "It gets down to a rather basic decision whether the party should be irrevocably damaged because of one person. . . . The fact is we are totally lacking in leadership and the Governor cannot lead since there are very few who will follow. He has no right to take the party, the legislature, and many local officials down with him."

The fact that this round-robin letter, after circulating without publicity for weeks, has now suddenly become public knowledge suggests that the *Newsweek* column may have been designed to bring the anti-Rockefeller movement out into the open where it can be analyzed, met, and perhaps destroyed.

Leaving LaGuardia Airport this morning for Washington, where he will support in debate and vote for the Democratic administration civil rights bill rather than the GOP-Southern Democratic substitute, Lindsay answered questions from reporters on the *Newsweek* column. There was "no basis at all," he said, for the story that Rockefeller persuaded him to run. As for the $500,000 guarantee, "no such promises were made." Would he accept $500,000 if it were offered? "I don't think so," he replied. "I don't think it would be right to accept that amount from two or three people."

One or two new angles developed. Lindsay said he traveled to Albany "about May 11" to tell Rockefeller about his projected candidacy but he made the trip "in a plane borrowed or chartered by Price," not in Rockefeller's *Beechcraft*, as reported in *Newsweek*. "I told the Governor I would want an independent campaign. I would want to go my own way and I wanted no griping. I'm not sure how well received that was."

Did he plan to invite Rockefeller to campaign for him?

"It is my intention to have New York Cityites do the campaigning," said Lindsay. "The Governor lives in Westchester whereas Javits lives in New York City." That was plain enough.

Gabe Pressman, having listened to the newspapermen, tried to sum up briefly in his TV interview.

"Was Governor Rockefeller the prime mover in your decision to run?"

"Not so."

"Did he promise to contribute $500,000 if you would run?"

"Not so."

"Then you don't have a friend at Chase Manhattan?"

"No and isn't it sad?"

Wednesday, July 7 — Sources of controversial information in this diary have generally been identified as I went along. For my slant on the present Rockefeller situation, however, I have cited no source. My reticence stems from an exclusive story I wrote a day or two before Christmas, 1963, which was copyrighted by the New York *Post*.

The story revealed that Mrs. Margaretta (Happy) Fitler Murphy Rockefeller, the Governor's second wife, was expecting a child in May. This was not keyhole gossip of the Winchell variety but legitimate political news. Rockefeller had divorced his first wife, the mother of his four grown children, to marry a considerably younger woman who had worked for him, who had been married to one of his employes, and who was herself the mother of four children she was leaving behind her. Every middle-aged mother of grown children who worried secretly about her husband discarding her for a younger woman was furious, at least for a while, over this revelation. The widespread feminine indignation affected even the male population and handicapped Rockefeller's prospects for the presidency.

The Governor reacted in a churlish manner to the *Post* story of an impending Happy event. "I never comment on gossip," he told Albany reporters, implying inaccuracy on my part as well as invasion of his privacy.

The Associated Press carried the story nationally, crediting the *Post* and adding the Governor's disclaimer. The manager of the rival United Press in Philadelphia remembered that Mrs. Rockefeller's mother lived there and congratulated her by telephone. "Isn't it wonderful?" cooed Mrs. Fitler, thereby confirming the story.

In Albany, Rockefeller was asked for a further statement. He confirmed pregnancy this time but said the expected month was June, not May.

Nelson Rockefeller, Jr., was in fact born May 30, a couple of days before the California presidential primary. The Governor of New York flew back from California to his wife's bedside while the Goldwater people took fullpage advertisements in the California newspapers showing the Arizonan with his happy family, an exercise in indirect morality which took care nicely of Rockefeller's vestigial chances of winning the convention delegates of California.

Under the circumstances it would not be sensible, even in a diary, to uncover my source of information within Rockefeller's official family.

Thursday, July 8 — Price has decided on a judicious disclosure of our financial situation as a way of counteracting the *News-*

week article. We are feeding reporters selected facts. Our campaign contributions to date, it is said, total $210,000 mostly in small amounts. A recent appeal for funds in a series of newspaper advertisements costing $9,000 brought in only $4,857 in contributions. For reasons ranging from poor health to lack of time, several influential Republicans—including Whitney and Thayer of the *Herald Tribune;* General Clay, who was recently named finance chairman of the Republican National Committee; and Horace C. Flanigan, a director of the Manufacturers Hanover Trust Company—have declined to serve as our finance chairman. The payroll at headquarters has been cut 25 percent and the purchase of office supplies has been suspended.

The payroll cut may be a Price device to trim deadwood from the staff. The temporary cutback in paper clips and typewriter ribbons may be a gesture for public consumption. Even the other details may not be as significant as they sound. I doubt that Price undertook the campaign without his required assurances of at least $1,500,000 in spending money.

There was earlier gossip around headquarters of a $100,000 Rockefeller loan. What happened to that? Moreover Lindsay is on closer terms with other members of the family, including the David Rockefeller who runs Chase bank, than with the the Governor. Since the Rockefeller clan and its banking and business satellites reportedly raised $600,000 for Louis Lefkowitz four years ago, a pledge of $500,000 for Lindsay would not be surprising. Rockefeller may be trying to take credit for the family effort. If so, we cannot call his bluff without emphasizing the extent to which the family is helping to meet the bills.

Raising $1,500,000 for a serious Republican effort to recapture the nation's largest city is not excessive. Way back in 1917, Mayor Mitchel raised $2,000,000 for his reelection campaign. Rockefeller himself spent at least $5,000,000 in his unsuccessful pursuit of the GOP presidential nomination last year. I suspect the poor-mouth act we pull in public need not be taken seriously. Certainly nobody is challenging my expense vouchers.

Friday, July 9 — When I contracted to work for Lindsay, Price promised me occasional evenings off to function as president of the New York Newspaper Guild and a week in July to attend the American Newspaper Guild convention in Detroit. Since the Guild presidency is unpaid and nominal, with real authority exercised by full-time paid officials, it mostly involves presiding at meetings. These average one a week. With the cooperation of Price and O'Donnell, my attendance record has been better than usual. However, when I reminded Price today that I was due in Detroit next week for the national Guild convention, he seemed surprised.

"You are president of the New York branch of the union, Local 1?" he said, recovering. I nodded. It's Local 3 but the difference did not seem worth mentioning.

"Who's going to be the new national president—you?" he demanded. I replied that we had a good national president and we were going to reelect him. Price lost interest.

"While you are in Michigan," he said, "you should look up Tom Clark, Governor Romney's Robert Price, and perhaps have a meal with Lieutenant Governor Milliken who is too good to remain Lieutenant Governor." He gave instructions on how to achieve these visits before turning to other matters.

Saturday, July 10 — Because Avice believes airplanes are dangerous, I am traveling with her by train to Detroit with very little to think about except the New York campaign. Tim Costello's clumsy start bothers me. He is such an inherently decent soul that everybody instinctively wants to help him. One of his assistants worked out a nice opening—a handshaking trip on the Staten Island ferryboat which the good doctor has been riding unnoticed for years. By some mischance the reporters and photographers got on one ferryboat and Costello on the other.

"And he has six children!"

They were reunited, but the day did not class as a success. The next day Costello tried to combine handshaking with a family visit to the World's Fair only to be rudely rebuked by an official who said politicking on the fair grounds was taboo.

Harold Prince's theatrical division of our campaign staff has been providing a singer or a small musical combination to warm up street crowds from our flatbed truck. This show-business background encourages Lindsay in his not invariably felicitous master-of-ceremonies mood. The other day he introduced Dr. Costello as if he were a song-and-dance man. "Tim is a full professor at New York University," he said with a moue, as if a full professor at NYU were a native of Uganda. "And he has six children! When does he find the time? And he smokes a corncob pipe—he's angling for the farm vote. . . ."

Certainly Costello has no more serious concern in government than Lindsay himself, but he does smell more of academe.

He made the mistake of responding to the introduction in kind. He even imitated Lindsay's superficial picture of a New York which would be livelier, more responsive to public needs, etc. However, he replaced his corncob pipe with an ordinary black pipe.

Sensing restlessness on Costello's part I had a talk with two of his aides, Philip Finkelstein and Paul Greenberg. The rule in physics that two bodies cannot sit comfortably in the same place applies to politics, I argued, and Costello should therefore take a different stance than Lindsay. Finkelstein and Greenberg agreed that their candidate would do better if he stayed in character.

At the next street corner stop Costello spoke soberly but simply about necessary reforms in such areas as housing and transit. Abruptly Lindsay stopped kidding Costello. He was still a bit too breezy for my taste, but by the end of the day he and Costello were becoming an effective team. It will be interesting to see what happens when our yet-to-be-selected Democratic candidate for Controller joins the other two on the city fusion slate.

Detroit, July 11 — Lindsay is as much a sport in politics as Bobby Fischer is in chess or Artur Rubinstein at the piano. Anybody attempting a definitive biography of him will have to search for clues to his development. He could not endure the daily ordeal of campaigning unless it gave him considerable inner satisfaction. He seems to need assurances that he is helping and pleasing others. This hunger for approval is so transparent and insatiable that it must derive from early family life.

Lindsay's father was a man who rose from messenger boy to president of an international bank, an active outdoor man who sailed his own boat on Long Island Sound and who, almost to the day he died, skated regularly on the Rockefeller Center rink. As a person of consequence in the community, George Lindsay liked to hear public affairs discussed at the dinner table. He played a role in convincing his four sons and daughter that the bad guys of Tammany Hall must be met periodically in electoral combat and reduced to penitence by the good guys of reform.

Lindsay's mother was a former actress who persuaded her sons to take music lessons and participate in school plays. In these areas, as in all others, John had to compete unconsciously but steadily throughout boyhood with George, his elder brother by two years, and David, his fraternal twin. All three were cut from the same mold, tall for their age, rangy, blue-eyed, quick of mind and body, and intensely energetic.

Like the sons of Joseph P. Kennedy, the three older sons of George Lindsay inherited a tradition of intramural rivalry. They tested themselves daily against each other, strengthening their capacities to the utmost. With his advantage in age, George offered a constant target of excellence for the twins. He seems to have been more contemplative in youth and maturity than the others.

Whereas David often acted in an impulsive way, John exhibited a steady temperament. Certain open qualities seem to have made him the general favorite in the family. In no nambypamby sense he emerged as the good brother.

Rod, four years younger than the twins, never played much of a role in the fraternal competition. He was shorter, less athletic, more social than the others. If he needed protection, he turned to John. Whereas George, John, and David became naval officers and lawyers, Rod served in the merchant marine and then moved into his father's occupation of banking.

There is also a sister, Eleanor. She was named after their mother, who died in 1947. As the oldest child by two years, Eleanor helped her mother in keeping the three competitive brothers within bounds. When she married Cooper Schieffelin, the social and wealthy head of a boat-building company and had children of her own she named a son after her favorite brother, John.

The rivalry between John and David Lindsay was intensi-

The rivalry between John and David Lindsay . . .

fied by simultaneous attendance at the same schools: Buckley, around the corner from their home in Manhattan; St. Paul's in Concord, N.H.; Yale College and Yale Law School. The twins rowed on the freshman crew at Yale. Both tried out for freshman football. They belonged to the fencing club, the Elizabethan Club and the Yale Political Forum. Both accelerated and finished college in less than four years but David attained membership in Phi Beta Kappa, the national honorary scholarship fraternity, and Skull & Bones, the most prestigious of the campus societies. John had to settle for Scroll & Key, the second-ranking society, and missed Phi Bete altogether. David dominated several extracurricular activities, whereas John racked up only one presidency, that of the Berkeley Association, a religious group.

After equally meritorious naval service, John and David returned to New York. Both dabbled in politics. John exhibited the better personality for it and David had to be content to assist his twin's candidacy for president of the New York Young Republican Club in 1951. John and a few others incorporated Youth for Eisenhower the following year. After the General's election, Lindsay went to work for Attorney General Brownell as administrative assistant, whereas David rose a notch higher in Washington, to general counsel of the Treasury Department. However, John returned to New York earlier than David and embarked on the soaring public career which now enlists George, David, and Rod in supporting roles.

Detroit, July 12 — Things are beginning to warm up at the Guild convention here, but I have time to put down a few precise notes on how Lindsay became an elective official. Only a couple of weeks ago I ground out a new campaign biography of the candidate which was deemed acceptable, and which is currently being distributed in quantity from headquarters. The details are therefore fresh in my mind.

When Lindsay was mustered out of the navy in April, 1946, he found that his hero, Mayor LaGuardia, had stepped aside after three terms. LaGuardia had been succeeded at City Hall on January 1 by William O'Dwyer, a too-plausible Irishman who at this time enjoyed the support of the Mafia, the Democratic county machines, and a segment of the Democratic reform movement. Obviously somebody was due to be disappointed soon in Bill-O.

Of more immediate concern to Lindsay was a campaign from the right to unseat Joseph Clark Baldwin, the LaGuardia-type Congressman in Lindsay's district, often called the silk-stocking district because it includes many well-to-do people east and south of Central Park, though in recent years it has acquired mixed, less-well-off groups at its north and south ends. Lindsay joined the New York Young Republican Club, a heady group of mavericks who were warning the Republican county leader, Tom Curran, not to dump Baldwin. The ultra-conservative boss brushed off the Young Republicans as "a lot of punks and pinkos." In due time he carried out his plan to hand the Congressional nomination to State Senator Frederic R. Coudert, Jr., a premature Goldwaterite whose chief claim to attention was that he had conducted a legislative investigation of subversive elements in the city school system to such ill effect that Bertrand Russell was prevented from lecturing at City College.

John Lindsay was idealistic enough at the age of twenty-four to be outraged at the backwash from Republican liberalism. He and other Young Republicans pushed Baldwin into a hopeless fight against the machine. Baldwin received nominal help from a few prominent liberals like Mrs. Wendell Willkie, Newbold Morris, Stanley Isaacs, Mrs. Kenneth Simpson, and Angier Biddle Duke (later a Democrat), but the public seemed caught in a postwar mood of weariness and cynicism. Endorsement of Baldwin by the American Labor Party served merely to give the conservatives a larger stick to hit him with as a dangerous radical.

At his father's suggestion, Lindsay had taken a temporary clerical job in a bank. His quick mind, fluent tongue, boldness, and energy did not seem particularly appreciated in the financial district but these were qualities of immediate and conspicuous value in politics. Soon he was neglecting the bank for the Baldwin campaign. According to family tradition, the break came when he tried to conceal a surreptitious cigarette in a wastepaper basket at his father's approach. The basket burst into flame. The resulting fire and Lindsay's banking career were extinguished simultaneously.

Baldwin lost the Republican primary by a humiliating 5–1 margin, but Lindsay carried his election district for Baldwin. This small but certifiable achievement was widely acclaimed by his peers. It looked like an omen for the future. Lindsay felt the potential ascendancy within him. What would have happened, he wondered, if he had run the whole campaign, or if—intoxicating thought!—he had been the candidate?

Lindsay went to Yale Law School that fall but he kept in touch with the anti-Coudert stalwarts in the Young Republican Club. When Oren Root opposed Coudert in the 1950 Republican primary, Lindsay and other club members staged house parties for him, a new technique for reaching well-to-do residents of high-rise apartment houses. As an open opponent of the triumphant Coudert, Lindsay became president of the Young Republican Club. He worked for Ike in 1952 and went to Washington for his reward, but he never lost sight of Coudert, who was building himself up as a target for middle-of-the-road and liberal Republican opposition.

On one occasion Coudert tried to hamstring the President's power to handle foreign policy. On another he urged repeal of the federal income tax which supplies two-thirds of the country's revenues. Through carelessness or laziness or indifference he missed 60 percent of the House roll-call votes. Republicans opposed to him in his district cited the fact that the Democratic vote there was rising from election to election.

In 1957, when Lindsay felt the situation was ripening, he returned to New York. To expand his political contacts he managed a judicial campaign for one of his Young Republican Club associates, Joseph Macchia. Macchia lost. That winter Macchia, Price, and Lindsay began plotting the anti-Coudert insurgency which flowered in the spring. With help from Brownell, a long-time resident of the district, and other liberals, Lindsay forced Coudert into retirement, defeated the organization's substitute in the primary, and went on to win the general election. Boss Curran resigned after this repudiation of his county leadership. Later that same summer he died.

Detroit, July 13 — Harry Van Arsdale, head of the Central Labor Council of New York City, today's guest speaker at the

Guild convention, probably illustrates as well as anybody else what is wrong with the Wagner administration. Van Arsdale is a genuine power broker, a member of the Establishment. What he wants from City Hall he gets. When his construction trades department wants work for its members, it is able to persuade the Mayor to endorse the Lower Manhattan Expressway, a monstrosity of a project which would bisect the Italian parish of San Gennaro and Chinatown, two of the oldest communities of New York.

Van Arsdale hails from Local 3 of the Electrical Workers Union. Since the Department of Water Supply, Gas & Electricity licenses electrical workers, Van Arsdale has been helpful in placing the last three commissioners of this city department who were former business agents of Local 3. None of these gentlemen knew much about water and the city is currently facing a water shortage. Take another example. The Uniformed Firemen's Association, one of Van Arsdale's Council members, regularly contributes to Democratic mayoral campaigns. It has managed almost at will to shift members from one borough to another according to family necessities, regardless of the identity of the Fire Commissioner.

As head of the New York Local of the Guild, I was assigned to meet Van Arsdale today and escort him to a hotel suite for a chat over drinks until time came to produce him on the convention floor. I must admit that the stocky weatherbeaten old unionist proved unexpectedly affable in casual conversation which did not touch on the New York mayoralty. Subsequently Van Arsdale delivered a speech on the shorter work week in which his local of the electrical workers has pioneered. I am obliged to report that he proved effective as an orator and won more applause than any previous speaker at the convention.

Detroit, July 14 — According to New York newspapers available here, Brooklyn boss Steingut has persuaded O'Connor to step out of the race for mayor and run for Council President on the Beame ticket. O'Connor is a sufficiently good vote-getter to strengthen considerably the anti-Wagner forces led by Beame. Tim Costello will find it difficult if not impossible to defeat O'Connor for Council President.

On impulse I made a long-distance call to Costello. He believes O'Connor won a promise of support next year for Governor from Steingut and Bronx boss Charley Buckley. This sounds reasonable since Steingut was trying earlier to shape up an FDR, Jr.–Screvane–Beame ticket by promising Screvane that FDR, Jr., would run for Governor next year and thus, if he won, allow Screvane to inherit the city.

The third man on the Beame ticket will be Civil Court Judge Mario Procaccino, fifty-three, the Italian-born son of a shoemaker. Procaccino's chief claim to consideration was faithful service in Charley Buckley's Bronx machine.

Lansing, Michigan, July 15 — Following Price's suggestion, I slipped away from the Guild convention today for luncheon at the Capitol with Lieutenant Governor William G. Milliken. He turned out to be a personally attractive liberal business-man in his early forties. A friend and former classmate of Lindsay at Yale, he asked many questions about Lindsay's campaign which I answered as well as I could. He also described his own recent county-by-county tours in Michigan in which he made himself personally available to citizens for appeals, complaints, and suggestions.

From the tenor of his remarks I gather that Lieutenant Governor Milliken would like to run for U.S. Senator next year but does not expect to have the opportunity. He would still be able to run for reelection with Governor Romney. He expects Romney to roll over the opposition again and to grow greatly in national stature. He would not be at all surprised if Romney became the GOP presidential nominee in 1968. I enjoyed the visit but I am not sure what was accomplished beyond making a contact of possible use if Lindsay himself nurtures national ambitions.

Detroit, July 16 — The death of Lindsay's sister is reported in a front-page story in the *New York Times*, which is sold in considerable quantity at my hotel here. Mrs. Schieffelin's body was found floating face down in the swimming pool on her Long Island estate around 2 A.M. yesterday. Her son John, seventeen, returning home after a visit to friends, noticed a light burning in the library. The library light was always on when Mrs. Schieffelin swam at night, but the pool lights were out. John called his mother. When she did not respond he decided to switch on the pool lights. He pulled his mother's body to the edge of the pool. After shouting to awaken his father, the maid, and the butler, he made a futile effort at mouth-to-mouth resuscitation.

According to the newspaper account, Mrs. Schieffelin was a tall, outgoing woman of forty-seven, in good health except for an ulcer which had been responding to treatment. She had left a note in the kitchen asking to be waked up at 8:15 in the morning. According to friends she had an appointment with her dentist yesterday and another with some friends to play bridge. Nevertheless an initial autopsy by the medical examiner proved inconclusive as to the cause of death. There were no signs of injury or foul play.

To garnish the mystery, the reporter touched subtly on the family's wealth and social position. Cooper Schieffelin was a descendant of the Schieffelin family which settled in New York before the Revolution. In addition to running a boat-building company of his own he was the second cousin of William Jay Schieffelin, 3d, president and chairman of Schieffelin & Co., a wines and spirits importing and pharmaceutical concern. The Laurel Hollow, L.I., estate of the Schieffelins, the story noted, consists of eleven acres in a wooded section near Syosset "known as Nassau County's gold coast."

The twenty-by-twenty-foot swimming pool is located a short distance to the east of the twenty-room English Tudor house. Mr. Schieffelin last saw his wife alive in the library about 10 P.M., just before he went to bed. He and his wife used separate bedrooms in the summer, he told police, because he likes air-conditioning and she did not.

Since I knew everybody concerned, I pored over the details of the story with some shock and depression. Lindsay received a call at the Roosevelt from his twin David around 3 A.M. He collected his sister's children—Julia, twenty-two, and Lindsay, twenty, Schieffelin—who have been living with friends in New York while working in the campaign, and with his brothers George and Robert and Mary drove out in a borrowed car to Laurel Hollow. Lindsay cancelled all campaign engagements for several days.

Anybody can commit suicide in a spasm of depression but it would seem implausible for a woman of Mrs. Schieffelin's temperament. Despite the mystery story setting, murder can be ruled out. Everything points to an accident, but the uncertainty is unfortunate.

Late today, in connection with a request of Lieutenant Governor Milliken for copies of certain Lindsay campaign material, I had occasion to phone campaign headquarters in New York. I was relieved to learn that the medical examiner has concluded the drowning was accidental. The medical examiner apparently did not make public the reasons for his verdict. The funeral will be held tomorrow at St. John's Episcopal Church in Cold Spring Harbor, L.I.

New York, Sunday, July 18 — Lindsay is back on the campaign trail and I am back with him. He seems alternately absent-minded, cynical, and lazy—qualities which are not at all characteristic of him. Our morning schedule called for an invasion of Lincoln Terrace Park, the Botanic Gardens, and Prospect Park in Brooklyn. It was poor scheduling; the scenery was pleasant but the populace was absent. Fortunately we had no press coverage. The weather had been threatening but the sun unexpectedly broke through the clouds, warm and pleasant. We strolled.

Lindsay moved ahead at one point and I came on him staring fixedly at two caged bears in a small circular zoo whose existence I had never suspected. He started perceptibly at my approach. "I'm trying to figure out which of my Democratic opponents looks most like that big black fellow over there," he explained. I suggested Screvane. Others who joined us preferred Beame. One even fixed on Bill Buckley as the bear's look-alike. For some reason the resulting jollity rang a bit false.

The tropical-smelling Botanic Gardens were deserted. Our walk-through was about as relevant to a campaign as a waltz is to war. We actually got stuck in a neglected box-hedge maze. Whimsically rather than in anger, Lindsay asked: "What path shall we now follow in pursuit of the reluctant voter?" There was not a voter in sight.

Later we did run into a cluster of citizens. Since campaigning in a park is forbidden, we had no barker or signs. As soon as one woman realized who Lindsay was, she asked truculently: "Can I get a favor if you are elected?"

"Certainly, if it can be done," replied Lindsay, meaning I suppose that the favor would have to be reasonable. In an audible aside he added: "Ask not what you can do for your city but what your city can do for you."

Word came via car telephone and panting Raider that Javits wanted to talk to the candidate. Lindsay entered an open-air booth. He stood there in the oblique glare of the sun for nearly ten minutes. When he emerged his head, arms, and shirt were soaked with sweat. It looked as if the conversation had been an ordeal.

After the Javits phone call our political minstrels wandered into a meadow at the other end of which a crowd was watching a soccer game. Instead of striding toward the voters, Lindsay dropped to the grass and everybody dropped with him.

"I feel tired," he said, for the first time I can ever remember. He looked tired. There were fresh lines under his cheekbones. The campaign was half over. If he dropped out now, it occurred to me, the repercussions would be endless. Of course he could not drop out!

During the trip back to the Roosevelt . . .

The death of Mrs. Schieffelin was on everybody's mind but nobody knew how to broach the topic. The conversation remained inconsequential and halting. We all felt sympathetic and Lindsay managed somehow to convey acceptance of our sympathy.

After ten minutes or so, he struggled to his feet and led the way slowly toward the campaign cars, which were required to remain outside the park limits. During the trip back to the Roosevelt Lindsay decided to curtail his afternoon schedule. In the past he has lamented once or twice to me that he cannot seem to sleep during the day when he gets a chance, but when I checked at 2:55 P.M. to see if he would comment on something for John Reilly of CBS-TV, Barnie Patterson said it was impossible. The candidate was taking a nap.

Monday, July 19 — Javits has reason to be unhappy. He was not consulted about the choice of our finance chairman or even about Lindsay's capitulation to Rockefeller. Lindsay probably had to yield to Rockefeller. His campaign was being strangled by Albany's pursestring-pulling. To breathe, he declared that Rockefeller had been "a good Governor" and that he would "take no part" in the effort by some New York Republicans to persuade the Governor not to run for reelection next year. Lindsay completed his pilgrimage to Canossa by saying he will support Rockefeller for another term.

Somehow reporters heard about the $100,000 Rockefeller loan, which has been the subject of gossip at headquarters for several weeks. Lindsay's explanation is interesting. On June 1, he says, Price went to his own bank for a $525,000 loan to keep the campaign moving. The bank wanted guarantors—in my circle we say co-signers—of the loan.

"All kinds of nice people promised financial help when I was considering whether to run," Lindsay noted, "but these promises did not materialize into cash. We were in hock." Then Thayer of the *Tribune*—"the only guy in New York with guts," in Lindsay's words—began knocking GOP heads together. He lined up several guarantors before approaching Rockefeller, but the Governor offered a $100,000 loan in his own name instead. That cut the $525,000 loan down to $425,000.

Lindsay wound up his explanation by expressing hope that the $100,000 Rockefeller loan would turn into a contribution and that the reported $500,000 collective gift from the Rockefeller interests would become an actuality. He is waging an aggressive, expensive fusion campaign with eighty storefronts for volunteers already in operation and more expected to open soon. If he did less, he pointed out, those who raised questions about his campaign financing would be carping about "the usual feeble GOP effort to capture City Hall."

Lindsay is giving out more details on his financial balance sheet. Javits, he notes, promised to raise $250,000 but has produced only $4,000 so far. This sounds invidious to some reporters but it does not disturb the Senator. He knows precisely what he can do in the way of fund-raising and in his own sweet time he will redeem his pledge.

What does roil Javits is the appointment of Bernard J. Lasker as our finance chairman. Lasker, a heavyset stockbroker known incongruously as Bunny, has a reputation for raising money—they say he has raised $50,000,000 for various charitable causes—but he is not particularly hep in politics. "I hope to God that the feuding I've been reading about between Javits and Rockefeller is not true," he told reporters in an initial press conference. "If it is true, it makes my job an impossible one."

Nothing could have jolted Javits more. Rockefeller has announced he does indeed intend to run again for Governor in 1966. Senator Hughes' letter is still circulating. Without Lindsay's obeisance, Rockefeller might not have dared to throw down the gauntlet to his party critics at this time. Javits is now left standing alone outside the closed door of the Executive Mansion in Albany. No wonder he talked Lindsay's ear off over the telephone yesterday. One consequence of their discussion, I learn today, is that Bunny Lasker will avoid all interviews in the future.

Tuesday, July 20 — Our city ticket has been rounded out by the selection of Milton Mollen, forty-nine, Wagner's housing coordinator, as candidate for Controller. Politically he can be described as a Brooklyn Jew who owed his start in government to the Democratic machine, but who drifted away from the clubhouse boys as a result of a growing personal relationship with the Mayor. He has an acceptable family: a nervous, community-minded wife and two children. At his initial press conference he stressed that he has been, is now, and always will be a Democrat, but that he feels the need for a reform-minded fusion administration.

A rumor that Mollen would join the Lindsay-Costello

team hit Screvane unexpectedly during a TV panel show Sunday. Flustered and irritable—TV is such a revelatory medium at times!—Screvane said he could not, until he checked the report, decide whether Mollen was "the Brutus of this campaign" or merely "an ingrate." Later Screvane said Wagner and he had raised Mollen over a period of a few years "from a very low-paid Assistant Corporation Counsel" to positions of importance. He implied betrayal: Mollen had sat in on his own campaign strategy meetings.

"At least two intermediaries for Mr. Mollen approached me as recently as four days ago, asking for a place for him on my ticket," said Screvane. "I told them he was unacceptable."

Mollen met the outburst calmly. By agreement with Price he was not supposed to confirm his candidacy until our press conference but he told reporters: "I never sent intermediaries to Mr. Screvane and I never contemplated running with him."

Because Mollen is warp and woof of the Wagner regime— he still has not resigned as housing coordinator—half a dozen Democratic spokesmen are working him over verbally.

"When Mollen joins the Lindsay ticket he joins the Rockefeller-Nixon ticket," says Beame.

Lindsay had no comment on this for publication but he complained about it privately. "Why does he bring in Nixon? I could say Beame is running on the Sparkman ticket. He supported Sparkman for Vice-President in 1952. It's just as irrelevant."

It would be comforting to interpret the Democratic outcry as proof that Mollen's selection is a great coup. Unfortunately there are Republican complications. Mollen is committed to a variety of Democratic programs such as the Lower Manhattan Expressway which Lindsay has attacked.

Charles G. Moerdler, a campaign activist who is president of the New York Young Republican Club, came tearing along the corridor at the Roosevelt this morning with a wild look on his face. In five separate reports over a period of a year and a half, he said, the club excoriated the city's housing program and demanded Mollen's resignation. The final club report was read on April 14 into the Congressional Record by Lindsay himself! An impulsive man, Moerdler has already told at least one newspaper reporter how he feels about Mollen.

Another blast emanates from I. D. Robbins, the independent Republican whose name Javits had once proposed for our ticket. "Mollen is the least effectual person in the Wagner administration," he said for publication today adding that he might repudiate Lindsay as a result. Among friends, Robbins is quoting Price's cynical explanation of the selection of Mollen: "We already have the good government people. Now we are looking for the bad government people." That's the kind of thing Price does say sometimes for effect, only half meaning it. Unhappily some of our less flexible Republican workers who distrust all Democrats openly exhibit their disgust over Mollen. Hardly anybody at headquarters has a good word for our new Democratic running mate.

Wednesday, July 21 — More on Mollen:

To some degree he was a choice of desperation. Such businessmen and financiers as George Backer, Benjamin Buttenwieser, Orin Lehman, and Edward Warburg—all Democrats living in Manhattan—previously rejected overtures to join the Lindsay ticket. At one time Alex Rose offered the designation to Arthur Levitt, Jr., son of the State Controller, a Brooklyn Democrat. Junior, a lawyer active in all his father's campaigns, was interested in the idea but Poppa would not permit his partisan picture to be sullied.

Frank Meehan, a businessman friendly to Mollen, passed word to him two weeks ago that he was on a secret new list of Lindsay prospects for Controller. This list was compiled by Price after a dozen more conspicuous eligibles backed away. When the list was shown to Rose, he checked several names acceptable to him. Since Mollen always consulted Rose on city housing moves affecting Liberal policy or personnel, he was among those checked.

. . . Mollen did switch . . .

For one reason or another all those on the list except Mollen were eliminated. Friday before last, Price phoned Mollen, but Mollen declined to see Price on several grounds—one being that Wagner, who would have to be consulted on any such radical proposal, was vacationing in Denmark with his sons. It is possible that Mollen still hoped Wagner might back him for a spot on the Screvane ticket.

Rose took up the pursuit. Mollen tried to hide, but Rose tracked him down through his doctor and persuaded him by phone to come to the Hotel Astor for a conference, the Sunday before last. Mollen kept saying no somewhat less positively.

On Wednesday Mollen met Price but nothing was settled between them. For a total of eight hours on Wednesday, Thursday, and Friday, Mollen conferred with Wagner, who had returned from abroad. The Mayor said Mollen would be committing political suicide if he went over to fusion but that life is "a series of calculated risks" and he had a right to make his own decision. Wagner gave no solid advice one way or the other. In case Mollen did switch, he volunteered, he would say publicly what he thought privately, that Mollen was a fine man and a fine public servant. That did the trick. Mollen saw Price on Friday to declare he would run. Because of his sister's death, Lindsay missed most of the negotiations.

In his joint press conference with Lindsay, Mollen stressed his "very deep and affectionate regard and respect for Mayor Wagner . . . [who has] given unstintingly of himself in the interests of the people of our city despite the most trying political, governmental, and personal tribulations." The reporters converged on City Hall for the Mayor's reaction. Julius Caius Caesar Edelstein and Debs Myers prepared a blistering attack on Mollen, I am told, but Wagner refused to use it. His eventual statement went almost as far in praising Mollen as he had promised.

Today Lindsay had to answer charges that our enlistment of Wagner's housing coordinator implies endorsement of Wagner's housing policies. Not so, he said. Mollen obeys orders in his present job, which he is finally resigning today, and he was frustrated by red tape and lack of funds. If elected Controller, Mollen will be allowed to help make housing policy. Lindsay then outlined a partial housing program of his own which he said would be a great improvement over present policies.

Thursday, July 22 — Screvane has filled out his citywide slate by choosing Daniel Patrick Moynihan, a writer from Washington, to run with him for Council President; and Orin Lehman, the physically handicapped grandnephew of the late

Gov. Lehman, to run with him for Controller. Neither Moynihan nor Lehman has ever previously run for public office. They are so unknown to the general public that their selection, on the surface at least, provides an abject lesson in impractical politics.

Orin Lehman is handsome, wealthy, well-educated man of forty-five. Tragically, for a person of his promise, he lost one leg and the use of the other during the war. After the war he earned a Ph.D. at New York University and taught American history at the New School. He worked several years at Lehman Brothers, the family investment firm, and left it to buy five upstate weekly newspapers and four radio stations. Later he sold the newspapers. Three years ago he married the former Mrs. Jane Bagley Long and they now have an infant daughter plus a son by her previous marriage. Screvane reportedly worried over the possibility that marriage to a "shikse"—the Yiddish word for a non-Jewish woman—might alienate Jewish voters, but he evidently concluded that the Lehman name and fame and money outweighed this disadvantage.

Pat Moynihan is the son of a Third Avenue tavernkeeper. He was raised in New York, but saw little of the city after he grew up. He served in the Navy and studied partially at least under the G.I. bill of rights at Tufts College, the Fletcher School of Diplomacy, and the London School of Economics. I first met Pat in 1955 when I covered Albany for the *Post*. He was then a writer for Governor Harriman, a tall, red-cheeked fellow of twenty-eight, with a penchant for annoying traffic cops.

Early in Harriman's term, Pat married the Governor's pert and efficient secretary, Liz Brennan. They went to live on a mountain top miles from Albany in a house which was cut off from civilization whenever it snowed. They became great favorites of the Harrimans. When the Governor failed of re-election in 1958 he transferred his official papers to Syracuse University on condition that Pat Moynihan serve as curator with a teaching title on the faculty. Subsequently he arranged for the appointment of Pat as an Assistant U.S. Secretary of Labor.

Soon after their arrival in the District of Columbia, Pat and Liz did some trespassing on a large neglected estate in the course of a hike. They noticed an unused stable which could be made habitable. They located the lawyer for the estate and persuaded him to lease the stable to them and their three children. Since the lease carried with it access to many acres of property, the Moynihans were thereupon established as slightly seedy landed gentry.

Pat performed acceptably as a Washington bureaucrat, finding time on the side to write a book with Nathan Glazer on minority groups in New York City entitled *The Melting Pot*. The financing was provided largely by Mrs. Dorothy Schiff, publisher of the New York *Post*, who utilizes a private philanthropic fund for such purposes.

Last summer, during the Democratic national convention in Atlantic City, Liz Moynihan managed a hotel suite there which Harriman utilized to sell the personality and political prospects of Bobby Kennedy to other New Yorkers. Pat played an aloofly astute role in this same operation and can therefore be classified as an original New York Bobby Kennedy man.

I was relieved to discover in Atlantic City that the years as a faculty member in Syracuse and as a government official in Washington had not dulled Pat's creative kookiness. Around 9 A.M. one day during the convention, in a pouring rain, a solitary person appeared outside my hotel on the beach in a bathing suit. It was Moynihan. I can certify this because I joined him for a swim in the rain.

Friday, July 23 — My most exciting discovery in this campaign to date is how Pat Moynihan landed on the Screvane ticket. If I can believe what I hear privately and I am inclined to believe it because it fits the known facts, Wagner and Bobby Kennedy utilized Moynihan to make a far-reaching division of political power in New York State. Here is how it worked out:

As soon as he declared for mayor, Screvane realized he must somehow placate Kennedy, who had worked behind the scenes last winter with Steingut and State Democratic Chairman William H. McKeon against Wagner's choices for Democratic leadership of the state legislature. Screvane secretly offered a place on his ticket to Stephen P. Smith, the Senator's brother-in-law and campaign manager. Smith might have nibbled but Wagner, hearing about it, exploded in annoyance over not being consulted by Screvane. That ended Smith's prospects.

The next development was a *Times* dispatch from Washington that "associates of President Johnson" were grooming Moynihan for a large political role in New York City. The President denied any such purpose. Other sources suggested that Moynihan's real sponsors were Harriman and Bobby Kennedy. Screvane became interested. This time he consulted Wagner before he acted. Wagner said he would take Moynihan if Kennedy agreed to dump McKeon as State Chairman. Kennedy agreed to dump McKeon—last winter's ally—on condition that Binghamton Mayor John J. Burns become the new State Chairman. Wagner's choice for a successor to McKeon had been George Van Lengen of Syracuse, but after consideration he agreed to drop Van Lengen for Burns. The dickering freed Screvane to grab Moynihan as an attractive new personality who might also consolidate his own political position.

I can imagine some unwritten codicils to the Wagner-Kennedy agreement. If Screvane becomes mayor, he and Kennedy will support Wagner for Governor next year. If the entire Screvane ticket wins, a Kennedy follower will move into the Number 2 spot in the city. Even if Screvane loses, Kennedy will exercise state control through John Burns.

Saturday, July 24 — Our daily exploration of the sidewalks of New York continues without letup. My pockets are full of untranscribed notes. It's near midnight; I must be up again at 7 A.M. The sensible thing is to select one item and forget the rest, but the mind balks at the necessity of choice. I shall select several items under appropriate headings and so, as Pepys writes, to bed.

RATS. Shortly before dusk yesterday we made an unscheduled visit to a lot in Harlem filled with beer cans, mattresses, bricks, broken bottles, and garbage. Mary Lindsay had sense enough to remain in a campaign car. Lindsay was entering the lot from a rear door of a tenement when a marble stair collapsed under him. Luckily he wasn't hurt. The superintendent said the building had not been repaired or the lot cleaned in least a year. Local kids had left six freshly killed rats in a cardboard container for our inspection. That sight and the stench made a female magazine writer who was with us faint. Lindsay called for a cleanup, but from the hopeless demeanor of the residents I suspect no cleanup would last long.

HELICOPTER TOUR. The increasing sophistication of our campaign is indicated by this morning's inspection of the city from the air. A large group of reporters and photographers were on hand when Lindsay, two city planners, and the pilot returned around noon to the West Side Heliport. "I'm depressed by what we saw but exhilarated by the potential," declared the candidate, reading from clipboard notes. "Staten Island is being devoured by land-grabbers. . . . Breezy Point needs public transportation or most of it will be consumed in parking lots. . . . The post-World's Fair plans are a hand-me-down scotch-tape job. . . . A growing borough like Queens requires a master plan. . . . The only green we saw in Brooklyn was for the dead in cemeteries. . . . New York City is a saltwater city but the people have been barred from the waterfront." Next week Lindsay will take a more intimate look at the waterfront from the deck of a cruising tugboat.

RENAISSANCE MAN. This afternoon Lindsay made his delayed tour of Orchard Beach. On the way he spoke at a North

Bronx protest meeting over an exposed city garbage dump. When a group of equestrians came by, Lindsay borrowed a horse for a canter. At the beach he joined a group which was dancing the hora to music provided by two guitars.

FOREIGNERS. This week has seen a new rash of coverage from abroad, stimulated, I imagine, by the beach stories and pictures. These visitors include a fellow named Biaggi and an assistant with an unpronounceable name from *La Stampa*, an Italian magazine; Gerd Rugge and Werner Kohn, West German TV; David Magnus of Rex Features, London, a photographer; and Moursi Rajaa, an ultra-polite but somewhat bewildered United Nations correspondent from Beirut. My favorite was Elsa Arana Freire, editor of the weekend supplement of *La Prensa* in Lima. "He looks like the hero of a cinema," said Miss Arana. "And he is so lean. He must be an active sportsman. We in Peru are very interested in all world affairs but particularly in this country's and I wanted to see in person this Lindsay we hear so much about."

HONEYMOON. Wagner and Barbara Cavanagh will take a wedding trip to Marco Island off Florida, they told several hundred friends last night at a "late engagement party" at the 21 Club. Cardinal Spellman will perform the ceremony Monday in Saint Patrick's Cathedral. There will be a reception at the Cosmopolitan Club. The town has not witnessed the nuptials of an incumbent mayor since Bill-O espoused Sloan Simpson, the model, in 1949. The guest list at the Wagner reception includes Screvane and Beame, Mayor Burns of Binghamton, Bobby Kennedy, and President Johnson, and their wives.

Sunday, July 25 — At first sight, Sammy Davis is frail and small and screwed up so tight that you wonder whether he can do what he has to do. Then he gets rolling and concern vanishes in a wave of enjoyment. Making his twice-postponed beach tour with Lindsay, he unbuttoned his shirt, tying the

. . . tails in a knot across his stomach . . .

tails in a knot across his stomach to bare his ebony torso. He mugged, signed autographs, kissed babies, and exchanged irresistibly lame quips with his fans.

"Why isn't Frank Sinatra here? What a silly question. He's doing my laundry, of course."

To a handball player stripped to the waist at a Manhattan Beach court he said: "I don't care how long you stay out in the sun, baby, you aint gonna get my color."

When our man at the bullhorn intoned: "Folks, that tall, good-looking man with the blue eyes and sandy hair right behind me on the boardwalk is John Lindsay," Davis tapped him on the shoulder to say: "Hey, man, I'm right behind you and my hair aint sandy."

Sammy Davis and Lindsay ate corn on the cob, stuffed cabbage, and roast beef. They drank cream soda and orange pop. They dueled in Scooter cars and made speeches from our flatbed truck.

At Surf Avenue and 12th Street, Coney Island, where a rock and roll band had collected a crowd around the truck while Lindsay went for a swim in the ocean, Sammy shouted: "I don't care if you're black, white, yellow, or pink. So goes the Negro, so goes the Puerto Rican, so goes the white man. Let's get behind this man Lindsay."

When reporters started a press conference with Lindsay on Brighton Beach Avenue, Sammy piped up: "Doesn't anyone want to ask me about Alabama or Mississippi?" Taking over in the wake of laughter, he explained that Lindsay has "the same kind of people-to-people communication as the late President Kennedy," for whom, as a Democrat, he also campaigned.

The imperishable scene of the day has nothing to do with Sammy Davis. In the midst of a revolving crowd of kids of all ages and sizes Lindsay is crossing a concrete space near a swimming pool. A man-sized trash can stands directly in front of him, perhaps 20 feet away. Worried over the prospect of some youngster getting crushed against it, Ted Mastroianni, our most powerful Raider, lifts the can over a low hedge.

Unfortunately, the can drops on an unseen sunbather stretched out in a beach chair on the other side. Beet red from the sun or homicidal rage, the sunbather gets up—and up and up. The giant focuses on the approaching candidate and shouts: "Nobody can put an ashcan on my head! I can't even vote for the man. I live in Nassau . . ."

Sid Davidoff, the onetime wrestler who heads the Raiders, moves in front of the angry man. With a gentle chest-high revolving motion of both hands, palms outward, he slows the man down until a friendly lifeguard throws an arm around the man's shoulder and with cajolery and laughter leads him away.

Monday, July 26 — Rockefeller and Javits are now officially reconciled. They resemble the married couple that gets as far as a courtroom in a bitter divorce action before deciding on a fresh start. The two leading liberal Republicans in New York hope for a mutually satisfactory future but they cannot easily forget the insults they recently exchanged.

Speaking in Minneapolis yesterday at the annual Conference of Governors, Rockefeller vowed never to run again for President. He promised to push Javits for Vice-President in 1968. Javits responded today by pledging support of Rockefeller for reelection as Governor next year. Javits believes he has won a substantial victory. He tells friends he has been urging Rockefeller to pull out of the presidential sweepstakes so the moderate wing of the GOP can solidify behind somebody like Romney in 1968. A Romney-Javits ticket is not impossible.

There are perils in planning politically so far ahead. One is that nobody runs for Vice-President. A nationally known prospect with pockets full of cash and the backing of his home state strives with all his might for the presidential nomination and if he misses and is lucky, he becomes available for second place on the ticket. Whether Javits is prepared to mount such a campaign, or can count on Rockefeller's unreserved support if he does, remains to be seen.

Second, presidential fever, like malaria, is recurrent. If Rockefeller is reelected next year by a substantial margin, his national temperature will inevitably rise. James Desmond, the Governor's biographer and, I notice, the only reporter invited to ride yesterday with Rockefeller to Vice-President Humphrey's reception forty miles outside Minneapolis, says as much in a dispatch carried in the New York *Daily News*.

"Governor Rockefeller today removed himself from consideration as the Republican candidate for President," the Desmond story begins, "but he didn't mean it."

The headline in the *News* is equally explicit: ROCKY: NO '68 RUN; BUT IT'S NOT BINDING.

Tuesday, July 27 — Bill Buckley still refuses to become a streetwalker, as he puts it, but he says some striking things. If he is elected, he told one interviewer, he will depend on "the Lords Spiritual of the community." These, he said, were the "moral leaders, the aristocracy in Europe centuries ago whose duty it was to maintain the finest, most civilized standards of society." Apparently the man wants to restore the medieval Establishment.

This evening the major candidates for mayor were interviewed in round-robin style by the Committee of 100, an influential group of 200 Negroes which has grown since it acquired its original name. Since the group is heavily infiltrated with civil servants, Screvane received the warmest reception. Beame slid in and out without causing a ripple on anybody's mind. Lindsay got in trouble by remarking lightly that as an ASP he belonged to the "smallest minority group in modern New York." The chairman, a Screvane partisan, commented acidly that Klansmen in the South also refer to themselves as WASPS.

Inasmuch as the Lindsay contingent arrived just before Buckley spoke we were able to appraise him at close quarters. He began by denying that the Conservative party was hostile to "the legitimate aspirations of the Negro race."

"The Jew with his crooked nose, the Italian with his accent, these were nothing like the disadvantages you suffered," he told the uncomfortable audience, "but socializing is not the answer. Adam Clayton Powell is harming the Negro cause. Why do you continue to elect him?"

Somebody jumped up to say that Powell had worked to end segregation in the armed forces during World War II.

"Yes," said Buckley with an air of invincible superiority, "but he also wrote a column for the Communist Daily Worker and he called many of his colleagues in Congress Fascists."

When the man continued to argue, Buckley said: "I'm not

here to engage in a spitting contest with you but if any statement in the world is safe to make it is that Adam Clayton Powell is a scoundrel and an opportunist." Becoming more belligerent in response to growls from the crowd, he added: "I can't promise you a thing. The mayor of New York is a limited job. Why should people throw garbage out of their windows in Harlem? James Baldwin tells me that's a form of social protest but his answer is inexplicable. Self-help is part of the answer."

On the basis of his provocative attitude, Buckley achieved more radio, press, and TV publicity on this occasion than all the other candidates together.

Wednesday, July 28 — In the ethnic, religious, and geographic terms used privately by the political pros, the major contenders for control of New York City may be summed up as follows:

The Lindsay slate consists of a Manhattan WASP (ASP), a Brooklyn Jew and a Staten Island Irish-Catholic whose name sounds vaguely Italian.

Screvane, a Queens Italian, has chosen a Manhattan Jew and an Albany-Syracuse-Washington Irish-Catholic.

Beame, a Brooklyn Jew, has picked a Bronx Italian and a Queens Irish-Catholic.

The lesser slates are less traditional. Paul O'Dwyer has filled out his ticket with a Manhattan Negro and a Brooklyn Jew whereas Ryan has chosen a Manhattan Negro and a Queens Jew.

The Conservative ticket is the least balanced. Buckley's running mates are Rosemary Gunning, head of the Queens anti-school-busing forces, and Hugh A. Markey, head of the Staten Island Zoo. All three are Irish-Catholics.

Thursday, July 29 — Mayor Burns, of Binghamton, is the new Democratic State Chairman, at $30,000 a year. The succession was accomplished at a poorly attended State Democratic Committee meeting in Syracuse.

Professor Alan Campbell of Cornell University, the platform chairman of the state party, suggested recently that instead of a political tool like William H. McKeon, who was installed originally by Mayor Wagner and forced to resign after he turned against the Mayor, and McKeon's predecessor, Michael H. Prendergast, who was a projection of Tammany boss DeSapio's power, the state chairman should be an issues-oriented expert. Only by acquiring a new party image in this fashion, said the professor, could the Democrats overcome Republican gains.

Campbell had a candidate: Howard J. Samuels, a Canandaigua businessman whom he unsuccessfully advanced as a gubernatorial prospect in 1962 and who since then has been chairman of a state Democratic advisory council. Other influential upstate voices were raised in favor of Samuels, but all the powerful county bosses (except Brooklyn boss Steingut and Bronx boss Charley Buckley) were for Burns. The handful of state committee members who appeared for the Syracuse meeting and virtually all the proxies received for use at the meeting were also for Burns.

Samuels had not become an active candidate for chairman, but he was nevertheless disappointed at his showing. The next time, he told an Associated Press reporter in Syracuse, the party should be allowed to choose its chairman "in a free and open meeting as prescribed by the charter." Isn't a Wagner-Kennedy consensus enough for Samuels? The man must be a troublemaker.

Friday, July 30 — The fact that Lindsay has been guarded secretly against assassination for almost a month became known today. Without any real evidence I would like to blame this breach of security on a stalwart young man we call Colonel Abel. The Colonel has been riding in our press cars for weeks.

Though nothing under his name ever appears in the conservative weekly publication he represents, he phones Buckley headquarters daily with Lindsay schedules and quotes from Lindsay press conferences. By accident I heard him doing this one day when he stepped into a phone booth next to mine. Thereafter, we kept an eye on the ostensible reporter who was keeping an eye on us.

If Colonel Abel classes as an enemy agent, he is not terribly furtive about it. He often asks questions and makes comments in an argumentive manner. Two out-of-town writers of some distinction, John Cauley of the *Kansas City Star* and Nora Sayre of the *New Statesman* from London, who were observing us yesterday, teased him about his rightist views and found he could defend himself competently.

The story in the *World Telegram* about our police guard was written by a reporter who stayed with us only one day, during which he became chummy with Abel. The Colonel has been around long enough to draw some conclusions about the recurring appearances of Detectives Allen, Vecchio, and Wasylecow. I assume he tipped off his friend. He may have figured that breaking the news through a neutral source would complicate Lindsay's campaign without embarrassing Buckley. In any case, I am worried. Though there have been no new threats since the July 4th weekend, I keep wondering whether the revealed presence of bodyguards may not be taken as a challenge by the legion of urban crackpots.

Our walking tours in the St. George and New Brighton areas of Staten Island today were plagued by Conservative party pickets. They were no worse than usual but the additional reporters attracted by the *Telegram* story focused on every Bircher waving a SUPPORT YOUR LOCAL POLICE sign. Once again I found myself scrutinizing hecklers for possible homicidal intent, which is no easy road to peace of mind.

John and Mary Lindsay had planned a late-evening visit to the home of Timothy and Genevieve Costello, who live in the

Verrazzano Bridge area on a one-block street which is hard to
find. We got lost. Word came by car telephone that one of
the Costello children was sick. The visit was called off, but we
were still lost. The front car containing the Lindsays, Detective Allen, and Gil Robinson took an abrupt right turn
down a steep and narrow road. After pausing at the top because he questioned the route, the driver of the press car decided to follow the leader.

As our car headed down, the candidate's car, whose driver
had realized his mistake, came roaring up. The two cars
ground to a stop, radiator to radiator, no more than inches
apart. I found myself shivering over the narrowness of the
escape and a realization of the endless personal and political
repercussions which would have followed a fatal crash on that
dark little road. At least we would have had the satisfaction,
my mind noted with a flick of malice, of taking Colonel Abel
with us.

The Catskills, July 31–August 1 — We are up in the mountains hunting for voters. As many as 100,000 New York City
residents are said to be on vacation here in 400 hotels and
more than 1,000 bungalow colonies. Louis Lefkowitz did some
modest handshaking through the big hotels four years ago but
that was nothing compared to what we are doing. Blue and
white posters announcing Lindsay's visit began to appear several days ago on every available telephone pole, fence, and
parking lot stanchion in the area. Since local ordinances forbid
such posting, village officials in Monticello and Liberty
shrieked outrage to the press and went around tearing down
individual posters. That attracted additional attention to the
remaining posters. Then in the dark hours before dawn Saturday our Raiders put up 3,000 new posters.

Lindsay reached Grossinger Airport by small plane from
New York around 9 A.M. Saturday. Between then and 4 A.M.
Sunday, when he went to bed at the Concord on Kiamesha
Lake, he ranged through a dozen of the largest air-conditioned

NEW YORKERS!
JOHN LINDSAY
CANDIDATE FOR MAYOR
IS COMING TO
SULLIVAN COUNTY
TO SAY "HELLO"

Under the Lindsay touch . . .

pleasure domes. A large press-radio-TV contingent had come up with me by motorcade from New York Friday evening and stayed overnight in a South Fallsburg motel. The TV cameras were particularly useful—at any given resort a certain percentage of the guests would jump into our act in hope of seeing themselves later on the screen—and the radio-press men added to the candidate's entourage.

Under the Lindsay touch, apolitical and airy, the crowds in the big hotels—Grossinger's, Brown's, Evans', Flagler's, Gibber's, Kutcher's, the Pines, the Laurels, and one or two others—opened up like speed-filmed flowers. There were only occasional holdouts. Poolside at Brown's, Lindsay obliged a middle-aged woman with a kiss.

"Hey, that's my mother," objected a skinny youngster.

"Your mother!" said Lindsay. "I thought she was your sister."

To another woman, dunking herself in the pool, he asked: "How's the water?"

"Wet," she replied unsmilingly.

Since Jerry Lewis and Jayne Mansfield were on the weekend entertainment bill at Brown's, Lindsay opened a small speech of greeting there with: "Hi folks, I'm Jayne Mansfield."

A solemn little girl looked him over. "No you're not," she said.

Throughout the day Lindsay kidded his staff as well as the public. He roared with laughter at the sight of me in wet trunks, carrying clothes and shoes in a mad dash for the campaign cars when his hurried exit from the Evans pulled me out of the swimming pool. Later he had fun with Pat Vecchio, our police protector, who stayed too long in the steam room, became dehydrated, swayed and fainted as he emerged into the locker room. Only Pat's feelings were hurt.

Our press release promised Lindsay would participate in the entertainment program at the Concord. On the way up he rehearsed an old Richard Rodgers song from the Garrick

Gaieties for possible use in a duet with Jane Morgan. Jim Clarity of the *Herald Tribune*, Murray Schumach of the *Times*, and the local AP man filed stories in the afternoon reporting the scheduled duet in the past tense on my assurances that it positively would take place. Smith even quoted the new lyrics starting: "We'll take Manhattan, the Bronx and Staten Island, too/And Brooklyn Queens with you and you . . ."

Lindsay waited expectantly at ringside in the evening but Jane Morgan became concerned lest he spoil the mood of her French love songs and did not call him up. When Jane's act ended at midnight without any duet I complained to the hotel publicist, to Jane's manager, and finally to Jane that it must be sung publicly before dawn or somebody would be guilty of perjury.

Lindsay came into the Night Owl Lounge at 1:30 in the morning. "I'll take care of it," he said after I explained the situation. He headed for Jane Morgan's table. They talked briefly and retired to a spot behind the bandstand for rehearsal. In due time—2:11 A.M. by my watch—they sang the duet. As an encore they danced a watusi. Everything after that was anticlimax.

☆☆★ *August*

Monday, August 2 — Categories of campaign do's and dont's seem clearly defined in Lindsay's mind. During our weekend in the mountains, he posed with a knife over a challah at Grossinger's but he did not cut the ceremonial bread and he did not eat such delicacies as gefilte fish and herring in sour cream for the benefit of the reporters. All he actually ate during breakfast with Jenny Grossinger was an ASPish dish of blueberries and he glared at the hotel photographer who caught him doing that.

For reasons of dignity, I suppose, Lindsay hates to be photographed with food in his mouth. During street tours in the city he accepts food which is offered by storekeepers but he quickly passes on to an aide any conspicuous or messy item like watermelon or a chunk of pastry. On the other hand if he is hungry and others are eating or if the photographers are not looking he may grab anything edible which strikes his fancy.

Small courtesies like wearing a yarmulka in a synagogue are extended to ethnic and religious groups by Lindsay as a matter of course. Periodically during his weekend in the Catskills he wished vacationers "a good Shabbos." He even gave a Jewish twist to his anecdote about the group bound for an asylum with whom he rode by accident on a train from Washington to New York. In the new version after Lindsay says he is a "candidate for mayor" the keeper exclaims, "Another meshugina," or lunatic, and resumes his head count. The use of "meshugina" heightened the laughter.

Lindsay does not like to be manipulated. At Evans' hotel, he watched the poolside dancing lessons, joking with the in-

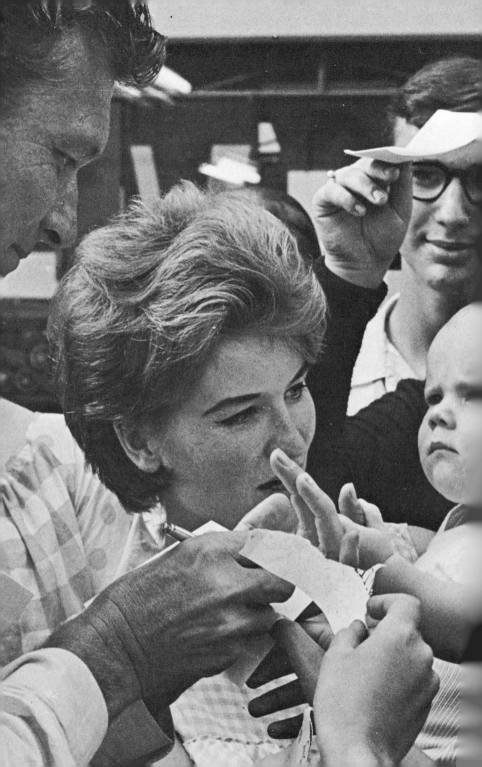

structor until the instructor tried to draft him to judge a bathing beauty contest. Then he left in a hurry.

In a political sense this decision may have been sound since there can be only one winner, and many losers, in a beauty contest. Again, Lindsay's sense of dignity may have been involved. Soon after he kissed a matron at Evans' he declined to kiss a baby. He never kisses babies for publicity.

During a recent sidewalk excursion in Brooklyn, a *Daily News* photographer explained that a picture with real "schmaltz," or popular appeal, consists of a baby, a dog, and a nun greeting the candidate simultaneously. Obviously this is hard to find in nature. Soon thereafter we encountered a dog placed precariously on the hood of a car by its owner who was proud of its capacity for shaking hands. Lindsay stood alongside the dog for a picture but he would not shake hands. When one of our advance men arranged for photographs of him imprinting his hand on some newly laid cement in front of a store, Lindsay ignored this opportunity for immortality.

On another occasion a rug dealer rolled out a red carpet on the sidewalk for Lindsay to walk on as a way of getting some publicity for himself. The candidate posed alongside the carpet but he did not tread on it.

At a conclave of Indians in a Queens park early in the campaign, Lindsay was presented a beautiful headdress. He posed for pictures holding it but he would not wear it. Similarly he refuses to be photographed in a cowboy hat or any other fancy headgear. Only last week a *Times* photographer who would die rather than be considered corny asked Lindsay to pose in front of City Hall pointing symbolically up toward the dome of what may conceivably be his official home next year. Lindsay shook his head and walked away.

Tuesday, August 3 — Since they can't get a rise out of Lindsay, Screvane and Beame are clawing each other. Screvane has renewed Wagner's old charges of bossism against Stanley Steingut and Charley Buckley. Beame deplores such "gutter tactics." Screvane, he says, is a "former rubber stamp for Wagner now trying to be city boss." Ryan is siding with Beame, declaring that Screvane "stands squarely in the tradition of boss rule. . . . He has backing from the most reactionary elements in the Democratic party, the old-line leaders of Tammany Hall and the Roe machine in Queens. He has lived on the bosses and for the bosses throughout his career." O'Dwyer, with impish wit, takes the position that Screvane and Beame are both right.

The target is too tempting to be missed, Price suggested at a headquarters conference this morning. Lindsay waited until he was in the middle of a street tour in the Washington Heights section of Manhattan to climb to the shaky top of a sedan to shout to a crowd of 200 persons that two of his Democratic rivals are involved in an open fight for control of the local Democratic party.

"Each has a half piece of the machine," said Lindsay. "It's 50–50. Each is fighting for the whole machine to take control of the city for another four years and perhaps another quarter of a century. We've had enough of it, enough of clubhouse rule! "

During a subsequent street tour in Brooklyn Lindsay spoke of Screvane and Beame—still without mentioning them by name—as "two wings of the same evil bird." He also suggested a statement on bossism (Democratic brand) which we are now preparing for morning paper release.

Wednesday, August 4 — Our block parties are primarily a device for putting volunteers to immediate and effective use. Inaugurated a couple of weeks ago, they will continue throughout the summer two days a week. Each block party is planned and handled by a single storefront. It lasts from 3 P.M. to 10 P.M. or later. A considerable area, several blocks as a rule, rather than one, is barred to motor traffic by police order. Our flatbed truck rolls in with Lionel Hampton's All Stars or some other musical combination to play for atmosphere and occasionally for street dancing.

The storefront hires various small mobile amusement park devices—everything from tiny "whips" to miniature Ferris wheels—to come and give free rides to the small fry who wait anxiously in line for their turn. Purveyors of amusement park-type food—spun candy, hot dogs, and the like—are allowed to take position along the edges of the blocked area, charging their customary prices.

Lindsay is supposed to arrive toward the peak of activity around 9:30 or 10. He struggles through the mob of kids to the speaking platform, delivers a campaign talk gauged to the caliber of the audience in the background, and leaves in a blaze of mob hysteria. The effectiveness of the block parties varies. The first one was a debacle because the too-numerous kids swarmed over everything like warrior ants. They roughed up everybody, including Mary Lindsay, who never was able to reach the speaking platform. They made so much noise that Lindsay could not be heard over the loudspeaker. At one or two later parties, Birchite pickets proved troublesome.

Last night's block party, held at Electchester, a middle-income housing project in Queens, was sponsored by the city and Harry Van Arsdale's Electrical Workers Union. Because the percentage of visible adults was high the "new Lindsay" was unveiled on this occasion.

For several weeks David Garth, a publicist, associated with C. J. LaRoche & Co., an advertising agency helping Lindsay on an unpaid basis, has been analyzing his street style and suggesting improvements. The chief changes noticeable last night were greater voice, more sweeping gestures, and the use of parallel, contrasting, and solidly affirmative sentences.

Lindsay used to repeat some dialogue with an imaginary citizen. "Don't you have to be crazy to run for mayor of New York?" "No, but it helps." That and the similar head-count in the train from Washington to New York joke have been banished from the campaign. Last night he shouted: "I *want* to be your mayor. I *want* . . ."

Lindsay hit the Electchester crowd with his regular pro-labor talk—what I call his Liberal party speech—plus the new tricks and the reception was good, very good indeed.

Thursday, August 5 — Our radio-telephone system is a continuing marvel to me. By utilizing the Empire State Building tower in some fashion, two specially equipped campaign cars can communicate with headquarters and with advance men all over the city. Lindsay often uses the telephone to decide whether to hurry or delay his arrival at a meeting. He can learn something of the tenor of a meeting in advance or pick up what happens at a meeting after he leaves. While moving from one engagement to another in the field he can keep abreast of developments elsewhere through campaign officials at the Roosevelt. He can even use the radio-telephone occasionally for relaxation.

On the theory that somebody may overhear our phone conversations, a partial and rather elementary code is employed. Headquarters is known as MANSION—a hopeful reference to Gracie Mansion. "MANSION calling BENJAMIN" means that somebody at headquarters wants to talk to Lindsay, who chose BENJAMIN as his alias because his political hero is Benjamin Disraeli. "MANSION calling ABE" means that somebody at the Roosevelt wants to talk to Gil Robinson, who has charge of the radio telephone system. His political hero is Abraham Lincoln.

Mary Lindsay is JUNO on radio telephone and Price is ADOLF. These are whimsicalities of Lindsay's. Mary is an outdoor girl, though to me she seems more Diana than Juno. Price is an orthodox Jew who sports no mustache. Otherwise the comparison to Hitler is not without justification.

Today's schedule called for a tour of six beach clubs in North Queens. It was a weekday and the tide was out. Nobody was bathing in Long Island Sound. Nobody was even sunbathing on these beaches. No reporters were on hand. At one beach club we found precisely five persons picnicking in the sand. Back in the car after shaking hands with all five, Lindsay accepted a radio telephone call from Price.

ADOLF: How have things been going?

BENJAMIN: Fine, fine. Enormous crowds!

ADOLF: That's odd. The AP and UP report sparse crowds.

BENJAMIN: Oh we're counting the rocks and the birds. By the way why aren't you out ringing door bells?

ADOLF: I'm trying to figure who is the best candidate for mayor.

BENJAMIN: You're fired!

Friday, August 6 — Six feet tall, black and white posters have suddenly blossomed in every New York subway station. They show Lindsay on the campaign trail. Over his tousled head runs a quotation from a column by Murray Kempton in the *World Telegram:*

HE IS FRESH AND EVERYONE ELSE IS TIRED.

Lindsay is in shirtsleeves and he has a broad smile on his face. Behind him to the left are some ecstatically grinning Negro children and a shopkeeper who looks Puerto Rican. Ten paces behind Lindsay is a white man trudging along in a dark suit carrying papers. That's me—THE TIRED MAN, as I am known jokingly at headquarters. Some trash cans, garbage cans, and street signs are also visible.

David McCall, head of the La Roche Advertising Company, sent out a half-dozen different photographers over a period of weeks to take "the official campaign picture." This presumably is it. I phoned McCall today. He believes the photographer was Nick Samarge, the time late June, and the location Bedford Avenue and Fulton Street in the Bedford-Stuyvesant section.

Inasmuch as the posters have brought me renown as the foil to Lindsay's freshness, I will confess that I am tired. An ordinary city campaign gets going about this time but Lindsay

has been running since early May. I hear he is planning to take a few days off next week. He does not show it, but he must feel some weariness.

Speaking of posters, a letter to the editor of the *Times* earlier this week suggested that Lindsay's campaign workers, having plastered the Catskills with notices which local officials are not equipped to remove, go up there again to take them down. I passed the clipping along to Price. The Raiders were consulted and they sent a detachment reluctantly into the Catskills Wednesday night to perform the chore.

In this Catskill mountain matter, I violated my vow not to interfere in anybody else's business at headquarters lest I encourage campaign paranoia. There have been other violations. They could reflect a greater commitment on my part to the Lindsay cause. Realistically, I suspect that it's the heady sense of power in a campaign headquarters which blows up everybody's ego, including my own.

Horace Carter, a smart, short, fat, cigar-smoking Negro who does research at headquarters, came into my office recently with the text of a proposed release putting Lindsay in opposition to the confirmation of the appointment of former Governor James P. Coleman of Mississippi as a Federal Circuit Court Judge. I remember Coleman from a 1956 conference of governors which I covered as a reporter. He and LeRoy Collins of Florida were then the only Dixie governors recognizing desegregation as the law of the land. All the older civil rights groups still rate Coleman as a moderate, but the newer Student Nonviolent Coordinating Committee (SNCC) (SNICK) has been campaigning violently against him. To my friend Horace Carter I therefore said: "Nothing doing. I won't pass the release."

Carter does some work for Javits. "Javits wants it," he said.

"And who is Javits?" I inquired.

Later it occurred to me that I had been abrupt and even insulting. I went down the corridor to talk things over with

Horace and perhaps to apologize. To my surprise he had lost interest. "You may be right," he said.

Saturday, August 7. — Milt Mollen is the Cinderella of the Lindsay–Costello–Mollen ticket. Much is expected of him as the Democratic standard-bearer in a fusion campaign yet his actual resources are small. He does not possess the machine put together by Price for Lindsay or have an independent political entity behind him like the Liberal party which backs Costello. Mollen has been assigned an office two doors down the campaign corridor from the press room and about the size of the press room. There he has a small staff headed by his campaign manager, Werner H. (Wyn) Kramarsky, thirty-nine, a gruff and competent veteran of Democratic reform skirmishes ranging from the Columbia University section to Greenwich Village. In theory Mollen can use all the facilities at headquarters but this does not always work out in practice.

Because of my own inclinations and my union interests I have generally been hospitable to newcomers and kind to those under pressure in a city room of a newspaper. Similarly and without conscious intent I have become a Lindsay ambassador to Costello and particularly to Mollen. He tells me his troubles. He complained bitterly the other day, for example, that he cannot seem to obtain Lindsay's campaign schedule sufficiently in advance to make his own plans. He does not yet possess campaign cars of his own and he needs all the exposure he can get with Lindsay.

At a direct request from Mollen which did not go through O'Donnell or Price I have prepared his campaign biography. It starts in the usual way: "Milton Mollen, forty-five, a Democrat who had risen to a key position in Mayor Wagner's cabinet, declared his candidacy on such and such a day . . . 'I am a Democrat, I have been a Democrat and I intend to remain a Democrat,' he said. . . . He promised to pull no punches on the issues . . . 'I will avoid personalities in this campaign,' he said."

With his customary concentration on larger matters, Lindsay did not change a word in the campaign biography prepared for him. Mollen on the other hand has quibbled over almost every phrase, despite the fact that the draft followed his own formula. He objected to one statement, for example, that as a Democrat he did not class as an organization man. The statement was true, he said, but he still hopes to attract machine Democrats. What an optimist!

Never having run previously for public office Mollen tends to be prosy and self-conscious on the stump. He overdoes his familiar "I have always been a Democrat" pitch, whereas the audience wants something concrete to indicate that things will improve under Lindsay as mayor. Mollen will not say a word which can be construed as criticism of his mentor, Mayor Wagner.

In his first introductions of Mollen during joint street appearances, Lindsay—by instinct, I guess—emphasized Mollen's war record, telling how his running mate was a flier shot down over Germany during the war, imprisoned in Stalag this and Stalag that, and finally the leader of a dramatic and successful prison break which brought him and other prisoners through the Nazi lines to allied territory. Mollen seems to have been an authentic war hero but he now has a soft, withdrawn appearance which does not suggest heroism. He may have realized his own incapacity to live up to the Lindsay introduction because he handed me a summary of his civic credits one day for possible use. I passed this along to Lindsay who modified his introduction with considerable gain in general crowd reaction.

Mollen does not look like a major candidate for public office. Last night, at a county Republican dinner in Staten Island, he was almost overlooked. Introduced as an afterthought following lively talks by Lindsay and Costello, who lives in Staten Island, Mollen droned on and on, dulling an aroused crowd. Unfortunately, Wyn Kramarsky was not present. To John Cahill, a friend who always travels with

Mollen, I suggested as tactfully as I could that in any similar future situation, the candidate should say a few words and take a bow.

Today Mollen's attitude toward me has been reserved and almost unfriendly. I don't know how Cahill translated my well-meant advice but if this keeps up it may impair my standing as self-appointed missionary to the lonely and discomfited at headquarters.

Sunday, August 8 — Having chased voters north into the Catskills last weekend, it was probably inevitable that we pursue them east on Long Island this weekend. Advance publicity that Phyllis Diller would be along blew up our radio-press-TV coverage and that in turn attracted larger crowds. We visited Lido Beach, Long Beach, and Atlantic Beach in Nassau County. Lindsay's pretext for this expedition is that he wants to meet even those who are not city residents on vacation, since he will try, if elected, to make Gotham so attractive that many will move back from the suburbs.

The candidate was in character today—he swam at Lido Beach in his boxer-type trunks, he threw four baseballs at a pyramid of wooden milk bottles in a boardwalk concession without hitting a bottle, he ate pizza, he joked and he shook hands—but he was upstaged by Miss Diller. For boardwalk walking the protean comedienne has oversized octagonal black and white sun glasses and a fright wig. Wearing a chenille shift, white Courreges boots and an Alice-in-Wonderland bow at the Shelborne Beach Club, she announced that her name was Timothy Costello.

"I don't know what John's talking about, this fusion mess," she said making a horrible face. "All I know is I'm on his wagon wherever the hell it's going."

After a quick change of clothes she appeared at the Colony Beach Club as Milt Mollen in a turquoise piqué shift with a ruffled hem and short boots. "John's been talking to me about what he's going to do for New York," she said. "I wonder

On impulse . . .

what he's been smoking." She made her climactic appeal as herself—in orange slacks, a yellow ruffled blouse, and those long white boots again at the Sands Beach Club, saying:

"John wanted a First Lady type along for the day but he couldn't find any so he brought me, haw, haw, haw."

She earned more applause than Lindsay and she signed five times as many autographs.

Screvane denounced Lindsay for exhibitionism this morning on radio, saying: "All these antics . . . jumping in swimming pools and the big grin and the big smile are very nice things but very frankly I think the public wants more in a candidate for mayor."

Lindsay listened to this by radio telephone in a campaign car. Later one of our advance men reported that Screvane and Beame were talking this afternoon at a rally of the Student Struggle for Soviet Jewry at Rockaway. On impulse Lindsay decided to attend the same rally on the way back to headquarters. He had a big grin and a big smile on his face as he leaped to the top of a station wagon to talk. He said more or less what his rivals had said but whereas they received only perfunctory applause he was mobbed by a wildly enthusiastic crowd before and after his speech.

Monday, August 9 — John and Mary Lindsay and Johnny left by plane this morning for a week's vacation in the Virgin Islands.

The candidate will not be missed for a while because the opposition is still howling over injuries inflicted by our weekend releases on water supply and the war against poverty. The Lindsay campaign, I begin to realize, has developed a kind of military pincer operation. One jaw consists of the field trips which consume so much of my time and attention. The other jaw consists of long statements on basic issues which march forth at regular intervals from headquarters, after being researched by George Lindsay's staff and processed for the media by Harry O'Donnell. George has managed to tap the town's best brains ranging from Professor Donald L. Shaughnessay of New York University, a labor arbitrator who also qualifies as an expert on the industrial basis of urban areas, to architect Philip Johnson and city planner Jane Jacobs. The statements, of course, are issued in John Lindsay's name.

The weekend releases which aroused so much excitement are scholarly documents, respectively 3,000 and 5,000 words long. The one on water supply did not mention Screvane but it stressed the absence of adequate planning for water in recent decades and the fact that New York's supply is presently in the hands of a man named Armand D'Angelo, who was secretary of Local 3 of the Electricians Union for 16 years before he joined the city as Deputy Commissioner of Water Supply, Gas & Electricity in 1955, becoming Commissioner two years later. D'Angelo never managed to obtain even an electrician's license. Since he knows little in a professional sense about water he is a remarkably qualified scapegoat in the city's present water crisis.

The other release names Screvane twice. He is described as the New York "poverty czar" who frustrated the federal concept of "self-help and involvement of the poor." He is blamed for "booby-trapping the program with devices to keep clubhouse politicians in control." Though the rest of the release is about legislative history and analysis, it must have hit Screvane hard because he is still sputtering. Lindsay, he says, has suddenly discovered the poor "the way Cortez discovered Mexico." Lindsay, he adds, is playing "brass-knuckle politics" and "dragging the poverty program down into the mire to gain a headline."

Screvane challenges anybody to name a single clubhouse politician in the anti-poverty program. That leaves him wide open. I could name a few right now.

Tuesday, August 10 — The drafting at Rose's request of a proposed Liberal party letter kept me at headquarters today. The letter will go to upper-case Liberals, particularly members of the International Ladies Garment Workers Union who are inclined to be suspicious of Republicans, lower-case liberals, and independents in a small test area. If the reaction there is good, Rose will mail the appeal citywide. The ostensible purpose of the letter is to recommend Lindsay to open-minded voters but it must also boost Costello and Mollen by associating them with the more popular Lindsay.

My draft begins: "We would like to share with you our thinking about the need for a nonpartisan city administration headed by JOHN LINDSAY, and why it is important to elect him and his running mates, MILTON MOLLEN and TIMOTHY COSTELLO. The Conservative candidate—a Goldwater Republican—William Buckley, is concentrating his fire primarily on JOHN LINDSAY. As reported by the *New York Times* on August

5, 1965, '. . . Mr. Buckley said Mr. Lindsay's voting record and pronouncements place him left of center of the Democratic party. . . .'

"Mr. Buckley is denouncing Mr. Lindsay for his well-known liberal record in Congress. Here is part of that record: As one of the House group that managed the drive of the 1964 Civil Rights Act, John Lindsay helped bring about its passage in committee and on the floor of Congress. He has been one of the outstanding fighters for civil liberties. His voice and influence helped pass the rent subsidy provisions of the new housing bill. He supported and voted for medicare and voted for the repeal of Section 14B of the Taft-Hartley law. He supported a high percentage of the liberal legislation of the Kennedy-Johnson administration."

A reminder that the AFL-CIO endorsed Lindsay twice for Congress, a suggestion that the nation's strength in a democratic sense depends on the strength or failure of local government, and then a final appeal. The copy went by messenger to Mary Kaplan, the knowledgeable and amiable switchboard girl at the United Hatters, Cap & Millinery Workers Union. Rose soon phoned to say thanks, the draft gave him something to work on and he would finish the letter. If I know Rose, he has solicited a half-dozen other drafts besides mine from which he will distill something peculiarly his own. Then the letter will go for final revision to the Reverend Donald Harrington, a vice-chairman of the Liberal party, and David Berg, chairman of an independent committee for Lindsay-Mollen-Costello, who will sign it.

Rose plays an unexpectedly large role in our fusion campaign. He heads the dominant faction in the Liberal party, which is willing to cede considerable control over the Costello operation to Price. (A lesser faction wants to keep the Costello campaign relatively independent.) Price, on his part, has established once-a-week breakfasts for the three major candidates and their chief advisers. (I am not invited to these breakfasts but I hear what happens.) Two such breakfasts have been held.

At the first breakfast, Rose insisted that Costello and Mollen be given a regular share in Lindsay's news conferences. This was acceptable to Price. At the second one, they discussed a proposal by Alfredo Vidal, head of our Spanish-speaking voters division, that we set up a Puerto Rican party to give Lindsay another line on the ballot.

Rose objected vehemently to the idea as divisive. If you start with a Puerto Rican party, he said, you may wind up with an Italian party, a Catholic party, and goodness knows what else. Dr. Frank Arricale, a social worker who manages Costello's campaign, said Costello would not run on a Puerto Rican line and that he personally would resign unless the idea were dropped. The Mollen representatives apparently took no decisive stand one way or the other, but Price decided to forget about the new party to please the Liberals.

Wednesday, August 11 — A list of political appointees in the city's anti-poverty program was awaiting me today at headquarters. It comes from an idealistic official within the program who is appalled at its overload of drones. The list specifies salary, title, previous record, and sponsor of sixteen individuals. Most of them were recommended by City Hall on the basis of an expressed political claim to attention. Some of them are quasi-competent but that does not lessen their clubhouse odor or the obvious central control of the program.

Several of the appointees hail from the pro-Wagner Voters Clubs in Brooklyn run by Louis Hernandez. One comes from Powell and another from Tammany boss J. Raymond Jones. There are emigrés from Bobby Kennedy's senatorial office and the Democratic Nationalities Committee. David Ross, majority leader of the City Council, placed one follower in the program, possibly as a reward for his impartiality between

Wagner and Bronx boss Buckley, his county leader. Joseph DiCarlo, head of Wagner's anti-Buckley Bronx Reorganizing Committee, placed one of his people, perhaps as a consolation for losing the top spot to Ross' man. On the list also are the wives of two influential judges. They were sponsored by their husbands.

After some consideration I turned over the list to a friend of mine who has recently been promoted to the city desk at the *Post*. If he publishes a proper exposé it will set up poverty czar Screvane for a roundhouse right by Lindsay.

Thursday, August 12 — Imagine running for office as the candidate of a Non-Partisan Party. Isn't that more piquant than just being a fusionist? My friend Harry Uviller suggested the idea at lunch in connection with Lindsay's search for a third line on the ballot. A Non-Partisan Party "will dramatize the ordinary citizen's stake in nonpartisan government," said Uviller. I relayed the idea to Price in a memo as soon as I returned to headquarters. It came back with a scribbled addition: "Alex (Rose) likes Independent Citizens Party better."

I would be inclined to argue against the shopworn Independent Citizens Party label except that everything seems to be settled. Price has assigned his two troubleshooters, Jim Marcus and Sam Kearing, to direct the collection of signatures on the designating petitions of the new party. They will work through the storefronts, which now number ninety. This, plus the holding of block parties, should keep our volunteers busy until they start canvassing by phone, by letter, and in person. Price made a phone check the other evening and found more than 1,000 volunteers busy in the storefronts. For any given moment, that's a goodly number of workers. Price wants 35,000 signatures on the new petitions and I will not be surprised if Marcus and Kearing produce them.

In another development today, Frederic R. Coudert, Jr., the former Republican Congressman whom Lindsay forced into retirement in 1958, has emerged as chairman of a new

Buckley-for-Mayor committee. This must be an effort by the Conservative party to reach disaffected Republicans. What I cannot understand is why Coudert made the break now, since there has been no recent open clash between him and Lindsay.

Richard Lewisohn, the businessman whom Lindsay installed as Republican district leader in his home assembly district after he upset the county machine, has carefully refrained from reprisals against the conservatives who stayed inside the Republican party. Lewisohn actually kept Coudert and several of his followers on the county committee! The only explanation for the new split which makes sense is revenge. It took Lindsay twelve years of watchful waiting and planning to oust Coudert. Now, eight years later, it's Coudert's turn to pounce.

Friday, August 13 — In the absence of the Lindsays, headquarters takes on a social air. Colleagues who were once businesslike or faintly hostile now gossip like old friends. All campaigns and some businesses pretend to be families. I'm dubious about such pretensions as a rule, but the Lindsays go farther in this direction than most. Mary Lindsay is consistently informal. The sight of her padding along the campaign corridor in stocking feet at 11 P.M. in search of volunteers for a mailing is reassuringly homely. John himself is always visiting the families of campaign workers. A couple of weeks ago, he dropped in on the telephone-answering service for doctors run by Price's mother. More recently he made a three-hour detour to see the wife and children of his Negro aide, James W. Smith.

This same spirit has filtered down to some extent at headquarters. Several days ago I was amazed when one of the Raiders, Richie Russo, and three of our drivers, Paul Kuisisto, Al Belli Bovi, and Trent Lemoine Inigo Jones, took me downstairs for a ceremonial drink in honor of my birthday. I must have mentioned the birthday but I cannot in a long newspaper career recall any similar ceremony. I was almost touched.

My daughter Betsy, twenty-four, having been laid off some weeks ago as an assistant producer at Channel 13, the educational channel, flirted with the idea of spending the summer as a volunteer in Mississippi with the Student Nonviolent Coordinating Committee (SNICK). To divert her from this worthy but hazardous course, I brought her around to headquarters. By calculated mischance we encountered Price's troubleshooter, Jim Marcus, who explained to Betsy the need for idealistic volunteers in our Bedford-Stuyvesant and Harlem storefronts.

Betsy accepted the challenge. After she served for a while in the black zones, she was shifted by Marcus to headquarters to work on an indoctrination course for all volunteers. Now she has fallen into a temporary job with Barry Gray, the radio commentator, and has been assured of renewed employment at Channel 13 in the fall. At this moment I am sensible of true family affection for Uncle Bob Price, Uncle Jim Marcus, and Uncle John and Aunt Mary Lindsay, in absentia in St. Croix.

Saturday, August 14 — Secretary of the Interior Stewart L. Udall today wound up two days of local hearings on the water supply of New York and other areas in the northeast. The city's inadequate planning alleged by Lindsay has been amply documented by the testimony. As the Secretary's experts made one embarrassing revelation after another, Commissioner D'Angelo's countenance acquired such a rueful cast that the omnipresent Bobby Kennedy was moved to request: "Smile, Commissioner, please smile at least once in a while."

After the hearings, a reporter on the *Herald Tribune* phoned our press room for clarification on "how Lindsay stands on water?"

Harry O'Donnell grinned with delight. "Jesus Christ did that a long while ago," he said. "Maybe our candidate can also do it."

Price cabled Lindsay today in the Virgin Islands: "Stay another week. We do better without you."

There is some truth in the jest. Not only are things going our way in such matters as the war against poverty and the water supply question, but Screvane and Beame have managed to entangle themselves in an ethnic hassle. Screvane accuses Beame of using "the big-lie technique of Hitler" and Beame has found a rabbi and former prosecutor at the Nuremberg war crimes trial to testify that Beame cannot be Hitlerish because he is Jewish. The Anti-Defamation League of B'nai B'rith is begging both boys to "refrain from appeals to bigotry" but they seem hard of hearing.

Napoleon had an appropriate slogan for such a situation: never interfere when an enemy is in the process of destroying himself.

Sunday, August 15 — William Haddad, a brilliant young man in a hurry, has been very much in evidence at headquarters this weekend. Sometimes he walks along our campaign corridor in close conversation with Mollen. Other times he appears with Mollen's campaign manager, Kramarsky. I know Bill well, because he was at one time a prize-winning investigatory reporter for the *Post*. He worked for Senator Estes Kefauver, for the Peace Corps when it was new, and he has run twice unsuccessfully as a Democratic reform insurgent for Congress in the downtown district of Manhattan. Recently he has been Inspector General in Sargent Shriver's Office of Economic Opportunity, an opportunity he may soon lose, according to newspaper reports, as a result of pressure from his old enemy, Representative Leonard Farbstein.

Ever since the Democratic national convention in Atlantic City last Summer, Haddad has carried shirts for Bobby Kennedy. Inasmuch as conversion to the Lindsay cause would make news, I asked Kramarsky whether Haddad was joining our family group.

"Bill is a genius in some ways," said Kramarsky, shaking his head in dissent, "but he does not think in normal fashion. I'd be glad to have him help Mollen but I have no intention of letting him ride around Manhattan on Mollen's shoulders in order to build himself up for another Congressional race as a Democrat next year."

A dark look crossed Kramarsky's face. "Did you ever see a paper-cutting machine work?" he asked, making an abrupt slicing motion with one hand. "That's what happened today to Bill Haddad. I CUT HIM OFF. . . ."

Monday, August 16 — Five years or so ago, after my first encounter with Herman Badillo (pronounced Bah-DEE-yo), I remarked that he was the kind of man who might become the town's first Hispanic mayor. Though he was then rather unknown, he exhibited the public magic shown by such diverse personalities as LaGuardia, Ryan, and Lindsay. It's a combination of drive, intellect, magnetism, and some other qualities. You can't define it but you recognize it.

Badillo will be thirty-eight within a few days. He is tall (six feet one), angular, and rather stern-looking. He was born in Caguas, Puerto Rico, orphaned at the age of five and brought to the mainland at the age of eleven by an aunt. Growing up in El Barrio, the Puerto Rican section of East Harlem, he earned a living as a pin boy in a bowling alley during his school days. After establishing himself first as a certified public accountant and then as a lawyer, he decided to do something about the political situation in East Harlem.

The population, once almost solidly Italian-American in that area, had gradually become 80 percent Spanish-speaking and Negro without any corresponding change in the regular Democratic organization, whose captains were still exclusively of Italian descent. Because of the Mafia presence it took courage on Badillo's part in 1960 to open a club for Negro and Puerto Rican voters.

Despite periodic wrecking of the club by vandals who were

never caught, Badillo's insurgent group elected one of two Democratic district leaders in 1961. That year Badillo also fought valiantly for Wagner in the primary and general elections in an area where the Mayor enjoyed little other support, and in 1962 he was rewarded by appointment as Commissioner of Relocation at $22,500 a year.

As the ranking city official of Puerto Rican background, Badillo took a long look. Then he moved from the still partly hostile slum of his youth to the well-to-do Riverdale section of the Northwest Bronx. Simultaneously he organized a Voters Club in the poor, predominantly Negro and Puerto Rican area in the Southwest Bronx. He made no secret of his ambition to climb as far as Hulan Jack, the first Negro to become a borough president in New York City, and perhaps farther, as the spokesman for the city's increasing Spanish-speaking population.

Now Badillo's chance has come. Screvane has chosen him to run for Bronx Borough President along with his citywide slate. Beame's candidate for Bronx Borough President is State Senator Ivan Warner, a capable Negro from Boss Charley Buckley's machine. This is the first boroughwide political test between a Negro and a Puerto Rican in the history of the city. Since these two minorities are increasingly jealous of each other, the Badillo-Warner primary contest has a significance second only to the citywide contest.

Tuesday, August 17 — Lindsay looks so relaxed and healthy after his vacation that Barnie Patterson wants him to pose immediately for pictures with his running mates. The HE IS FRESH AND EVERYONE ELSE IS TIRED posters must soon be replaced with posters showing the citywide slate.

In an early morning pep talk to the staff which preceded 12 hours of pavement-pounding all over town, Lindsay revealed that he did some scuba diving in the Virgin Islands. On one occasion, he said, a helpful stranger attached twenty or thirty pounds of weight to enable him to go deeper than usual.

Tanned and Spry, Lindsay Renews Hectic Campaign

...Daniel Weiner, may that in 315 years of Judaism in American life, neither has read of a

bernstein, he said, the local chapter of B'nai B'rith, got the police cracking. They put a 24-hour guard

the Bronx, mostly an young people, has already started to work for him.

Lindsay Battle Plan Holds To Step-by-Step Schedule

By Paul Weissman
Of The Herald Tribune Staff

Somewhere in Rep. John Lindsay's Roosevelt Hotel headquarters are 16 pages of handwritten legal foolscap containing the campaign battle plan.

Drafted 48 hours before Rep. Lindsay announced his candidacy by Mr. Lindsay's permanent campaign manager, Robert Price, the plan

(as befits a campaign manager), has made only one official visit.

In a campaign budgeted at $1.5 million, no one likes to talk about money or discuss fund-raising problems. But one Lindsay financial authority said last week:

"Lasker (Bernard J. Lasker, Lindsay finance chairman) hasn't raised a dime and Jack Javitz

You do a little bit every day."

In nine weeks of campaigning, Mr. Lindsay, who returns from a week-long vacation in St. Croix tomorrow afternoon, has shaken hands with more voters than any mayoral campaign in history.

The schedule has followed so closely to Mr. Price's "book" that the candidate is almost fully scheduled to

"I was barely able to struggle to the surface," he said. "Only later did I realize that the stranger was closely associated with one of my Democratic opponents!"

"I'm grateful for the six days in which to recharge my batteries," he continued amid the laughter. "*Time* magazine was with me three days out of the six. I must have waded through sixty pounds of research material on the campaign. I hope I understood it. . . ."

Indicating Costello and Mollen, Lindsay said: "The three of us out front have the more dangerous roles but also more fun. The volunteers are in back and you are in the middle . . . everyone doing his job. This is a family, a close family, too. It's difficult at times for all of us to grasp the entire picture. We need confidence in our neighbors. Nothing is more depressing at times than headquarters work but by a miracle and Bob Price everything comes into focus in the end."

Price took over. "The opposition is already combing the Lindsay record," he said.

"In last year's congressional race, our Democratic opposition did the same thing. It picked four out of Lindsay's thousands of votes in Congress, one being a time in 1959, as I recall, when he voted against a bill to put restaurants in airports or something like that. . . .

"It's bound to be a dirty campaign," Price warned. "Nonenlightened Democrats can feel the power structure crumbling!

"Between now and September 20 is the crucial part of the campaign. Anything not done by September 20 will be too late, take my word for it!

"I honestly believe we are still the underdog because after the primary the Democrats will bind together.

"We must be leading by a quarter of a million votes by October 1, because we will have to give back that amount of votes.

"I expect the President, the Vice-President and Senator Kennedy to join in the campaigning after the primary. I just checked Madison Square Garden for the last week of the campaign. It's reserved for the horse show so it doesn't look as if they can exhibit the President there. I worry about that a little. Don't you worry, I'll worry for all of us . . ."

Wednesday, August 18 — Wagner is now formally supporting Screvane. On the basis of his endorsement, the experts generally give Screvane a safe lead over Beaume. They may be wrong. The fresh but nonspecific charges of bossism made late yesterday by the Mayor at a news conference are hardly convincing. Wagner faced five hostile Democratic county leaders in the primary in 1961. Now three of the five county leaders—those in Manhattan, Queens, and Staten Island—are aligned with Screvane. The list of hostile bosses mustered today by Screvane consists of Charley Buckley of the Bronx, who is ailing; ex-Tammany chief DeSapio, who does not even control Greenwich Village these days; and Powell, whose standing in Harlem is second to that of Tammany boss J. Raymond Jones. Out of excess caution, Screvane omitted from his list the only really functioning pro-Beame county boss, Stanley Steingut of Brooklyn.

Among the mayoral contenders only Screvane takes any comfort from the Mayor's declaration. Beame says Wagner has a right "to support anybody who supports his own policies." That sounds as if he will now blame Screvane for all of Wagner's mistakes. Ryan says Wagner "endorsed his own inept administration." O'Dwyer describes the new charges of bossism as "hollow as a drum" and Lindsay expresses pious regret over "such feuding among the clubhouse factions in the city." In effect Wagner now seeks party vindication behind an inadequate front man against the combined opposition of Beame, O'Dwyer, and Ryan, with Lindsay hooting from the sidelines.

If he had acted earlier, Wagner might have whipped the Central Labor Council into line for Screvane before the primary election. It's too late for that now. Some political leaders who have been holding off may now back Screvane on the theory that Wagner is a likely Democratic choice for Governor next year, but I doubt that the rank and file will be greatly affected.

The more obvious developments in the Screvane-Beame tussle may be summarized as follows:

Pro-Screvane. A saturation campaign of radio spots stressing experience in government is helping the Council President. Organizationally he has done best in the Bronx, utilizing reform groups behind Badillo and his own citywide slate. He is taking advantage of mistakes by Victor Campione, who is operating the Buckley machine during the boss' illness. One such mistake was the selection of a practicing Rabbi to run for State Senate against a pro-Screvane member of the Rabbi's congregation.

Pro-Beame. Charges that the "unconscionable" 5 percent

city-state sales tax is based on a "private arrangement between Wagner and Rockefeller" is helping the Controller. Organizationally, he has done best in Brooklyn. He has initiated a truce there between pro-Screvane and pro-Beame district leaders which leaves both groups free to harry independents and reformers. Steingut's promise not to challenge the designating petitions of Beame's rivals pleases machine men all over town. Yesterday Steingut filed more than 100,000 signatures for Beame to 50,000 for Screvane.

With Manhattan, Queens, and Staten Island Democrats split in various ways, the crucial difference between Screvane and Beame may prove to be their running mates. O'Connor is a source of popular strength for Beame. Procaccino is the prototype of party workers everywhere. Orin Lehman makes a pleasant appearance and pulls in some campaign money, but Pat Moynihan seems to be developing into a political catastrophe. Take, for example, the radio tirade delivered by Moynihan after Beame's campaign chairman, Paul P. Rao, Jr., charged that *The Melting Pot* was more anti-Italian than a former TV program about the Mafia called "The Untouchables."

Instead of arguing that his book was a sociological treatise and not a campaign document, Moynihan said: "He (Rao) is a small little man. His Daddy is a Judge, his Daddy got him lots of nice soft political jobs all his life. He has too many wives but not enough principles. . . . I was a stevedore on the North River piers before Mr. Rao got his first jar of hair pomade and if he thinks he can run me out of my town, he's wrong."

To which Rao replied: "I remember once reading that when Socrates was booted by an ass he did not think it proper to return the kick." Rao went on unnecessarily to cite his high I.Q., his earning of a law degree in two instead of three years, and various high spots in his political career. Even so, he can afford the mistake. Unlike Moynihan he is not presently running for public office.

Thursday, August 19 — We were walking in the Chelsea section of Manhattan this morning when Detective George Wasylecow began saying goodbye. Price has apparently asked for a lifting of the police watch against assassination which began secretly during the July 4th weekend and became known to the public toward the end of that month. The other two detectives, Barney Allen and Pat Vecchio, will not return. As integral parts of our daily campaign existence they will be missed.

Birch Society pickets appeared in force during our afternoon street tours in Brooklyn. Their tone seemed uglier than usual, as if they had stored up venom during Lindsay's vacation and realized that he no longer possessed special police protection. He met them head on. Overriding the clamor by loudspeaker from a flatbed truck at the southeast corner of Bushwick Park, he said: "This demonstration reminds me of some of the worst moments of history. It ought to alert New Yorkers that the city is beset with extremism of a dangerous kind."

Turning to the non-Birch segment of the swelling crowd, Lindsay said: "If you are satisfied with the inept downward slide of New York during the past twenty years you will vote for the other guy. If you are satisfied with poor housing, you will vote for the other guy. If you are satisfied with crime in the streets you will vote for the other guy. . . . If you want a fresh start you will vote for me."

Since the candidate's phrasing and delivery seemed exceptionally sharp, I made additional notes:

"They used to say New York was a great place to visit but that they wouldn't want to live here. Now they don't even want to visit here. They charge you so much at the World's Fair it isn't worth going. . . .

"I say to New Yorkers, don't let your vote be taken for granted this year. Vote independently this year. I ask you to take my hand and be prepared to sweat a bit. You can have what you want, do what you want, if you think of reform.

Look high and remember that New York City belongs to the people and not to the clubhouses. . . .

"Are we New Yorkers or something less? If you are willing to ride a wave of reform you'll vote for the Lindsay team and start all over again. If you'll give me a chance, I can help this city to grow. It doesn't make any difference if we put 1,000 men on the moon, if we can't run a city here at home, we're finished—everything is finished. If New York is ungovernable, we're all through.

"I say to New Yorkers, rise up. Let's go, New Yorkers. We shall overcome our troubles. Let's go to work, let's go; let us build a new city."

At a Queens street rally in the evening, he said: "I came to this neighborhood a month ago and again two weeks ago. I'm here now and I'll be here after the election. Say to your neighbors that at least I care enough to come. Begin with that. If you are willing to join a revolution, a new movement in New York City to break open the existing establishment, then come with me."

For a Republican, he sounded almost subversive.

Friday, August 20 — The official inner circle of the Lindsay campaign came into existence today. Those invited by Price to breakfast for this purpose were George, John, and David Lindsay; Barnie Patterson and Connie Eristoff; Dick Aurelio, John Deardourff, and Harry O'Donnell. This constitutes the tighest possible functioning unit. Javits was not included because Dick Aurelio serves as his alter ego at headquarters. Similarly speechwriter Deardourff may represent Rockefeller. As O'Donnell's assistant, I was not needed. Nobody from the area of campaign financing, not even the fourth Lindsay brother, Rod, is listed. There is no expert on minority problems or labor. If the list had been longer, James Carberry, a dour but brilliant speechwriter, and one of the field men, Gil Robinson or Sid Davidoff, might have been included.

The precise membership may not be important. Price is

forever setting up groups to accomplish an oblique purpose or smooth a ruffled set of feathers. When the purpose is achieved or the feathers are smoothed the group tends to dissolve. Price once remarked that he sets up many campaign committees "but in the end John and I usually do the work." In interviews he usually asserts with undue modesty that he has no more say at headquarters "than any one of twenty other full-time volunteers" but when a campaign aide charged recently that his idea of a policy meeting was "to kick everybody out of the room and close the door," Price beamed unexpectedly and said: "You sound just like Lindsay."

Price's purpose in creating the inner circle may be to refute charges—emanating from such different sources as the *Wall Street Journal* and the state political editor of the United Press—that he is a campaign dictator. As soon as the existence of the inner circle proves he is not a dictator he can resume being one.

Catskill Mts., August 21–22 — Negro and Spanish-speaking residents of New York City have developed vacation resorts of their own in Ulster County in imitation of the celebrated Jewish ones in Sullivan County. I imagine many middle-class New Yorkers do not know of the existence of these places. I had never heard of them until we invaded them for campaign purposes this weekend. The accommodations are more modest and the prices lower than in the original pleasure domes but the basic appeal is the same: good food, fresh air and sunshine, indoor and outdoor games, dancing, some entertainment, and romance—above everything else, romance.

There has been a hurried, niggardly feeling about this second expedition into the Catskills. No sleepover was scheduled. This meant that the cars for reporters and photogaphers which left the Roosevelt around 9:30 A.M. Saturday did not get back to town until 4 A.M. Sunday. Campaigning in the mountains being old hat by this time, the *Tribune* and the *Times* did not cover, but the AP sent a reporter and the *Daily*

News a photographer for part of the trip. Professor Joseph Illick, of San Francisco State College, who plans to write about the campaign for a San Francisco paper, traveled with me in the first news car, along with Robert Kee, of TV Rediffusion of London, and his assistant, Norma Woodstone. They were delightful companions. The British TV technicians and their equipment traveled in a separate truck.

The British TV equipment, including a long black sleeve used by a sound man, rivaled Lindsay as an attraction in the Negro resorts around Kerhonkson and the Puerto Rican "Las Villas" near Patekill. Arrangements had been made for dinner at an expensive Jewish resort in the area. A misguided Lindsay assistant had the nerve to suggest to Kee that a show of TV activity might repay our hosts for their generosity. Kee said he was running low on film. It was then proposed that he shoot with empty cameras for effect.

It was at this point that Kee stalked over to me to say he did not mind paying for the meals of his men but he did mind asking them to work during mealtime when they were tired. I begged him to do no false shooting and promised to pay for everybody. I did try to pay later but the hotel declined payment. Kee and his crew left after dinner.

The rest of the trip was a quagmire. An American TV crew had been hired by our Spanish division to cover specified Puerto Rican resorts during the evening. The schedule was overloaded but nobody could be omitted without causing offense. Lindsay's manner gradually became edgy. He would dive into a place, shake a few hands, say a few words and dive out again.

Our news car driver, Trent Jones, the son of Mrs. Nina Jones, Mrs. Happy Rockefeller's press secretary, showed signs of weariness. Jones is a scholarly offbeat youngster who returns as an undergraduate to the University of Pennsylvania in the fall. He had been suffering from a cold and the effects of a night on the town when he left New York in the morning. By midnight his long-haired head was nodding ominously at the wheel. Since he refused to abandon his post of trust, we made a special stop—after Lindsay left us to fly back to town—to pour a quart of strong hot coffee into Jones. On that fuel he managed to convey us safely to New York.

Monday, August 23 — I'm in bed with one of those 24-hour viruses. The illness prevented me from attending a fund-raising "swimming and frugging party" last night at the Linden Beach Club in Whitestone, Queens. The guests included Johnny Desmond, who is playing opposite Barbra Streisand in *Funny Girl*; Carol George, a blues singer; Richard Terry, another singer; Carmen Cavallaro, who plays the piano and leads an orchestra; the Three Sisters from *Fiddler on the Roof*; and that well-known raconteur and mountain-climber, John Lindsay.

Since I am psychosomatic in the extreme I have been wondering what brought on my minor ailment. Worry over the newspaper situation may have contributed to it. Last Tuesday evening I ducked a Lindsay block party in the Canarsie section of Queens in order to preside over an emergency Guild executive committee meeting. On the recommendation of our executive vice-president, Thomas J. Murphy, we voted unanimously to strike the *New York Times* during the week of September 12. Ever since then the thought has been hitting me with increasing force that in the event of a strike I may have to drop out of the campaign to avoid embarassing Lindsay. If so, the *Post* will not want me back since my leave of absence runs until January 1. As a reporter on leave from the *Post* I will not even be eligible for strike benefits. A fine prospect!

Tuesday, August 24 — The temptation is strong in keeping a diary to note high spots rather than low ones. Actually the slips in a campaign are just as intriguing as the successes. Lindsay concedes that we have made mistakes but he usually argues that we haven't, in the immortal phrase of Yogi Berra, "made any *wrong* mistakes."

Perhaps the most basic blunder to date was the issuance in early July of contradictory explanations about Rockefeller's past and intended contributions to the campaign, which I think I mentioned awhile back. Lindsay has subsequently emphasized his political independence from Rockefeller on specific issues but a hazy impression persists in many quarters that he is the favorite of the GOP plump cats in the state.

Our most conspicuous recent flop was the presentation of a "Ten Point Program for the Economic Rejuvenation of New York" before a joint luncheon of Rotarians and Kiwanians in Brooklyn last Thursday. Lindsay was waiting for me when the campaign cars unloaded outside the Hotel St. George.

"I can't read this," he said, indicating a 3,000-word text prepared by a new speechwriter. "It's just words. Has it gone to the newspapers?"

It had gone to the papers for noon release and it was past noon. Lindsay shrugged and went inside. He started off by describing an incident which happened, he said, at a previous Rotarian-Kiwanian luncheon. He complained to the chairman, a Kiwanian, that somebody had stolen his watch. The chairman sidled over to a Rotarian, spoke confidentially and returned with the watch. How did he persuade the thief to give the watch back? "Shush," said the chairman, "He doesn't know I took it!"

After two similar anecdotes, Lindsay began to throw chunks of his sidewalk routines at the audience. At the end the audience seemed reasonably appreciative. Though he never delivered the ten-point speech, the newspapers have generally chided him for it. Wagner dismissed the program as "full of water and air" and Bill Buckley termed it "utter nothingness." Both are right. Our research staff is still working on a substitute program.

A spurious Barry Goldwater issue was created a couple of weeks ago. Charles (Lulu) Constantino, a retired lightweight who once lost fights to Beau Jack and Willie Pep, sponsored a pro-Lindsay rally near the hero sandwich and spaghetti house

which he and his brother Jimmy—the Hero King of Brooklyn
—operate outside the Brooklyn Navy Yard. In mailing invitations and press notices Lulu used leftover envelopes with
GOLDWATER VICTORY RALLY in scarlet letters in the upper left
hand corner. Since Lindsay did not support Goldwater last
year, this created consternation. The rally was cancelled.

The first batch of our HE IS FRESH AND EVERYONE ELSE IS
TIRED posters was printed in Chattanooga, Tenn. Because the
local printing industry is sensitive about losing business to the
hinterland, a newspaper exposé on this created a storm. The
skies cleared when we were able to establish (a) that the order
had been given to a New York firm which passed its overflow
business—without notice—to a Southern subsidiary, and (b)
that the same firm was filling poster orders for Screvane and
Beame down South.

Even Price nods. He made an error, I believe, in pulling
off our police guard. Those hate-filled Birchite pickets sound
nastier by the day.

Price also erred in trying to bring Lindsay back from vacation without public attention. His theory that the first publicity should be something positive in a campaign sense can
be defended, but an alert *Daily News* reporter, realizing that
only one plane arrived each evening from the Virgin Islands,
bushwhacked Lindsay at the airport for a damaging interview
on the "pretty boy" issue developed by Screvane. Since then
Bill Buckley has been referring to Lindsay as "the Cecil B.
DeMille candidate for President," "The Grecian Profile" and
"The Gorgeous Hunk of Man with the Gift of Mellifluity."

We all make mistakes. My most recent one involved a list
of political appointees to the anti-poverty program. My friend
on the city desk of the *Post* turned this over to a nonpolitical
woman reporter who did not realize that appointment in such
a situation depends primarily on the political muscle of the
sponsor. By placing stress on the candidates' supposed qualifications she managed to disinfect a valid story of political infiltration.

. . . the West Side Congressman . . .

Wednesday, August 25 — Ryan is being taken more seriously as a mayoral contender on the strength of finding leaks in the city's water supply system. Bill staged a dramatic press conference last Saturday while the Lindsay caravan was combing the Ulster County countryside for vacationing voters. Standing barefoot in water, his slacks rolled knee-high, the West Side Congressman pointed to a small waterfall inside a grotto not far from the West 100th Street entrance to Central Park.

"Look at that, it's a Niagara Falls," exclaimed Ryan, estimating the loss from the Central Park Reservoir, five hundred yards to the South, at thousands of gallons a day.

Because of legitimate public concern over a drop in the water level of the city reservoirs upstate from 80 percent of capacity a year ago to 40 percent now, Ryan has become an overnight hero. In Staten Island, Brooklyn, and Queens, homeowners are drilling wells on their property, not for drinking water but for pools, lawns, and car-washing. Complaints are being heard in lower Manhattan that the quality of water from the billion-gallon Central Park Reservoir has deteriorated.

Ryan has taken every possible advantage of his opportunity. His office has established a Leak Bureau with a special phone number to receive tips on mysterious effusions of water. By this device he learned about a geyser in a subway station in Brooklyn and a small stream at 93d Street and Fifth Avenue in Central Park.

Water Commissioner D'Angelo's confusion has helped Ryan. At first he denied any leak at the grotto. Later he said his engineers knew about the leak all along. After further delay his office announced that he was investigating.

D'Angelo and Ryan stood by on Monday while divers inspected a sluice gate in the reservoir. As soon as the corroded gate was repaired, aides of the Commissioner said, the leak in the grotto would stop. Yesterday D'Angelo reversed himself. For technical reasons, he said, the flow at the grotto would have to continue for some months at least.

For many years I've been living near the West 100th Street entrance to the park. Once a week at least, on my regular Sunday morning walk, I have passed the now-celebrated grotto. The waterfall looks contrived to me. Certainly the way the stream ducks almost immediately under a path for pedestrians is artificial. The stream runs 150 feet into an exquisitely shaped small pond created by a man-made dam at its easterly end. From the bottom of this second waterfall, a stream meanders into the hills, traveling a good three-quarters of a mile to a large boat basin at the northeasterly tip of the park at 110th Street and Fifth Avenue.

Without being a water expert or even a former secretary of Local 3 of the Electrical Workers Union I can see that the grotto and the waterfall within it, the waterlane to the pond and the longer stream through the hills to the boat basin are parts of a cleverly concealed "natural" design dating back decades to a time when Father Knickerbocker had more water than he knew what to do with and could spare a little for scenic beauty.

Unless Ryan wins the Democratic nomination, which is unlikely, there would be no gain to Lindsay in disputing the validity of the discovery at the grotto so I shall keep my opinion to myself. I do not expect that D'Angelo will dare to tell the public in its present semi-hysteria that he let a deliberate leak continue into a period of water shortage. On the other hand he cannot stop the flow from the grotto without destroying much of the charm of the north section of the park. He is in a difficult position.

Thursday, August 26 — Lindsay drew 2,000 persons to a rally last night in Forest Hills, a section of Queens County which is 75 percent Democratic. The size of the turnout disturbed some of the followers of Queens Democratic boss Moe Weinstein. A half-dozen Democratic captains formed a claque to shout "Rockefeller stooge" whenever Lindsay paused. A spectator picked up the cry sufficiently to ask what the candidate's attitude was toward the Governor.

"Rockefeller was wrong on the Condon-Wadlin Act," Lindsay replied, referring to a Rockefeller veto of a bill which would have softened the present unduly harsh and unenforceable penalties under the law prohibiting strikes by public employes.

"Rockefeller is wrong on mandated free tuition," Lindsay continued, referring to oblique efforts from Albany to break the free-tuition tradition in the city university. "He is wrong in not giving $200,000,000 more to the New York City school system. Why should the 35 percent of the students in the State University who live in the city get only 25 percent of the school revenues? I think the Governor is wrong on many issues. I vote independently."

The hecklers quieted down, but Jack Barnes of the Associated Press, the only reporter covering us, had been taking careful notes. Since AP copy goes to all the papers and this was exciting enough to be generally used, the discussion was resumed on a wider plane at our morning news conference today. Lindsay made it clear that he does not reject Rockefeller support. "He is trying to help and I think he is helping. I am in agreement with the Governor on many things and in disagreement on other things. I have never hesitated to disagree with him publicly on an issue."

It had been said before, but under the persistent questioning of the reporters it had to be said again: no dates have been set for Rockefeller appearances in the Lindsay-Mollen-Costello campaign.

"Our job is to present our position ourselves and there isn't anything anyone else can do," said Lindsay.

Asked if he agrees with those who think Rockefeller would be a liability in his campaign, Lindsay replied: "I don't think so at all." He looked positively shocked at the idea.

Friday, August 27 — Two books on Lindsay will appear next month. Daniel E. Button, executive editor of the Albany *Times-Union*, is the author of one entitled *Lindsay: A Man for Tomorrow*. Button had accepted an advance for the book from Random House and had researched it but he had not reached the writing stage. The day Lindsay declared for mayor, Bennett Cerf wired Button to get moving. Button obtained a leave from his paper, holed up in a motel outside Albany for thirty days and emerged with a manuscript. He is a scholarly fellow, a former assistant to the President of the State University, so his opus will undoubtedly be a superior campaign biography.

The second book is a monograph on politics from 1918 to 1965 in the congressional area south and east of Central Park entitled *John V. Lindsay and the Silk-Stocking Story*. It's by Casper Citron, a radio commentator formerly active in Democratic reform politics, who knows the subject since he once ran unsuccessfully for Congress in this district.

There have been rumors of a third book. Leonard Lyons' newspaper column carried a recent item that "Theodore H. White, who wrote *The Making of a President,* is in town to write a book on 'The Making of a Mayor.'" White has his home here so being in town is not necessarily significant. His secretary, Dana Benenson, recently requested a file of our releases. White himself took me to breakfast yesterday. Most of his questions, such as the precise source of contributions to our increasingly expensive campaign and what Lindsay will do with his 35,000 volunteers if he is elected, were over my head. White will go out with our press caravan after some preliminary talk with Price. Though he has agreed to do an article for *Look* magazine, he has no present intention, he says, of writing a book on Lindsay.

Cornell Capa is already taking photographs for the *Look* article. Since he is famous for close-ups with a wide-angled lens he wants to be in Lindsay's car all the time. This creates a problem. Ordinarily the candidate's time is rationed among photographers covering him to avoid jealousy. Today I gave Capa permission to ride in the lead car on two legs of our many-legged schedule but that did not suffice. Finding a niche facing Lindsay a few inches in front of the candidate's nose, Capa remained there alert but impassive as a Buddha while we traveled from point to point. Moreover he pulled into the overcrowded car his caption writer, Giovanna Breu, a charming girl married to Joe Breu of the UP.

The situation became impossible after a block party in Trump Village, a housing project near Coney Island. As Lindsay pushed through the dense crowd after his speech, his shirt was ripped again and again, deliberately and with malice, by a Conservative party picket. Mary Lindsay was close enough to catch the man a resounding slap across the cheek. Then our three most powerful Raiders, Teddy Mastroianni, Norman Samnick, and Sid Davidoff, charged the picket simultaneously from different directions. The man collapsed like a tackling

. . . the shirt-ripping incident . . .

dummy. He was yanked to his feet and turned over to police. Lindsay reached his car naked from the waist up and bleeding from a long scratch across his chest.

Because his flash bulb failed Capa had missed a picture of the shirt-ripping incident, but he held his usual vantage point in the Lindsay car when it stopped for a conference a few blocks from Trump Village. By this time everybody was sitting in everybody else's lap in that car. Lindsay struggled out of the car and stood on the sidewalk listening to contradictory advice on how to obtain a new shirt.

Since the Lindsays were due next at a private meeting with some potential campaign contributors collected by Mollen, I asked Capa to move back into one of the two press cars. He ignored the request.

Turning to Giovanna Breu I said loudly that there was no longer room enough for Capa or her in Lindsay's car.

"We were invited to ride here," snapped the lovely Giovanna.

"You were not invited by me," observed Mary Lindsay. Capa's hearing improved. He and Miss Breu left for seats in the press car where I was not riding. They gave every indication of being insulted.

Our motorcade of reporters, photographers, advance men, field men, observers from headquarters and volunteers—five or six cars in all—proceeded to a new Lindsay headquarters on Southern Boulevard in the Bronx, called Bronx Democrats for Lindsay. There we waited an interminable hour for the Lindsays and the Mollens to arrive. During the waiting period Capa bought me a pizza and a beer. I interpreted this as a sign of forgiveness on the part of the renowned photographer, but his colleague, the lovely Giovanna, still will not speak to me.

Saturday, August 28 — The latest wave of immigration in New York City—later than the Latin-Americans who followed the influx of Puerto Ricans—is that of Chinese from Hongkong and Taiwan. These new arrivals are pouring by the tens of thousands into the downtown area known as Chinatown, pushing the Italian-Americans farther north and the Jewish residents farther east. Simultaneously, not a few second, third, and fourth-generation Chinese-Americans are gaining courage to desert Chinatown in favor of orderly sections of the city like Washington Heights, Flatbush, and Forest Hills. It may be the Chinese passion for law and order which makes them conservative in American politics. Certainly they are the only minority in New York City that is demonstrably pro-Republican.

All this is preamble to the fact that we opened an Independent Citizens party clubhouse in Chinatown this evening. It was supposed to be a regular storefront until somebody got the idea of using the new catchall party name. The occasion was enlivened by the presence of a dragon, an undulating skin over five or six cavorting Chinese. Everybody tossed strings of tiny firecrackers at the dragon until Pell Street was full of noisy flashes and acrid smoke. One firecracker went off in the hair of James Ryan, the Associated Press reporter, but, as Lindsay observed in one of his buoyant moods, no firecracker stood much of a chance in collision with an AP man's head.

Three dainty, elaborately dressed Chinese girls had been elected Queens to preside over an oriental smorgasbord in the second-floor headquarters. A man named Mok played a harmonica solo composed for the occasion and a man named Wei delivered a two-sentence speech in praise of "responsible nonpartisan government."

After Lindsay responded appropriately, we all descended into the street again where the dragon revived among fresh bursts of firecrackers. Lindsay decided to drive the Queens home. All three of them got in the back seat of his car. By this time Kee's British TV crew and Cornell Capa, who had been taking pictures earlier, were gone. Only Ryan remained with me in the back seat of the press car as we followed the candidate's car slowly through the narrow winding streets of Chinatown.

The Queens got out in front of a spacious white apartment house facing Manhattan Bridge Plaza. They were roundly kissed goodnight in turn by Lindsay. As they disappeared inside he shouted back at the press car in mock indignation: "Why don't you fellows get lost?"

The two Lindsay campaign cars rode side by side along the Bowery. A small object flashed through our open window missing Ryan's nose and landing on the floor at my feet.

"Look out," yelled Lindsay from the other car. "It's lit!"

The object was a chain of Chinese firecrackers. Since they can explode unexpectedly I stamped vigorously until I realized I had been fooled. The firecrackers had not been lit. I should have picked them up like an unexploded hand grenade and tossed them back at the other car, but it was too late for that because Lindsay's driver had speeded up to the sound of jubilant laughter and gotten away from us.

Sunday, August 29 — I am resting at home today with O'Don-

The girls might have been friendly visitors from another planet.

nell's permission. I read Norman Podhoretz' laudatory article about Pat Moynihan in the *Herald Tribune* Sunday magazine. Podhoretz quotes Theodore White as saying Pat has "one of the most luminous minds in Washington." No doubt this is true but Pat continues to embarrass his ticket. His latest gambit, as a Bobby Kennedy man, is to refuse conspicuously to attack Bronx boss Charley Buckley, the chief target of Screvane's charges of bossism. He is as blind to Buckley's defects as Mollen is to Wagner's.

Monday, August 30 — Negro children in the urban slums are fascinated by blondes. This was brought home to me one day when two fifteen-year-old Norwegian-American girls were al-

. . . clinging like barnacles . . .

lowed to ride in the luggage area of one of our press station
wagons at the request of their father, our Bay Ridge storefront
manager. In every Brooklyn ghetto where we stopped a silent
semicircle of black moppets gathered at the rear of that press
car to stare solemnly at the transparent skin and cornsilk hair
of our pretty guests. There was no hostility, just admiring
curiosity, in the stares. The girls might have been friendly
visitors from another planet.

Negro children give Lindsay his most enthusiastic welcome. He treats them like his own children. That helps. His
light blue eyes and generally Nordic appearance may also help.
According to Pat Moynihan's *The Melting Pot*, many Negro
children in the cities grow up with a need for a substitute
father because their own fathers desert the home. The substitute image is provided by the white press, the white magazines,

and TV. Perhaps Lindsay corresponds to it. I don't know for sure but I do know that the gratifying frenzy of the Negro small-fry often cuts the candidate off from adults whom he is trying to reach.

This thought must have occurred to Lindsay one afternoon when he was walking through Fort Greene Houses, a low-rent housing project in Brooklyn. Three or four Negro youngsters were clinging like barnacles to each arm and others were clustered so heavily around his shoulders, waist, and legs that he had difficulty moving. In the middle of a square paved area he paused, noting the adults watching from windows, balconies, and fire-escapes of the high-rise buildings on each of the four sides.

"Let's play a game," said Lindsay, smiling at the youngsters. "Everybody face this direction." He faced south.

"I'll count one-two-three and at three everybody wave. Understand? I'll count one-two-three and then everybody wave. One, two, three, WAVE!"

Somewhat raggedly, the children imitated his waving. Some adults in the south building waved back.

"Right face, everybody," ordered Lindsay, facing west. "Do it again, one, two, three, WAVE." This time the waving was more solid and the reception improved. "Right face again, everybody. One, two, three, WAVE. Keep waving. Right face again. One, two, three, WAVE. Wonderful. Now let's go around the whole circle again . . ."

Gradually the applause and delight of the children on the ground and their friends and relatives in the buildings intermingled until the whole project was one applauding, waving crowd.

Since then Lindsay has tried his group-waving trick in two other low-rent housing projects, one in East Harlem and one in Queens, with identical exhilarating results. Unfortunately no reporter or photographer has been present on these occasions. The interaction of children and adults has to be seen to be believed.

Tuesday, August 31 — At a news conference today, Bill Buckley kept referring to Lindsay as "the ecumenical candidate." That's a religious way of saying fusion, I suppose.

"Lindsay is trying to become mayor by doing nothing," continued Buckley. "A victory for Lindsay would be a victory for the left wing of the Democratic party. If Lindsay were any more liberal, he'd be in a zoo!"

Somebody asked: "Why aren't you out campaigning on the streets, like Lindsay?" Buckley replied that he found crowds "rather an ordeal." He added: "I sometimes wonder how Lindsay really feels about crowds."

Well, this afternoon we were moving north along Fourth Avenue in the Bay Ridge section of Brooklyn with an entourage of Buckley pickets. In addition to the familiar signs they had a new one reading: LINDSAY LOVES COMMUNISTS. Armand Starace, the Republican leader of Bay Ridge, was walking with me a pace or two behind Lindsay, when a shower of ripe tomatoes came from across the street.

One tomato caught Starace on the right side of his neck. Another smashed against his right leg. Two boys, almost out of sight, were dodging south through the sidewalk crowd. A third was scampering east toward Fifth Avenue along a side street empty enough to allow a clear look at the way he was dressed.

Lindsay kept walking as if nothing had happened. Friends clustered around Starace. Assuming that this third boy would try to rejoin us as soon as he felt safe, I asked a couple of Raiders to wait with me just around a corner one block to the north. The boy did not appear.

We waited in ambush again another block to the north. This time the boy came skittering along and we grabbed him. He couldn't have been older than twelve or thirteen. He was carrying a paper bag which still contained one tomato. One of the Raiders removed the tomato.

Though the boy was defiant he looked frightened when the Raiders began talking of getting a cop. I said we would let him go if he explained why he threw the tomatoes. He said a man with a SUPPORT YOUR LOCAL POLICE sign approached him with a bag of three tomatoes and gave him 50 cents to throw them at Lindsay. . . .

The Raiders and I looked at each other in silence. Then the Raider holding the tomato placed it carefully inside the boy's shirt and flattened it with a slap before telling him to be on his way.

☆☆★   *September*

Wednesday, September 1 — Lindsay has accepted a CBS-TV invitation for an hour and a half debate on September 19. He has also agreed to debate on Barry Gray's radio program over WMCA as soon as a date can be arranged. His acceptances are contingent on the appearance of his Democratic and Conservative opponents. He will not meet either one separately. This arrangement gives him one big advantage. Beame and Screvane are now scrambling frantically toward the September 14 primary election. Whoever wins will find it difficult to turn around and face Lindsay on TV only five days later. As for Bill Buckley, who has been howling for an exclusive debate with Lindsay, he is suddenly left without a case.

The preliminary maneuvering for position is worth noting because a revolutionary change in American politics was wrought by the Kennedy-Nixon TV debates of 1960. President Johnson did not debate Barry Goldwater on TV in 1964, but the 1961 mayoral election in New York and many other elections across the country were decided by confrontations in the Kennedy-Nixon manner. Since the ordeal by electronics gives any underdog a chance of becoming an upperdog overnight, even the relative willingness of the candidates to debate becomes important.

Screvane's advisers, I hear, want him to avoid any video-jousting with Lindsay. On the basis of a supposed Quayle poll of 1,500 Democrats in five boroughs taken August 23, which allegedly shows Screvane receiving 51 percent of the straws to 33 percent for Beame, they believe they have Beame licked in the primary. Screvane will then, they say, be in Nixon's 1960 position—the better-known, more experienced public figure—and he must therefore not repeat Nixon's mistake of building up his opponent through TV exposure. They can be wrong on two counts.

Beame and Screvane debated last night on Barry Gray's late-evening radio show. I caught the tag end of it. Except for a Screvane charge that Beame has "gotten in bed" with Bronx boss Charley Buckley and a Beame charge that Screvane is being "demagogic" it seemed dull. Beame, for instance, mentioned the *Post* article about politicians grabbing top jobs in the anti-poverty program. Screvane replied that the article "did not say we hired anyone on the recommendation of a political leader." Screvane was right but they were both too polite.

According to Marshall McLuhan, radio is a "hot medium" favoring strongly individualized presentation. Once Screvane and Beame learn to act naturally they will do all right on radio, but I believe Lindsay—and Bill Buckley, too—will do better in the "cool medium" of TV.

Thursday, September 2 — Lindsay, who frequently gets snappy with reporters, had a better excuse than usual for ill-temper last night. He was tired from a long day of campaigning which had begun with a 9:30 A.M. news conference and included a supermarket opening on the lower East Side of Manhattan, a Catholic carnival in Brooklyn, two long walking tours in Queens, and a Citizens Committee reception in Forest Hills. By the time we reached the First Unitarian Church of Brooklyn Heights it was raining and the rain seemed to sum up the dull resentful mood into which our campaign caravan had fallen.

Lindsay read a 3,500-word position paper on education as his speech of the evening. The paper ranged widely over existing defects in the school system and urged the expenditure of an additional $100,000,000 to recruit new teachers and reduce class size. He then asked for questions. These were on the whole intelligent and well-phrased. However, one persistent questioner on the subject of school-busing for purposes of in-

tegration attracted the attention of Mort Dean, a CBS-TV reporter who had gotten permission to set up his equipment in
the church vestibule for an interview with Lindsay on the way
out.

Dean did not appreciate the fact that Lindsay has been
using a complicated formula on school busing ever since it
was the chief issue in the 1964 Congressional campaign. No
matter how Dean framed his questions, he could not get the
Congressman to venture outside the formula. In his frustra-
tion Dean began to charge on the air that Lindsay was evasive.
The candidate contained himself until the interview ended.
Then he exploded. "You don't know what you're talking
about, you son of a bitch," he told Dean in a low tone. "Don't
try to interview me again."

That was last night. This morning Dean joined me at
breakfast at my invitation in the Hotel Roosevelt coffee shop
so we could discuss the incident quietly. I mentioned several
incidents of aggressive and tricky behavior by radio and TV reporters which have bothered Lindsay recently. While conceding that Dean's behavior did not belong among the cases cited,
I pointed out that the interview, which was not prearranged
and hence represented a concession on the candidate's part,
came toward the close of an arduous day on a sticky subject.
Dean in turn mentioned various complaints of the radio-TV
fraternity against Lindsay. In his own case he had no complaint except that he did not think he deserved a rebuke for
trying to make some news.

After explaining the school-busing formula, I told Dean
that Lindsay considered him one of the top men in his field.
Despite the remark he made Lindsay has no blacklist, I said,
and Dean will be as welcome as ever at our news conferences.
I then invited Dean to the morning news conference which
had been postponed until 10 A.M. to let Lindsay finish posing
for a *Time* magazine cover portrait by Henry Koerner. Dean
did not accept today's invitation but the air was considerably
cleared without apology on either side.

. . . highly charged individuals create an atmosphere . . .

Friday, September 3 — After a while you take life at headquarters for granted. If you look at it with foreign eyes for a few minutes, you realize it's an anarchistic place where highly charged individuals create an atmosphere which is usually energetic, often gay, and occasionally tragic. An unguided tour of a few rooms across the campaign corridor from the press office will demonstrate this.

... on a billboard overlooking Bryant Park ...

Start with Harvey Rothenberg, a former commander of LCT 1234 against the Japanese in World War II, who now presides over the 60 paid employes and 250 regular volunteers at headquarters. Our office manager is a camera fiend. The wall behind his large, centrally placed desk is covered with snapshots of colleagues in surrealistic poses. He caught me, for example, standing inside a large empty metal trash can alongside Harry O'Donnell's desk. How he induced me to climb into that trash can I do not know.

Harvey has a whim a week. Recently he handed out HAPPY and SAD buttons to the staff, with a request that one or the other be worn at all times. On the basis of the buttons he conducted a daily survey of office morale until he was thwarted by iconoclasts who insisted on being HAPPY and SAD simultaneously. The least colorful aspect of Harvey's room is Mary Lindsay's desk, facing a side wall exhibiting a few pictures of the Lindsay children, taken by Katsy Thomas, our athletic and enterprising campaign photographer.

Moving along that same side of the corridor brings you to the room of Ken Duffes, a soft-spoken, silvery-haired promotional genius. Ken is credited with the sixty-foot-long illuminated message (taken from the film "Mary Poppins") on a billboard overlooking Bryant Park in midtown Manhattan: LINDSAY IS SUPERCALIFRAGILISTICEXPIALIDOCIOUS, which may well be the most original sign of the campaign.

The next room belongs to Gil Robinson and his electronic equipment. Anybody walking in here is likely to hear Debbie Thomas, the radio telephone operator, intoning some message in partial code: "MANSION calling RAIDER GENERAL. MANSION calling RAIDER GENERAL. JUNO will join BEN at Coney Island in the afternoon." The room itself is dominated by a large wall motto: ASSUME NOTHING—which I assume came from the Washington office of former U.S. Attorney General Brownell, for whom Lindsay once worked.

Finally comes the room reserved for the 75 school-age volunteers called Raiders. Those in charge are Sid Davidoff, the Raider General; Sid's secretary, Lynne Goree; and Dotty Marks, the Den Mother. This noisy place with its stuffed bunnies and doggies hanging from the walls, its pennants and posters and blue-and-white silk sashes resembles nothing so much as a prep school version of a day nursery. One wall exhibits a campaign schedule on which gold stars are pasted for Raiders who have been arrested for campaign exploits or who have escaped arrest in a diverting fashion.

Beame threatened at one time to sue over a picture of him in the Raider room with hair drawn over his face under the title ABE BEATLE. Candidate Beatle is quoted as saying: "I shall use the full power of the bosses to back the sales tax." Until his advisers talked him out of it Beame claimed this was libelous. Another photo shows Bill Buckley with a Hitler mustache. Buckley may not like this, but he has not threatened to sue.

The most conspicuous banner in the Raider room, in letters two feet high, reads: BREAK A LEG, JOHN. This derives from a theatrical maxim that it is bad luck to wish anyone good luck before a performance. Since Lindsay has a genuine feeling for the theater, he often grins when he strides along the campaign corridor and catches a glimpse of that friendly malediction.

No talisman is perfect. Last Sunday afternoon a young Raider called Weasel, in accordance with the group's fondness for obnoxious-sounding but proudly-borne nicknames, darted across the street on an errand as our campaign cars were preparing to leave the Roosevelt. A speeding taxi hit the boy and threw him almost twenty feet. He was taken to hospital in pitiable condition. I was off Sunday and because of tight scheduling could not get away to see him until today. I found Weasel well-attended in his hospital room, cheerful, and clearly on the mend. His worst injury turns out to be a broken leg.

The Poconos, September 4 — Campaigning in the mountains of Pennsylvania can be conceived as an extension of our previous visits to the Catskills and Long Island. Yet it is farther than we have gone previously in search of voters. If the summer were longer I suppose our next trip would be to Atlantic City or Sun Valley.

The logistics of our invasion of the Poconos required two small planes. Lindsay, the Mollens, and Costello took one plane and the reporters covering us took the other. The press plane had no trouble but the candidates' plane veered off course and bounced around violently in the air. Lindsay bent over to touch the ground gratefully when he emerged from the plane at Mt. Pocono Airport. Mollen, who had turned green, was so sick he went to bed for a couple of hours in a nearby hotel.

Though there were earlier stops, including a dude ranch in Milford, and a recreational and cultural resort in Forest Park known as Tamiment, our objective was Unity House, the vacation haven of the International Ladies Garment Workers Union. Approximately 1,200 union members were enjoying themselves when we arrived. We swam in the lake, attended a cocktail party under the trees, dined in the Unity House dining room and attended a rally in the Unity House theater.

The British appetite for views of Lindsay being insatiable, we were joined at the cocktail party by a BBC-TV crew under David Webstein. David Dubinsky provided plenty of action for them. Blowing a whistle fiercely at intervals to summon subordinates for instructions, the seventy-five-year-old union president took his visitors on a tour of lakeside cabins and along the way gave his uninhibited views on the future of New York politics.

Not until dinner time did the reason for our excursion become apparent. Louis Stulberg, the union secretary-treasurer and heir apparent to Dubinsky, was present, along with such vice-presidents as Charles (Sascha) Zimmerman, Shelley Appleton, Ed Kramer, and Matthew Schoenwald. I had never seen so much ILGWU brass in one spot. When I commented on the turnout, Zimmerman explained that the executive board is meeting there Monday and Tuesday.

For weeks there have been reports that elements in the union hierarchy were dragging their heels over the Lindsay endorsement. Undoubtedly the question of financial support will arise at the board meeting. Since the ILGWU normally provides half the sinews of war for the Liberal party, the importance of the impending rally became clear.

Lindsay had only prepared "remarks." He made one or two mistakes in extemporizing, praising Dubinsky as the leader of the "textile union industry"—instead of the ladies garment industry—and citing the Liberal party record "over the course of a century," though the party was only formed in 1944.

Though Costello and Mollen spoke at too-great length, they were well-received. Dubinsky carried the show. The old man alternately bullied and caressed the audience, howling for quiet and shouting for the closing of curtains at the rear, conceding that union members cannot be told how to vote because they are too intelligent and telling them, with a glance at Stulberg, who shared the platform with him, that he was confident "this team will be the administration of the city of New York after January 1." I guess we'll get our money.

Sunday, September 5 — Monique Van Vooren (40–30–40 and 135 I.Q., so they say) joined our campaign tour today of

. . . chiefly concerned at first over possible wind damage to her intricate hairdo . . .

Marine Park, Jacob Riis Park, and the Rockaways. A very composed young woman wearing a pink scarf with a fringe over a pale green dress, she seemed chiefly concerned at first over possible wind damage to her intricate hairdo whenever she rode in a convertible with Lindsay.

Under urging from Richard Bricker, an advertising man who is a friend of Lindsay, Monique loosened up sufficiently in the afternoon to sing "Oh Johnny" at one stop, using the old lyrics instead of our campaign version. Lindsay congratulated her with a kiss and the audience surged forward for autographs which she signed with a will. Lindsay escorted her home from Fort Tilden in Rockaway to Manhattan by helicopter.

Monday, September 6 — Lindsay has a weakness for bright youngsters. Most of them at headquarters are recent college graduates with high I.Q.'s and lesser quotients of common sense. Several of them hail from out of town and are quite unfamiliar with local habits. Lately they have been having a field day with our "daily irritant." This is an idea stolen from Bill Ryan who followed up his daily discoveries of water leaks by citing a "daily broken promise" of the Wagner-Screvane administration.

Our daily irritants — which by implication the fusion team will eliminate if it is elected—include filthy subways, potholes in the streets, missing street signs, and "the bunching of buses." They went over well for a while but they have been wearing thin. The other day we belabored the daily irritant of waiting for a bus in an exposed spot on the sidewalk. Our proposal of ornamental umbrellas to shield bus riders from exposure to the elements aroused some reportorial snickers.

Lindsay was ailing today for the first time in the campaign, so Mollen and Costello conducted our regular news conference. At the customary briefing before the news conference, Mollen suggested that in presenting our daily irritant in the future we stress that it's a minor matter lest somebody get the notion that the Lindsay-Mollen-Costello ticket is "seeking election on a slatless-park-bench issue." Everybody agreed and at the news conference itself the daily irritant was omitted by common consent.

Tuesday, September 7 — I awoke at 3 A.M. with the name of Krakauer in my mind. I had never heard the name before but I understood at once that he is the imp at the base of my spine who objects to me sitting down before a typewriter after a long campaign day to write an entry in this diary or for that matter to write anything at all. I don't know why Krakauer bothers me in the middle of the night or even whether he is enemy or friend.

Since my wife Avice was also awake I tried to tell her about Krakauer but she was not interested. What she wanted to know was: what would we do for money when I lost my job with Lindsay? Curiously enough Krakauer had some opinion on this subject but it has already faded from my mind.

The inevitable Guild strike at the *New York Times* is now set for a week from Thursday. In retaliation, the Publishers Association will probably lock out employees on several other papers (excluding the *Post,* which withdrew from the association during the 1962–63 strike) and we will experience something approaching a citywide newspaper blackout. At a recent executive committee meeting of the New York Guild I repeated an earlier statement that I expected to leave Lindsay if any conflict developed between his campaign and my union duties. Today our Guild newspaper, *Frontpage,* carried an appropriately grim photograph of me under the headline: AT GUILD CALL/PILAT DROPS/LINDSAY LABORS.

If I have an enemy at headquarters—and how can I fail to have at least one?—that headline provides a fulcrum to pry me loose from a job which I find exciting in itself and doubly exciting in that at my age I can still handle it. I don't even need an enemy since I have notified O'Donnell that I intend to resign in the event of a strike.

Wednesday, September 8 — State GOP Chairman Carl Spad has set up a Republican committee in the Belmont Plaza Hotel under John A. Wells, former director of Rockefeller's drive to gain the presidential nomination in 1960, "to mobilize the efforts of 700,000 enrolled Republicans in the city campaign." This gesture will enable the Governor to say he did his share in case Lindsay by some remote possibility becomes mayor.

The honorary chairman of the Republican City Campaign Committee, according to Wells, will be Rockefeller. Who else could have been found for such an onerous job? The honorary vice-chairmen will be Lt. Gov. Malcolm Wilson, Attorney General Lefkowitz, former Senator Keating, and Wilma Rogalin, the long-stemmed blonde beauty who is vice-chairman of the Republican State Committee. With that bunch actively on Lindsay's side, how can he lose?

The Wells announcement, of course, damages Lindsay's chances by inducing a new spate of embarrasing questions. In theory at least our storefronts, which now number 106, are mobilizing every Republican, Liberal, Democrat, or Independent who wants fusion government. I suppose the necessity of saying that the new committee is superfluous is what bothered Lindsay yesterday. Today he was willing to face the music.

"Do you welcome the Wells committee?" he was asked at a news conference.

"It's unnecessary," he replied.

"Were you consulted about it?"

"No."

"Can a Republican run the city successfully after 20 years of Democratic rule?"

"A nonpartisan independent administration, not a Republican one, is needed to rebuild the city after 20 years of gradual deterioration. The city of tomorrow requires nonpartisanship."

Asked if he had received $100,000 from Rockefeller, Lindsay replied that the loan is still outstanding. He may be on uncertain ground. A rumor is circulating that the formation of the Wells committee is somehow linked to a promise by the Governor to convert his $100,000 loan into a campaign gift.

Certainly the Rockefeller presence haunts headquarters. Campaign aides enthusiastically circulate and earnestly applaud the feeblest possible jokes about the man in Albany. Sample: Rockefeller is about to sign a desalinization bill passed by the state legislature. He pauses, pen in hand, to ask: "When did New York run out of salt?"

Thursday, September 9 — Price filed pre-primary statements with the Board of Elections yesterday that the Lindsay campaign has already received and spent nearly $600,000. This slightly exceeds the receipts and expenditures of all four Democratic contenders put together plus Bill Buckley. As a result the newspapers are full of political analyses implying that Lindsay is trying to buy the mayoralty. By listing loans as assets instead of liabilities, one observer places the total of Lindsay's campaign contributions to date at $900,000. Another argues that the eventual capture of the White House must be envisaged since the capture of City Hall does not warrant such spending.

Screvane estimates the eventual cost of the Lindsay campaign at $3,000,000. Beame is more conservative in his arithmetic; he sets the figure at $2,000,000. A Lindsay spokesman (O'Donnell) tells reporters that the campaign was originally budgeted and is still budgeted at $1,500,000.

Since our news conference was scheduled for 2:30 P.M. we had time to prepare for the inevitable press onslaught. Alex Rose phoned in midmorning to suggest stress on the unusual length of Lindsay's pre-primary campaign. Others at headquarters urged emphasis on the expense of planting storefronts all over town, each with a dozen telephones, buttons, brochures, etc. In the briefing session before the news conference, Lindsay took a different tack. He resisted running for mayor, he said, because he was not sure a "campaign of deep penetration" could be mounted and he wanted nothing less. Friends still expect him to lose, he added, for want of $700,000 for TV.

Without any action on our part, the public relations climate began to change around noon as a result of an exclusive front-page story in the first edition of the *World-Telegram*. Under a banner heading: HATE TACTICS HIT LINDSAY, the story revealed, on the authority of a source "close to the Republican-Liberal candidate," that "vicious right-wing terrorism" was being exercised against Lindsay. The death threats in early July, which resulted in a police guard for a month and a half, were recounted. Incidents of harassment against storefronts and groups of volunteers, including infiltration and sabotage, robbery and assault, were cited in convincing detail. One or two cases of hooliganism in the streets on which I had filed memos with Price were also described. I imagine Price leaked the story to a favorite reporter.

When inquiries rolled in Lindsay said he was sorry the story had appeared since he did not wish to alarm his volunteers. A check with his operations men, he said, indicated that the story was substantially accurate. He declined to ascribe the terrorism to any particular political group but it did not take much detective work to follow the trail to the Conservative party.

Bill Buckley felt obliged to issue a disclaimer. "There are crackpots everywhere," he declared, "both on the left and the right, but I am a responsible rightist, just as Lindsay is a leftist." Unfortunately for Buckley his message did not reach his supporters soon enough. Our Queens walking tour today encountered a score of Birchite pickets in a rough mood. "Go home, Lindsay, you bum, go home," they shouted. They called him a "Commonist" and other names at short range.

Several cops and a sergeant were watching but they ignored my pleas that they keep the pickets far enough away to permit the candidate to communicate with the voters. After a half-hour of turbulence Lindsay entered a five-and-ten-cent store to shake hands. The Birchite pickets, kept outside by

"There are crackpots everywhere."

the police, began shouting: "We want Buckley." A number of Lindsay volunteers responded by shouting: "We want Lindsay."

With the help of a bullhorn, the Lindsay forces overrode the opposition. A Buckleyite grabbed for the bullhorn, but a Raider named Mark Schlachtman shoved him back and stuck out his chin provocatively. Sid Davidoff stood alertly alongside Schlachtman. Obviously a riot was in the making. One of the cops to whom I had previously appealed without success yelled: "Give 'em room, give 'em room!" and began pushing back the pickets. From that moment the police kept the Birchites at a reasonable distance.

Friday, September 10 — Price convened a small group at 11 P.M. to discuss Lindsay's schedule after next Tuesday's primary election. Those present included the candidate, his brothers

George and David, O'Donnell, and me. Starting Wednesday, Price explained, White Papers—which are expanded and pretentious position papers on basic campaign issues—will be issued on a daily basis. It was agreed:

1. O'Donnell will draft, not later than Sunday night, the statement to be used by Lindsay Tuesday evening. "There must be nothing negative in it," cautioned Price. "The Democratic victor deserves his day in the sun." The statement will pledge a constructive campaign and stress Lindsay's willingness to debate.

2. Lindsay himself will draft a restatement of his reasons for running for mayor for use at an 11 A.M. news conference Wednesday. This will include a "one-paragraph fist-in-the-face for Screvane or Beame and a one paragraph fist-in-the-face for Buckley," Price said.

3. John Deardourff will draft a statement to be issued at a Thursday news conference stressing the local quality of the fusion campaign and voicing confidence that the Democrats will not import outsiders. In this way it is hoped to discourage them from using President Johnson or Bobby Kennedy. Lindsay definitely will not use President Eisenhower or Rockefeller.

Somebody mentioned the WABC-TV panel show known as "Page One" on which Lindsay will appear Sunday. If one of the panelists—Ed O'Neill, Frank Lynn, and James Van Sickle —asks about Rockefeller's role in the campaign, Lindsay will be vague. "I'll say it's a matter of scheduling," he said. "I'd rather look naive at this point than slug."

If asked about the Wells committee, Lindsay will say he welcomes support from all groups. If the GOP wishes to participate, fine. "I will point out that my opinion was not asked on the formation of this Republican committee, which classes, however, as quasi good-government," declared Lindsay.

"If they push you in a corner," said Price, "don't drown, swim!"

If a TV panelist suggests that the fusion campaign seems to

have fallen off from the peak set at the time of the Liberal endorsement, Lindsay will answer that the reception he gets around town continues to be good. We now have 30,000 volunteers: 10,000 workers, 10,000 hangers-on and 10,000 drifters, Price offered. Better not be explicit on that, he suggested.

How about off-track betting?

Price: If people want it, you have no objection. Let the people decide.

Lindsay: I'm not against it on moral grounds. With the need for money so acute in government, if they want it, let them enjoy it, okay, but it must be well-policed.

Next Friday, said Price, we will file 35,000 signatures on our independent designating petitions. We will also issue a compilation of hate literature.

Weekend after next we will focus attention dramatically on the Kitty Genovese case in which a young girl was killed near her home in Queens while neighbors looked on without coming to her help. This will be followed by a White Paper on crime.

George Lindsay: Since lawlessness in the streets is becoming such a big issue, John should work in occasional references to public safety and the high morale of the police.

Lindsay: Yes.

He began to experiment out loud with phrases for his Wednesday morning talk. ". . . machine candidate of the old, tired, locked-in, do-nothing administration . . . a candidate with poor credentials who obliterated the true reform candidates, Ryan and O'Dwyer . . ."

Like Price, Lindsay seems to think Screvane will win the primary election, but he paused abruptly to say: "If Beame wins he will campaign on the sales tax. In which case we will drape him with a city income tax or a payroll tax."

Price: We may have to be downright demagogic on the sales tax. We may have to make some irresponsible declarations in the next six weeks. The name of the game is politics.

Lindsay: Rocky and the sales tax are where we're being

bloodied up most. How can you win an election if you're tied to Rocky and Wagner? If you're in bed with both of them and Wall Street you're unhappy. I'm unhappy but . . .

David Lindsay: You have to come up with an alternative to the sales tax, John. It's hurting the little fellow. You saw that editorial in the *Times* . . .

Price: No, he's got to duck it.

David: I don't like ducking. You have all sorts of expensive programs, John. You ought to say how you will pay for them. You owe that to the public.

Lindsay: Only the candidate has a right to shout in this room. Do you want to sit in my chair, David, and be the candidate? Will you take my place, David, and explain what you will substitute for the sales tax? Will you?

David subsided.

Saturday, September 11 — Bill Ryan is raging like a lion through the streets. He caught up with Screvane in Harlem this morning and accused the Council President of conspiring with Beame to avoid radio and tv debates with him. Screvane just walked away. Around noon, Lindsay was speaking to a crowd of three hundred from a sound truck outside Ohrbach's when Ryan ran across 34th Street. Mary Lindsay saw him first and nudged her husband. He stopped talking, nodded to Ryan, and climbed down to the sidewalk.

"What about a debate?" shouted Ryan, his throat quivering and his hands trembling with excitement.

Lindsay said he had accepted an invitation to debate Bill Buckley and "the Democratic choice" on September 19. "Replies from the Democrats have been slow coming in. If you win the primary, Bill, I hope you'll take part." He was quite calm.

"What about a debate right now?" pressed Ryan. "I represent the most Democratic congressional district in Manhattan and you represent the most Republican one."

Lindsay laughed explosively. "My district is more than two

to one Democratic in registration. I'm sure you do not want
to malign the district while you are standing in the middle of
it." Slipping into smoother gear Lindsay said he enjoyed Ryan's
statement that never in the history of New York City had two
men, the leading Democratic contenders for mayor, done so
little for so many.

"They're always talking about whose record is worst,"
grumbled Ryan. "It's time we had an independent."

Lindsay commented that he had often listened to Ryan
discuss issues on the floor of the House. He wished the discussion in the Democratic primary came up to that high standard,
he said.

Ryan promptly renewed his demand for immediate debate.

"I'll make you an offer, Bill," said Lindsay. "I have to go
on to another spot but there's my truck up there and my microphone. Go up and talk as long as you like."

For the first time Ryan's face eased into a smile. "I'll accept that offer," he said, "because I believe in sharing the
wealth." He went up and as we left we heard him referring to
Screvane and Beame as "Tweedledum and Tweedledee."

Sunday, September 12 — Lindsay is visibly upset over a story
in the *Times* that he hopes for a Screvane victory in Tuesday's
primary election. His position, he insists publicly and privately,
remains unchanged; he has no preference between the tired
halves of the old Democratic machine. Price blames the leak
on O'Donnell. I have not asked O'Donnell about it, but I
would not be surprised if he did suggest the story. He and the
reporter are friends; they were huddled confidentially at Harry's
desk the day before the story appeared.

To judge from a wave of wired and phoned protests, the
effect of the *Times* story is to drive a certain number of Pavlovian Democrats—to use a Price phrase—from Screvane to
Beame. This would be a smart maneuver on our part if it
could be demonstrated that Beame is the softer opponent. I

. . . visibly upset over a story in the Times . . .

do believe Beame is easier to beat. If Screvane wins in the primary, the machine men of Beame will have relatively little difficulty in accepting a new hand at the wheel, whereas if Beame wins many comparatively independent and liberal supporters of Screvane will fly into orbit and land in Lindsay's camp.

All over town the more devious Democratic politicians are working out arrangements for survival. In Queens, Beame and Screvane captains are talking up a mixed slate of Screvane for Mayor and O'Connor for Council President, a deal designed to protect both local candidates and their local lieutenants. In response to anguished appeals from Pat Moynihan, whose weakness against O'Connor inspired the idea, Wagner has publicly urged all his followers to stand firm for the full Screvane–Moynihan–Lehman ticket.

Herman Badillo, Screvane's candidate for Bronx Borough President, is not being opposed by Puerto Rican elements in the county Democratic machine who should be clobbering him in the name of Boss Buckley. There is even a secret non-aggression pact between the Hispanic followers of Badillo and Lindsay. John Flores, who is running our Spanish division during the illness of Vidal, mentioned this the other day. At first glance it looks fine for Lindsay. The thing to remember about political conspiracies, however, is that they cannot influence an appreciable number of voters without becoming apparent, in which case they may inspire a violent reaction.

The Badillo-Lindsay understanding—in which neither side attacks the other—is negative and almost invisible. If it continues past the primary it may upset Republican and Liberal supporters of Bronx Borough President Periconi, who is on Lindsay's city slate. I can even visualize a certain number of pro-Periconi Italian-Americans expressing their resentment by switching from Lindsay to a Democratic candidate for Mayor.

Monday, September 13 — Price looked scornful when I told him this morning about my ten-cent bet with Horace Carter that tomorrow's Democratic turnout will not exceed 650,000. "You'd be safe betting on 400,000," he said. Newspaper estimates range from 400,000 to 600,000 Four years ago, the vote was 720,000 but the issues then were more deep-seated and emotional. Even so, the present four-way contest cuts so oddly that it is hard to appraise. There may be an element of wish-fulfillment in my bet. Judge Max Bloom, former Bronx chairman of the Liberal party and one of the more astute politicians around town, convinced me when we met recently at Unity House that Lindsay's prospects can be gauged by tomorrow's Democratic turnout. Bloom cited the low figures in 1933 when LaGuardia won for Mayor and in 1950 when Rudolph Halley won for Council President. "No outsider or non-Democrat has any chance of becoming mayor," he said, "unless there is a low vote in the Democratic primary as a result of disillusionment or apathy. If the Democratic turnout in this year's primary exceeds 800,000, Lindsay is finished."

The Citizens Union, an allegedly nonpartisan organization which often takes a delicate hand in primary elections, is neutral this year. It will express no preference among the Democratic contenders, it says, because it sees "no clear-cut choice in the public interest." Javits says the Democratic primary is "irrelevant." I have avoided betting on the Screvane-Beame outcome not for any such reason, but because of uncertainty. Price is also cautious. He said this morning he expects Screvane and Beame to get about 40 percent each of the Democratic vote, with 16 percent going to Ryan. Murray Kempton, the columnist, gives 40 percent to Screvane, 37 percent to Beame, and 20 percent to Ryan, with the added comment that 30 percent of the Democrats voting in their primary will eventually switch to Lindsay.

The supposedly climactic Screvane-Beame TV debate over WPIX—with Ryan and O'Dwyer carefully excluded—settled nothing. Dick Lee of the *Daily News*, dean of New York City political reporters, terms it "a dull draw." Mary McGrory, the Washington columnist, says it exposes both candidates as "im-

plausible political personalities who fail to turn on the voters."
Harold Harris of the *Journal-American* scores the debate as
"nothing to nothing with both sides going hitless and runless
all the way," and our own baseball buff, Harry O'Donnell, is
reminded of the way he felt on the eve of the 1945 World Series between the Detroit Tigers and the Chicago Cubs. "They
were so awful I didn't think either of those clubs could finish,"
he says.

Tuesday, September 14 — We served food and drinks to a
substantial number of radio-press-TV reporters in the Roosevelt
Grill tonight as returns were tabulated in the Democratic primary election. Beame was the generally unexpected winner,
pulling 44 percent of the vote to 36 percent for Screvane, 15
percent for Ryan, and the rest for O'Dwyer. Beame's running
mates won, O'Connor by a larger margin and Procaccino by a
smaller margin than the head of the ticket. Moynihan was low
man on Screvane's totem pole. The only real winner on the
Screvane side is Badillo in the Bronx. Two indirect effects of
the election are the freezing of Wagner out of next year's
gubernatorial contest and an additional gain in state power by
Bobby Kennedy.

Lindsay congratulated Beame sweetly as planned and
urged him to take part in a series of debates in a campaign
"contributing to the revival of New York for people and for
living and not to its continuing decline." Mary Lindsay refused to kiss her husband for the cameramen. "We do our
kissing at home," she said. She confided later that her mother,
who is old Virginia despite a present home in Connecticut,
was horrified at a picture of the Lindsays kissing during a celebration of his victory in the 1960 Congressional election.

In his victory statement Beame said "the Rockefellers and
the Republican Old Guard are trying to buy City Hall, but
New Yorkers are not gullible." He also jibed at Lindsay as
"the candidate of Barry Goldwater and Richard Nixon." Bill
Buckley was not mentioned in Lindsay's wire or in Beame's

victory statement but he crowded into the dialogue. Beame's comment about Goldwater, he said, "is about as accurate as calling Beame the candidate of Chester Arthur and Grover Cleveland." He added that "as a Republican" he prefers "a Democrat running as a Democrat to an imposter like Lindsay."

Beame is willing to debate Lindsay but he cannot accept the time set aside by CBS-TV on Sunday because he is tired from his arduous campaign and needs a few days rest. "After all," he declares, addressing himself publicly to Lindsay, who has campaigned longer and harder than he, "you had a comparatively easy summer and, if I recall correctly, you also took a week's vacation in the midst of that summer."

More than ever I believe Beame will turn out to be a softer touch than Screvane. The turnout in the Democratic primary, incidentally, was 738,720. This means I lost my ten-cent bet with Horace Carter.

Wednesday, September 15 — During years of joyous servitude as a political reporter I watched many candidates for extended periods of time. Most of them gradually worked out a basic speech and a basic approach to campaigning which they then followed except for minor variations. Lindsay has remained more fluid, more experimental, than any of them. He has learned quite recently, when a wave of enthusiasm hits him during a street tour, to clap his hands together quickly over his head as a sign of appreciation. He will also occasionally smack his right fist loudly into his left palm while walking, to suggest excitement.

Lindsay is continually testing new phrases and new opinions, some his own, some acquired from Price or the research staff. During the last few days he has been emphatic in saying that "nobody who wants to go to college in America and who has the stuff should be denied a higher education for lack of money." He has been using an old Navy saying: "One hand for the ship and one for yourself," to suggest that listeners can look out for their own interests and still help in the campaign. To civic groups he has been stressing their need for greater access to government and promising that if he is elected they can have a "neighborhood city hall" in their area. This apparently answers Teddy White's question as to how volunteers can be absorbed after the election.

An unusually distinguished group of writers, reporters, and photographers, including Teddy White, witnessed Lindsay's promised restatement this morning of his reasons for running for mayor. The candidate spoke not as originally planned at a news conference but at a meeting of two hundred staff members in the foyer of the grand ballroom downstairs in the hotel. There was nothing particularly new in the four-thousand-word text, great quantities of which were run off in advance, but the staff reacted like an operatic claque, cheering each familiar phrase.

A sample paragraph: "The city is in my blood and I will not stand by while it slides deeper into mediocrity, despondency, and finally, civic lifelessness. One remains a bystander at such a time only at the peril of everyone. All must act before it is too late. I act by entering and leading a fight against all odds. I will carry the fight into the streets of New York as long as there is voice and power within me."

On the whole, it was sufficiently good theater to impress the outsiders. They included Willem De Graeff and David De Goede, a reporter and photographer from Elsevicks' *Weekblad* of Amsterdam, Holland; a West German TV director named Fredericks and his crew; Mrs. Suzanne Schiff, a photographer working for a Swiss syndicate; Jules Duche of the *Washington Post* and a larger-than-usual collection of local radio, TV, and press men.

As the day wore on, the exotic luminaries of the communications media gradually disappeared. By the time we made an evening rally on a street corner in the Flatlands section of Brooklyn, only Bob Monroe of the indispensable AP was still following us. Since Monroe was interested only in hard news,

Lindsay felt free, I guess, to put himself experimentally inside the not-too-well-dressed but respectable-looking members of the audience.

"You got a cranky boss, you got problems on the subway going home," he said in a sort of patter. "You do the dishes after supper and the wife does 'em over. You referee the fights between the kids . . .

"WHY ARE YOU HERE? Because you and I need to leave a legacy of some kind for our children . . .

"Costello and Mollen have been taking bloody beatings from their groups because they joined me in this crusade. So have I. WHO NEEDS IT?—to be whiplashed and harassed day and night? I do, because I want to be mayor.

"In all good conscience there is nothing better I can do and you have a right to expect nothing less than my best from me."

Thursday, September 16 — The Newspaper Guild struck the *New York Times* today. Since the craft unions are respecting the picket lines which Thomas J. Murphy, executive vice-president of the Guild, established at 8 A.M., the country's most respected newspaper cannot continue to publish. The next step, probably tomorrow, will be a retaliatory lockout of employes by five other newspapers represented in the Publishers' Association of New York leaving only the *Post*, which no longer belongs to the association, on the newsstands. Futile negotiations continued through the night over automation, job security, and a union shop at the *Times*. As president of the local, I was considerably involved but I managed to make Lindsay's 11 A.M. press conference at one of our largest and liveliest storefronts at Broadway and 72d Street.

In his prepared remarks, Lindsay called upon Beame and Buckley to run "without the crutch of outside help." Hopefully he added: "I am sure the national leaders in our country who are not residents and voters of our city understand that the formation of municipal government is a local matter for the people of the municipality to decide and that partisanship must be put aside in the larger interest of rebuilding a city in crisis." The effect of this appeal is already dubious, since Beame's people claim to have a promise of campaign help from Vice-President Humphrey and Buckley has been talking about former Representative Clare Boothe Luce and even Goldwater as possible barkers for the Conservative cause.

Back at headquarters, weariness and discouragement enveloped me like a cloud. Around 1 o'clock Lindsay bounced into my office with a query. Fortunately I knew the answer. Without conscious intention I found myself babbling: "It's been suggested I resign because of the Guild strike. I'm willing to quit if I'm an embarrassment to your campaign . . ."

Lindsay, who had been on his way out, stopped and stared at me with cold blue eyes for a good three seconds. All my campaign errors and inadequacies flashed through my mind. This was his chance—if he wanted it—to lighten cargo. "I don't think you need to resign," he said finally before he left.

Friday, September 17 — How does a political campaign operate without publicity? That's our problem at the moment and Price is working on it.

Only two reporters—David Murray of the *Post*, the sole mass-circulation daily still publishing in town, and Ted Knap, the Washington correspondent of the Scripps-Howard chain —showed up for our early morning news conference in one of the large downstairs rooms at the Roosevelt. It might as well have been held in a closet.

Lindsay made a conversational announcement about the filing of our Independent Citizens Party petitions and left for Washington. The rest of us drifted into the lobby. Murray asked whether the new party would be permanent. I offered a guess that it might continue legally if it drew 50,000 votes. Price, standing nearby, corrected me. The 50,000 votes required to establish a permanent party must be cast in a state-wide election, he pointed out. "This is just another line on the ballot," he said.

Murray and Knap decided to use the pressroom phones upstairs. While waiting for an elevator we gossiped about the *Times* strike which had led the Publishers Association last night to lock out the employes of five other dailies. Wagner is trying to mediate but I don't visualize any quick settlement of the strike-lockout and I said so.

"How will you fill the vacuum?" asked Knap.

Price answered. "We'll run two press conferences a day instead of one," he said.

Everyone laughed. The remark seemed particularly hilarious because Price used the old-fashioned "press conference" phrase instead of the more modern "news conference," which acknowledges by implication the existence of radio-TV.

Price is serious. He expects radio-TV to expand campaign coverage soon and he intends to take advantage of it, he explained on the way up in the elevator. As we walked along our fourth-floor campaign corridor with the reporters a couple of steps behind, Price asked what I thought about putting pro-Lindsay advertisements in the out-of-town dailies which have begun to creep onto the local newsstands. Off the top of my head I said small ads might be warranted.

"How about a Lindsay campaign newspaper?" pressed Price.

On this I had doubts. Producing a satisfactory paper on short notice would be impossible. Offering a shoddy substitute for sale would arouse resentment.

No, no, said Price impatiently. The paper would be free, a throwaway consisting of news bulletins—local, national, and international—and short factual articles on the campaign.

What about distribution? The Raiders, said Price as we passed the Raider room, could give the paper away at subway entrances in the late afternoon.

It is conceivable that Price did some preliminary brooding

over the problem last night or this morning, but my impression is that the gamut of his original thinking could be observed from 8:58 A.M., when the subject was broached in the lobby, to 9:03 A.M., when he left me at the pressroom entrance with a comment about finding some strike-idled reporter to put out the campaign newspaper. Add another half-minute to those five minutes—long enough to let Price reach his office at the end of the corridor—and I imagine the wheels whirring with increasing velocity inside that mighty balding dome came up with the name of the right editor of the Lindsay throwaway.

Saturday, September 18 — Since the primary, Edward N. Costikyan has become the dominant voice at the Beame hacienda. As a campaign manager, he makes a great deal of noise in public. Should we be intimidated? I doubt it. On the basis of long personal observation, I view Eddie as an overrated politician who will prove to be a hidden asset for Lindsay.

In terms of general achievement, Costikyan seems formidable. He is the second son of an Armenian rug dealer and a Swiss school teacher who met and married in Weehawken soon after their arrival in this country. He rose to become a law partner of Adlai Stevenson and the first Protestant boss of Tammany Hall since Boss Tweed. Except for a brief period when he tried to induce reporters to pronounce his name as "Costigan," Costikyan has accepted his rise with due humility as a triumph for the American melting pot. At the age of forty-one, he possesses an excellent reputation as a trial lawyer, a writer, and a musicologist. He is currently completing a book of reminiscences and he has been known to conduct groups of amateur musicians in performances of Handel's *Messiah* and Mendelssohn's *Elijah*.

In politics, Costikyan (pronounced kah–STICK–ee–an) periodically takes a giant step forward, sideways, or backward, leaving embittered colleagues behind him. He became active in 1953 with the New Democratic Club, a reform outfit organized by Casper Citron in East Manhattan. Citron was elected that year as a district leader, but Tammany boss DeSapio refused to seat him, under a technicality. Word came from Tammany that a more amenable representative of the club would be seated. Costikyan purged Citron, ran for leader himself, was elected and seated. He informed acquaintances whimsically that a Manhattan Democratic district leader should really be called a sachem. When he became embroiled later in a primary contest with another insurgent, the new sachem received DeSapio's formal endorsement and support.

After former Senator Lehman and Mrs. Eleanor Roosevelt brought fresh prestige and resources to the reform movement in 1959, Costikyan attracted attention as the first district leader to sign a petition for DeSapio's ouster. In 1961 he became the earliest advocate of the highly debatable eventual decision to turn over the idealism, drive, and personnel of the reform movement to Wagner as the tail on his anti-boss reelection kite.

If he won, Wagner promised, a reformer would be the next Tammany boss. When DeSapio's twelve-year regime did end in the fall of 1961, the Committee for Democratic Voters held 30 out of 66 votes on the Tammany executive committee. As the largest single bloc of Democrats in the county it deserved the leadership, yet Wagner temporized. He did not want a partner in power. He wanted a subservient boss.

By this time Costikyan had one foot in and one foot out of the CDV. He took part in the caucus of the reform district leaders but his club was not affiliated with reform. When the caucus chose somebody else (John Harrington, from Wagner's own Yorkville district) as its candidate to succeed DeSapio, Costikyan walked out, announcing that he would not be bound by the vote. After months of maneuvering Wagner got the old-line formerly pro-DeSapio clubs to support Costikyan. On March 2, 1962, without a single reform vote, the ostensible reformer became the new Tammany chieftain.

For two uneasy years Costikyan struggled with his responsibilities in the Wigwam. A minor achievement was to make one of his law partners, the man immediately above him on the office totem pole, a judge. He worked well with the regulars but he was never able to conciliate the reformers whom he had betrayed. When at last he alienated the Liberal party, Wagner's unshakable ally, his telephone calls to City Hall were no longer returned and he felt obliged to resign.

A new political luminary had streaked across the local sky: Bobby Kennedy. Sure enough, in the winter of 1964–65, Costikyan appeared in Albany as the tactician for the Kennedy-Steingut-Buckley axis in its long fruitless struggle against Wagner's choices for Democratic leadership in the state legislature.

Costikyan's present political prominence stems from the Albany association with Steingut. During the primary campaign, Costikyan seems to have given Beame's friend, Assemblyman Bert Podell, considerable autonomy at headquarters. It was Podell, rather than Costikyan, who mounted the attack against Wagner long before the Mayor endorsed Screvane. After Beame's victory in the primary, Costikyan changed public relations firms, put Podell in his place, and experimented with new tactics.

As a campaign manager Costikyan makes heavy use of the newspapers. He refers regularly to Lindsay as "Handsome John" or "Glamorous John," which is just a Madison Avenue variation of Screvane's pretty-boy theme. He promises loudly to end the Liberal party's "backdoor access to Gracie Mansion and City Hall." This delights machine Democrats who have long resented the Liberal veto over their party's policies and candidates, but it disturbs many independents and intellectuals. It certainly cannot please the Mayor, whose support is now needed to consolidate Democratic strength behind Beame. Even Harry Van Arsdale, who is working to rally the Central Labor Council for Beame, felt obliged the other day to defend Dubinsky and Rose as respected labor leaders after they were attacked personally by Costikyan.

. . . concentration on areas normally avoided . . .

It is Costikyan who has decided to placate Bill Buckley as an indirect ally against Lindsay. This policy alone is likely to estrange further the membership of fifty Democratic reform clubs around town who opposed Beame in the primary and who now regard Costikyan with utmost suspicion.

Sunday, September 19 — Toward the start of the campaign in May Lindsay used to hit Negro and Puerto Rican neighborhoods more than half the time. This concentration on areas normally avoided by Republican candidates for mayor lessened after a while but it has been renewed since the primary. Something of a peak was reached this afternoon at a two-hour rally in Harlem. The Lindsay camp mustered full effort in the face of a huge Beame–O'Connor–Procaccino sign in front of the Hotel Theresa. The Lindsay Lovelies, in sashes, outnumbered the inevitable Black Muslim newspaper salesmen. Jackie Robinson was there and the cream of Lindsay's theatrical troupe, from actresses Josephine Premice and Diana Sands to Sammy Davis, Jr. Reverend George Lawrence, a Bedford-Stuyvesant populist, helped to tune up a crowd stretching across Seventh Avenue and almost a block north and south of 125th Street. Faces leaned out of windows everywhere you looked. The *Harlem Daily*, one of a horde of temporary newspapers inspired by the press blackout, is allotting considerable space to the rally in consideration of its importance and the fact that Price has taken a full-page advertisement. The reporter for the *Harlem Daily* estimated the crowd at 7,500 persons which would make it one of the largest turnouts for any purpose in Harlem history.

Following Mollen and Costello, Lindsay spoke for 15 minutes. He stressed his independence in Congress. "Who knows what it means to stand alone in this business? How many of you have felt the lash on your back—as I have—for being independent and standing on your own two feet? Who knows about conditions in Harlem better than you? Who knows better about absentee landlords than you?"

The rhythmic quality of the phrases stirred voices near the platform: "Yeah man, tell 'em. Yeah man."

"Who knows better that there isn't enough protection in the streets? Who knows better about teenage kids without work and without hope walking the streets, getting in trouble with narcotics and crime?"

"Yeah man, tell 'em."

Talking in a loud clear voice, swinging his arms, swaying his body, and pounding his feet, Lindsay wound up with a promise to "break down the walls of discrimination in housing" and create a slumless city. "There must be no more colonialism," he shouted, "no more tokenism in housing, in schools, or in any other form of life here in New York City!"

The crowd responded emotionally. Among the cooler spectators, I am told, though I did not see him, was J. Raymond (The Fox) Jones, the astute Negro veteran of the political wars who was installed as Tammany boss by Wagner after Costikyan's retirement. Since The Fox supported Screvane, there may be no love lost between him and Beame. If he does his duty, he will tell the Democratic candidate to mend his fences with Negro voters or be prepared for electoral surprise.

Monday, September 20 — Lindsay's official purpose in going to Washington Friday was to back the Mississippi Freedom Party in its futile effort to unseat that State's lily-white congressional delegation. His unofficial purpose was to chat with Bill Ryan. Unlike Screvane and O'Dwyer, Ryan did not pledge support for his party's choice after the primary. On the pretext of exhaustion he refused to take calls from Beame and Costikyan. He would not even talk over the phone with Lindsay. In Washington, he and Lindsay, who often vote alike, were among the small group of supporters for the Mississippi Freedom Party. When they met on the House floor, Ryan loosened up sufficiently to say he will watch the progress of the campaign a while before he decides what to do. I understand he made the same comment over the phone to Bobby Kennedy, acting as Beame's peace envoy.

While most of the ardent reformers went for Ryan in the primary, a number of union-minded reformers favored O'Dwyer. Ryan and O'Dwyer together polled 150,000 votes. Many reform votes were also included in Screvane's total of 269,000. Price has already made a pitch for these votes by inserting small ads in newspapers right after the primary—before the press blackout—suggesting that any Democrat dissatisfied with the results should call a certain telephone number. The response has been good. Our volunteers follow up every call. Where membership lists of reform groups can be obtained, the volunteers canvass the members by phone or personal visit.

One of the early Ryan volunteers for Lindsay was my wife.

Avice got permission from Alex Rose and James Huntington, head of the local Lindsay storefront, to coordinate the fusion drive in Park West Village, where we live. Our daughter Betsy, now a part-time Lindsay volunteer, is helping Avice. They find that many Ryan stalwarts, including Mrs. Eugenia Flatow, the female Democratic leader in our district, are openly pro-Lindsay.

At our morning press conference—we now have a morning and either an afternoon or evening news conference every day—Lindsay was asked if he had talked recently with Ryan. On his recent trip to Washington, Lindsay replied, he did exchange a few words with Ryan as well as with James H. Scheuer and Jonathan Bingham, the reform Congressmen in the Bronx who backed Badillo and Screvane in the Democratic primary.

"I congratulated Bill on the fight he made in the primary," said Lindsay, "and told him he had done a constructive job in the campaign. We had very little time to discuss the mayoralty but I wanted him and his reform colleagues to understand that if the Lindsay team wins, the city will have a completely nonpartisan government."

To make his point doubly clear, Lindsay added:

"The reformers have a home on the Lindsay team. Many of these young men and women joined the reform movement because they were not given opportunities by the machine. Mayor Wagner and the late Governor Lehman joined them for years in battling the machine but the machine is now triumphant. There is a great reservoir of talent in the reform movement which has never been tapped. That talent would be of great use to the city. If we win we will use it."

The deliberate intensity of our effort to net disgruntled reformers became more apparent later in the day. We were joined on three Bronx walking tours by Donald H. Elliott, thirty-three, a tall, handsome lawyer from Ryan's Riverside Democratic Club. Elliott has agreed to set up a local issues department at headquarters. Before Lindsay appears in one of the neighborhoods which collectively comprise New York City, Elliott will hand him a typed sheet citing local grievances and needs. An introductory reference to the annoying triple shift at a local school or a traffic hazard down the street should wake up the audience and make it receptive to larger truth.

In street corner talks on University Heights, and in the Fordham and in the Pelham Parkway sections, Lindsay emphasized his support for the direct election of district leaders, which happens to be the chief reform currently demanded by CDV.

"If elected mayor," he promised, "I will not rest until reform is brought to both political parties. Why should we tolerate tired old methods when we are reaching toward the twenty-first century? The time has come for this reform in the Bronx so that people may choose their district leaders and choose wisely. I put the direct election of district leaders up to Charley Buckley and Paul Fino!"

By naming GOP boss Fino as well as Democratic boss Buckley in the presence of reporters Lindsay made news. It happens that both major parties in the Bronx, unlike the other boroughs, still cling to the old-fashioned indirect county committee method of picking district leaders, which gives an entrenched machine great advantage. Lindsay's nonpartisan approach tends to prove his sincerity. No better appeal to the reformers could be found. I only wish I could claim credit for the idea. Ryan, Bingham, and Scheuer, as Democratic Congressmen, cannot afford to break with their party. In the end they will have to go along with Beame, but every day they delay should loosen the Democratic allegiance of their followers and accelerate the trend to Lindsay.

Tuesday, September 21 — Beame is prompt, modest, conscientious, and thrifty. He rides around town in an ordinary black Public Works Department car which contrasts sharply with the flamboyant Lindsay motorcade. Reporters used to complain during the primary campaign that they had to provide their own transportation while covering Beame. Because of the newspaper strike-lockout this no longer occurs, but Beame's accommodations for the press are still elemental. Out of anxiety, perhaps, he often arrives ahead of his schedule. This evening, for example, Beame reached PS 232 in Howard Beach, Queens, twenty minutes before any official of the Lindenwood Community Civic Association which had invited him to a "candidates' evening." Beame took a seat at a table on the auditorium stage and waited stolidly for the meeting to start.

During a street tour Beame concentrates on handshaking. "I don't miss a hand," he told an interviewer recently. "I like to go out there and meet people. It's the most effective thing a candidate can do." Beame's hand-pumping at a subway exit was so determined one day that a boy came over and told him he was working too hard. On a sidewalk-pounding expedition he tends to move faster and faster if the crowd is thin, stopping only when somebody asks a question. Then he is likely to bog down in a semi-speech on government or taxes instead of answering with a sentence or a phrase. He gets lost easily in a crowd.

There is no exhilaration or drama in Beame, but he is determined and he possesses an excellent memory. He can produce facts and figures galore on almost any problem. His preoccupation with finances often makes him sound conservative. It is fair to say that on the most issues he is definitely more conservative than Lindsay.

Beame takes advantage of his handicaps. When somebody mentioned that he used a stand during his TV debate with Screvane to look taller than his five feet two inches, he commented that it was better to have a platform of some kind than no platform at all. Lately he has taken to saying that he does not see eye-to-eye with Lindsay. Can a candidate, I wonder, win an election by corralling the small-person vote of those who stand under five feet six and therefore resent the tall ones of this world?

On radio last night Beame was explaining again why he ran uphill for mayor when he was assured of reelection as Controller. "I wanted to cap my career—make my mark," he said. "I'm going to do it because I owe this city a debt. I was brought up on the lower East Side and we didn't have the privileges. I couldn't afford to go to college so the city gave me a free college education. It gave me the opportunity to be a teacher and to enter public life and to reach high office. The city has given me everything I have and I want to pay it back." In some ways that's an effective platform.

Wednesday, September 22 — Fire swept our citywide headquarters for volunteers, destroying the card-filing system used by 114 storefronts around town. Damage to the nerve center of our activities in the closing weeks of our campaign may be serious. Apparently the fire started around 8:30 in the evening but word did not reach us until 10:30 when we arrived, an hour behind schedule, at the Bayside Jewish Center in Queens. Our radio telephone system has been annoyingly out of order all day.

Paul Serafini of the AP hurried into a phone booth at the Jewish Center to report on Lindsay's previous Queens appearance, only to step out of the booth almost immediately with news of a three-alarm blaze at our 9 East 42d Street headquarters in Manhattan. Lindsay was standing nearby listening to a Rabbi explain that part of the audience had left because of the lateness. When I interrupted to mention the fire Lindsay fixed on me the expressionless stare which sometimes masks intense irritation. He had two questions: was the fire bad and what caused it. It was bad, I said, but I did not know the cause. The city desk of the AP wanted to know if the candidate would inspect the ruins; if so, they would assign a photographer. "I don't know what I'll do," said Lindsay curtly, going inside with the Rabbi. Later he said to tell the AP he would try to reach the scene of the fire by midnight.

It had been a long wearing campaign day—with news conferences at 9 A.M. and 1 P.M., three afternoon walking tours in Queens with Mollen and Costello, a cocktail party of women buyers in Manhattan's garment center, a stewards meeting of the International Union of Electrical Workers in Brooklyn, and several other stops. Since the schedule allowed no time for meals, those who did not have access to the refrigerated boxes in the candidate's station wagon had to forage along the road.

Our coverage during the day included Mrs. Barbara Carter, an established writer who plans a book on the future of New York City; Lucy Howard of *Newsweek*; Ed Bell of the *National Review*; a New York University professor of political science, a reporter from the *Columbia Spectator* and Katsy Thomas, our campaign photographer, but only Serafini of the AP and David Murray of the *Post* were with us when we reached Bayside.

The fire was out when we got to the volunteer headquarters but the firemen were still watering down. Three out of the four floors used by us in the building were gutted, all windows broken, all signs destroyed. Lindsay was allowed to go inside to join several campaign officials, but the rest of us were kept outside by the police. Lindsay stayed inside a good 20 minutes. He was tired-looking and grimy when he emerged, but in good spirits.

"Did you notice those Buckley buttons inside?" he asked Murray. "No, this is all I found," the reporter replied, pulling some Buckley campaign literature out of his pocket.

Seriously and on the record after the joking ended, Lindsay explained that a volunteer caught a whiff of smoke at 7:45 P.M. A fire marshal was summoned. He found no fire and left. At about this time a man who refused to give his name phoned the East 51st Street police station to warn: "There's going to be trouble at Lindsay's headquarters." Police went to the Roosevelt Hotel and were searching the headquarters there when billowing smoke betrayed the fire at the other headquarters a few blocks away. One volunteer was overcome by smoke, treated at Bellevue Hospital, and sent home.

The master card file is largely burned or water-soaked, but there should be considerable duplication in the storefronts. The likely cause of the fire is the wiring of a Xerox machine or the air conditioning system. No signs of sabotage have been discovered.

Thursday, September 23 — Lindsay did not do well in the first triangular radio debate of the campaign. He fielded issues less adroitly than Beame and his presentation was obscured by the pyrotechnics of Bill Buckley. To make matters worse Buckley and Beame ganged up on him. Take this truncated bit of dialogue:

Beame: Lindsay is ashamed of being a Republican.

Buckley: I'll buy that. Under the circumstances, I share your exasperation. His running mates have long records of attachment to the Wagner administration.

Beame: He's much more pro-Wagner than I am. . . . He has a fusion of persons, not parties.

Buckley: It's confusion, not fusion.

When Lindsay asserted that he "began by taking on the whole Democratic organization and ran alone" Buckley registered laughter for the studio audience and said: "I wish I could run alone with a million bucks and with the press engraving my every word on Mt. Rushmore—run with Siamese twins AND a rump Republican party AND the press AND Barry Gray!"

Barry Gray was the moderator. He is a Lindsay partisan but his role in presiding over WMCA's hour-long debate was restricted to telling the candidates when to begin and end their opening statements, rebuttals, questions-and-replies, and closing statements. If Lindsay needed help he did not get it from Gray.

. . . statements, rebuttals, questions-and-replies . . .

Beame made the only news, by challenging Lindsay to appeal to Rockefeller to roll back the state sales tax which requires city residents to pay 5 percent and upstaters 2 percent on most purchases. "I'd be delighted to," said Lindsay when Beame asked him to join in demanding an immediate special session of the state legislature.

Lindsay soon realized that the legislators are in the midst of campaigns for reelection and would not welcome any call for a special session even if the Governor were foolish enough to reopen his pandora's box of taxes. Unfortunately Lindsay's tardy mention of legislative campaigning sounded like a retreat from a commitment.

Beame forced Lindsay, who was generally on the defensive, to join him in arguing for mandated free tuition in the city colleges. He urged elimination of the gross receipts tax, expansion of the community college system, and ending "the void between government and the citizens." As I expected, he struck a responsive chord among listeners with his humble explanation as to why he preferred a contest for mayor to uncontested reelection as controller.

Curiously enough, my notes contain rather few remarks by Lindsay. Most of the things he said are things he has been saying right along. They therefore did not strike me as particularly newsworthy. On the other hand I was fascinated by the phrasing of Buckley.

Charging that he had been treated as a "non-person in this taffy-pull" Buckley said: "I hate to be a boor but I beg Lindsay and Beame on bended knee to say whether a couple of hundred people can deprive a city of its newspapers. What are they going to do about it?" It developed that they favored the orderly processes of collective bargaining. "Labor unions are changing the economic life of the city," continued Buckley, prodding Lindsay to say why he voted against the section of the national labor law which allows states to prohibit the closed shop. He said economists agree that an increase in the minimum wage does not in the end improve living conditions and he called welfare a racket.

"I read Lindsay's program for the economic rejuvenation of the city," said Buckley, "and I wondered if I was reading Gertrude Stein. To discuss an issue is not to catalog wiggled ears.

"Lindsay and Beame are routine human beings ruled by high motives, but unfortunately very little of what they say relates to New York City. Lindsay worries over crime, but endorses the civilian review board. He attacks bosses, but he doesn't attack Powell. . . . I never know whether Lindsay is in Albany or Washington or Tokyo. It's impossible to remember any Lindsay position—it's like jelly in the hand. If he came out in favor of blue instead of green, I'd consider he was on the road to reform."

Occasionally and without too much effect Lindsay tried to puncture Buckley. When he accused the Conservative candidate of being "against progress" Buckley scoffed: "Once again we march into demagoguery!" Beame, on the other hand, avoided criticizing Buckley. During the entire debate the least favorable thing this City College graduate said about Buckley was to link him with Lindsay as "these pleasant men from Yale who are so rarely seen around City Hall."

Friday, September 24 — Headquarters is in a state of nerves. It's been building up for some time; the radio debate merely brought it to a head. Nobody wants to concede that the debate was a disaster. Since no transcript seems to be available and the *Post's* coverage is newsy and laconic, I have prepared a cautious summary of my notes.

To the annoyance of Barnie Patterson, who keeps the candidate's appointment book, the favorite scapegoat is over-scheduling. At noon yesterday Lindsay opened city headquarters of a new organization called Democrats for Lindsay–Mollen–Costello, run by two members of the reform movement, Reverend Howard Moody, pastor of Judson Memorial Church in Greenwich Village, and Mrs. Werner H. Kramarsky, daughter of Mrs. Dorothy Schiff, publisher of the *Post*, who is an enthusiastic supporter of Lindsay. The schedule also included a news conference, a speech at a convention of state employes, and an evening talk at a school in Forest Hills, Queens, only an hour and a half before the debate. The morning had been left open for briefing, but at the last minute Lindsay had to give more than two hours to answering loaded questions before the Central Labor Council most of whose members were committed in advance to Beame. With proper briefing and more rest he might have done better in the debate; the question is: how much better.

With Lindsay tension sometimes shows in lapses of restraint. Monday evening, at a banquet of the New York State County Officers Association, he asked for a drink of Scotch,

. . . *the favorite scapegoat is over-scheduling.*

downed half it and began an impromptu account of his campaign difficulties, including the drought and the press blackout.

"Fortunately," he concluded, "I know how to make news and I know how to make water."

After a pause over the final phrase—the reaction to which could have been chilled silence—that highly starched group of rural politicians and their wives burst into delighted applause.

During a recent afternoon rally in Bensonhurst an oddly dressed middle-aged woman began whining in a nasal voice: "Why don't you SING, Lindsay, why don't you SING?" from a position directly below the loudspeaker.

Lindsay endured it a while then leaned over to say: "Later, dearie. You and I will make sweet music together as soon as it gets dark." The howls of laughter from the crowd forced the woman to flee in such confusion that I felt a little sorry for her.

In the course of several walking tours in Queens Wednesday Lindsay left his jacket in a campaign car along with a fresh shirt and some other clothes he needed in order to proceed directly to a Manhattan cocktail party. Unfortunately Gil Robinson sent that car on an errand and replaced it with another car. Though the day had turned cool, Lindsay had to ride to Manhattan in a sweat-drenched shirt.

The first I knew about this minor catastrophe was when Lindsay exploded—that's the only word for it—between Harvey Rothenberg and me as we stood talking in the middle of the campaign corridor at the Roosevelt. He was dashing to his room, far behind schedule, to dress for the cocktail party. Infected by the candidate's obvious agitation Rothenberg quarreled with Price over scheduling that very afternoon and resigned his unpaid post as office manager. Today he is back at work as if nothing had happened.

Even Mary Lindsay has seemed distraught at times. Today she flared up at me because a Brooklyn Assemblyman whom I did not introduce failed to stand when she dashed into my office with a message from her husband that he was ready for a radio taping. Later in the day she was scheduled to open a Spanish branch of Democrats-for-Lindsay. Since she was to be dropped off by the campaign caravan, she was stepping into the lead car outside the Roosevelt when Lindsay said: "Maybe you should let it go and stay with Kathy. Barnie can take your place."

Mary did not say a word but her face was dark with annoyance as she turned and hurried into the hotel to find Barnie. Lindsay explained that Mary had driven up yesterday to Miss Porter's School in Connecticut to bring back their oldest daughter who has developed mononucleosis. While I sympathize with Kathy whose illness is apparently not serious I am obscurely relieved that the Lindsays have objective reason, over and beyond the campaign, for being jittery.

Saturday, September 25 — All politicians were instructed to march together at the head of the annual Steuben Day parade this afternoon and then to sit together in the grandstand, but Lindsay decided to be different. Not until our advance men placed Rockefeller, Javits, Wagner, and Beame safely in the grandstand did he start walking up Fifth Avenue from 60th Street. At each street intersection he made a production of shaking hands with the cops on duty, who were not generally favorable to his cause but who had to be polite. Sid Davidoff and Jim Smith moved along the sides of the marching column, pointing periodically at the candidate in the middle of the street and saying: "That's John Lindsay," with a resulting ripple of friendly shouts and applause all along the route. I ran ahead to alert reporters and photographers at the grandstand that Lindsay was coming.

"How's that for one-upmanship," was the enthusiastic comment of radio reporter Stu Klein. "I knew he'd do it!" Gabe Pressman of NBC-TV led a stampede to Willie Schoeps, the parade chairman. "It's unfair," said Willie. "He should be with the other politicians."

Lindsay compounded the sensation by not going into the grandstand at all. Waving and grinning, he walked past his political colleagues. He marched to the end of the parade route at 86th Street, then turned East to find our campaign car on Park Avenue. When everybody—there must have been eight or nine of us, including Barnie Patterson, who schedules the candidate but rarely goes out with him—had piled into the car in a somewhat hilarious mood, Lindsay asked seriously: "What can you do about a city as crooked as New York, Ollie?"

Lindsay's question-asking technique is notorious at head-quarters. He has a way of focusing on some broad topic: "How do you balance the budget of a city like New York?" or "How do you make the streets safe in a city like New York?" and trying it on one presumably competent person after another until he has the whole range of possible solutions.

Lindsay's "crooked city" remark was slightly different. In a small, temporarily vacant room at headquarters yesterday, during the taping of a radio interview to be aired tomorrow, Lindsay had commented that crooked building inspectors and other grafting city employes often played a role in driving businesses out of town. I remember nodding, smiling, and reminding myself to point out later that the building code, a jungle of accumulated and uncorrelated rules, which only two or three persons in the entire city are supposed to understand, makes grafting almost obligatory. I never did get around to suggesting revision of the building code, which has been needed desperately for decades, but Lindsay must have noticed something in my behavior because he gave me this tardy opening today. The perceptiveness of the man is often amazing.

Sunday, September 26 — Briefing sessions were held yesterday morning and this morning in preparation for the first triangular TV debate today. Lindsay stood at a lectern in a corner of Price's room, while his brothers George and David, Price,

O'Donnell, Deardourff, and I, sitting around the room in comfort, threw questions up at him. David objected violently to one reply couched in standard campaign language.

"That stinks," he shouted. "You're not answering, John, you're not answering! You're making a speech."

"Don't get upset, David," Lindsay admonished his twin and tried again.

"That's better," said David.

Price insisted on yes-or-no answers. Gradually he got them. I made several suggestions, including a challenge to Buckley on the Birch Society, which were shrugged off. In addition to these sessions there was a shorter last-minute briefing at which three of our canniest storefront managers—Daniel Hoffman, Joel J. Tyler, and Franklin R. Weissberg—described the stir of the sidewalk to Lindsay.

CBS had provided stools around the rim of a semicircular wooden frame for the three candidates; Mort Dean, the moderator; and two other Channel Two political experts, Jim Jensen and Tom Dunn. When we arrived at the studio, Beame was already standing at the spot where he was supposed to sit. Throughout the debate he remained standing, chunky as a Maillol piece of sculpture, thereby attaining equality of height with his taller sitting rivals. Unfortunately the cameras remained alive for a couple of minutes after the end of the debate. As the candidates began to stroll about the studio Beame's shortness was disconcertingly revealed.

To some extent the debate had a repetitive quality. Lindsay held himself out as the best hope for change and new vigor in the city, Beame said there was no substitute for experience, and Buckley pictured them both as "picking petals from daisies" instead of facing basic necessities such as a twenty-cent subway fare and a residence requirement for relief.

There were some shifts in position. When Beame reproached Lindsay for failing to join in his demand for a special session of the state legislature to roll back the sales tax, Lindsay called him a demagogue for resorting to an obvious gimmick. When Lindsay charged that Beame, if elected, would bring back the political machine "against which Ryan, O'Dwyer, and Screvane broke their skulls in the primary," Beame replied that he and Lindsay both belonged to political clubs. Lindsay's was on Park Avenue among the bluebloods of the silk-stocking district, Beame added, "whereas mine is in Crown Heights—just the little people."

On several occasions during the 90 minutes of opening statements, rebuttals, surrebuttals, questions-and-answers, and closing statements Beame and Buckley did not use up their full time. Eating a larger slice of humble pie than ever, Beame said he was sorry not to be able to "speak as glibly as Mr. Lindsay." Buckley took the opposite tack. Under prodding from Mort Dean to resume speaking he replied grandiloquently: "No, I think I'll just contemplate the great eloquence of my previous remark."

Beame was less modest in describing his political career. He had been, he said, "at the nerve center of city government for the past 20 years, as Budget Director and Controller." Lindsay promptly blamed him for all the mistakes and insufficiencies of the Wagner administration.

Following the Costikyan line, Beame presented statistics on achievements during the Wagner regime. He accused Lindsay of "bulldozer tactics" in criticizing conditions in New York. Buckley agreed that "bulldozer" was a good description of Lindsay.

The hand-holding of Beame and Buckley was not as conspicuous as it had been during the radio debate. Buckley charged that Lindsay was not interested in the city until he decided to run for mayor. "Destiny called when he sat down and figured that he had $1,500,000—enough money to run this caper." Beame suggested that Lindsay's campaign expenditures would actually exceed $3,000,000.

Buckley's phrasing was as sharp as ever but the TV cameras caught the restless shifting of his body, his eyeball-rolling, and grimaces. The cameras also revealed the glumness of Beame in contrast with the animation of the other candidates. Lindsay's poised directness was perceptibly appealing.

On an old-fashioned point-scoring basis, Buckley may have done as well as he did on radio, but on the basis of influencing votes through visual impressions—recalling Marshall Mc-Luhan's view that "the living room has become a voting booth"—the Conservative candidate lost ground. Though Beame's people are slightly apologetic—he was angered by Lindsay's thrusts, they say, but he "held himself in"—they are reportedly planning to accept invitations to two other debates.

The most accurate barometer was provided by Mary Lindsay. At the conclusion of the debate she rushed across the studio to shout at her husband: "Hey, you were terrific!" Despite her rules against the public display of affection, she then kissed him.

Monday, September 27 — The *Herald Tribune* resumed publication today after withdrawing from the Publishers Association. This unexpected crack in the united front of the publishers puts four other newspapers under greater pressure to settle with the unions. Indirectly it eases my personal situation in the Newspaper Guild. Various members of our union executive committee have been urging a special meeting to get a report on our precise bargaining position from Thomas J. Murphy, the Guild's executive vice-president. Several days ago I threatened to force such a meeting by petition. Today Jack Deegan, secretary-treasurer of the local, phoned to say that Murphy is calling an executive committee meeting for Wednesday evening. Naturally Tom is more obliging now that his truculence has had triumphant results.

The first issue of the Lindsay Campaign Reporter has just appeared under the editorship of Robert Laird, a *World Telegram* reporter now on strike, and M. J. Cadgene, the blondest and smartest of Price's three smart secretaries. An augmented staff of Raiders attended to the distribution. This four-page

This four-page throwaway . . .

throwaway is an attractive piece of journalism, with large pictures, some sports as well as news bulletins, and a variety of campaign articles. My contribution was an article on Lindsay's demand for the direct election of district leaders which I thought would appeal to Democratic reformers. The most effective thing in the issue is a cartoon by John Pierotti, reprinted by permission of the *Post,* showing a tall, smiling Lindsay between two small scowling figures, Boss Buckley, holding a placard calling Lindsay DIRTY REPUBLICAN, and Bill Buckley, holding one calling him DIRTY LIBERAL. The title is: BUCKING THE BUCKLEYS.

Tuesday, September 28 — Because of Rosh Hashanah, Beame has done no campaigning since Sunday night. Lindsay has been in Washington to support a bill giving voting rights to District of Columbia residents. Before returning he will attend a ceremonial signing of the federal aid-to-the-arts bill at the White House. He will probably receive another pen to add to those he received from President Johnson at the signing of the medicare and civil rights bills. Lindsay's boasting about these presidential pens, which are issued in carload lots, makes me uncomfortable but I suppose it impresses Pavlovian Democrats. In any case, the present lull allows me to record my role in the great *Esquire* exposé of Lindsay.

When Noel E. Parmentel, Jr., first strode down our campaign corridor, more than a month ago, I greeted him in friendly fashion. I know him fairly well and find him interesting. We covered the Senator Case-Robert Morris primary fight in New Jersey together and we have met at Conservative party dinners in New York. Parmentel is a tall, rawboned, middle-aged freelance writer, a bachelor, erudite and eccentric, conservative in his thinking but independent enough to pen a searing analysis of Bill Buckley about a year ago. When Barnie Patterson saw me with Parmentel, she beckoned me over to say excitedly and quite loud enough for him to hear: "Don't talk to that man! He's doing an axe job on John for *Esquire* magazine." I returned to Parmentel to ask if he were doing an axe job. When he cheerfully admitted the charge I continued to chat with him without providing classified information.

Parmentel's "John V. Lindsay: Less Than Meets the Eye" appeared about a week ago. It caused consternation at headquarters chiefly because the staff has been spoiled by the prevailing adulation given the candidate in magazines and books.

Price recently littered headquarters with free copies of campaign biographies of Lindsay by Daniel Button and Casper Citron. On a single day not long ago I noticed a puff account of Lindsay's naval career in *Bluebook* magazine and a more literary but equally complimentary report on him as a White House-bound politician in *Cavalier* magazine. *Esquire* differs from magazines like *Bluebook* or *Cavalier* in that it specializes in a glib hybrid of fact and fiction which Dwight Macdonald calls parajournalism. The burden of Parmentel's complaint is that Lindsay does not measure up to the late President Kennedy in intellectual brilliance or sophistication. "He thinks like Nixon, talks like Eisenhower, goofs like Goldwater."

"John Lindsay is one of the most bourgeois people alive," continues Parmentel, as if being bourgeois is sinful. "He is as oblivious to the high gloss as he is to the Locust Valley Lockjaw spoken by so many of his peers. He could easily pass muster as a scoutmaster in Peoria, a Lutheran (Missouri synod) layman in Wichita, a vice-chairman of the civic-affairs committee of the Toledo Lions Club, a 14th degree Mason (York rite) in Sioux Falls. His rather determined egalitarianism smacks more of George Babbit's Left period than of Philippe, duc d'Orleans.

"One would not cast him in either Mr. Smith Goes to Washington or Salome. He would get the old Jeffery Lynn roles and his best girl would be Lola or, more probably, Rosemary Lane, while Ronnie Reagan waltzed off with Priscilla. His aloneness and aloofness appear the result of a failure of imagination rather than a triumph of introspection. . . . And his mild hysteria and bouts of profanity are certainly no more than the neurosis of dissatisfaction, an affliction of the American middle class becalmed in a sort of social Saragossa with no more new words to conquer."

When I was reckless enough at headquarters to suggest that such exploding paper-bag phrases do no damage to the candidate, I was accused of defending "my friend Parmentel." Two or three days after the article appeared, I ran into the opposite criticism. Arriving home at midnight, I found a message asking me to phone Jill Stern, the daughter of J. David Stearn, former publisher of the *Post*. I have known Jill for years so I returned the call as requested. She explained that Parmentel had been at her apartment that evening and had expressed concern over my reaction to his exposé.

Too tired to be diplomatic, I began by saying that my reaction would have been more favorable if Parmentel had inquired instead of sending a deputy by phone. The article treated Price brutally, I said, and it showed no understanding of Mary Lindsay's character. I excused some touches of malice as required by the medium but I could not forgive the sneering references to a Lindsay I.Q. of "at least 110, with an attention span of at least 28 seconds" and his "stupidity problem." After watching Lindsay in operation almost daily for months, I said, I thought he had one of the finest functioning intelligences I had ever observed. Jill hung up in annoyance.

Twice the next day Parmentel tried to reach me by phone at headquarters. Each time I was out. The first time he promised to call back and the second time he left a message with Edie Radley: "Tell Ollie Pilat to go to hell." Two days later he made another call. Again I was out. This time he told Edie he was going to vote for Bill Buckley but he expected Lindsay to win and he was betting on Lindsay the $1,160 he received for writing the *Esquire* article!

Wednesday, September 29 — A meeting between Rockefeller

and Republican National Chairman Bliss in New Jersey to discuss national GOP problems was brought up in our morning
news conference.

Lindsay: I have no comment on the meeting. I'm out of
touch with national Republican problems.

Q.—Have you spoken recently with Chairman Bliss?

A.—No and I have no plans to speak with him.

Q.—Do you expect help from him?

A.—No. The national officials understand the New York
City election is nonpartisan.

Q.—What if Ike wants to come in?

A.—I have received no application for a visa.

Q.—Your campaign chairman says Rocky will be invited to
speak for you.

A.—Jack Javits is our senior Senator. He lives here in the
city. He is entitled to say anything he wishes. I stand on my
previous statements.

Q.—Do you often disagree with Javits?

A.—We agree most of the time.

Q.—Who will decide on Rockefeller, you or Javits?

A.—I'm running the campaign. I make all the decisions. I
believe the voters want to judge me by myself. I think the
same should be done regarding Beame and Buckley.

Though Lindsay privately and now publicly has overruled
Javits on Rockefeller, the senior Senator will take a leading
role in our street campaigning during the next few weeks.
Plans for this already have been made, starting with a walk
with Lindsay Saturday through the diamond center around
Canal Street.

I have always believed that Bobby Kennedy is jealous of
Lindsay's similarities to the late President Kennedy—minor
things like their joint fondness for Ian Fleming novels and
major things like their athletic stride and vigor, their common
legacy of grace and style—and that sooner or later he would
take a large role in this campaign. Now he has done so in a
manner which even I did not expect.

At open air rallies . . .

Bobby Kennedy walked the streets with Beame this evening. At open-air rallies in the Brownsville, Bedford-Stuyvesant, and Williamsburg sections of Brooklyn, he asked votes for "Abe Beame, a great Democrat" on the unscrupulous ground that a Democratic mayor would receive preferred treatment from a Democratic administration in Washington.

"Give Beame the opportunity to work with President Johnson and Vice-President Humphrey in Washington," said the Senator. "The Democratic Congress will also work better with a Democratic mayor."

Though Congress and federal agencies obviously should not discriminate between cities because of the political complexion of their mayors, Beame carried this unprincipled approach one step farther.

"The city depends on Washington for aid in housing, education, and the anti-poverty program," he stressed. "The new city administration will have to work with Washington and with Senator Kennedy." Beame also warned against the "possibility of a rejected Republican party capturing City Hall this year, the State next year, and the nation in 1968."

Thursday, September 30 — J. Raymond Jones will continue in control of the ancient and now perhaps honorable institution known as Tammany Hall. The Fox won reelection easily and quite unexpectedly today as Manhattan Democratic leader for a full four-year term.

Since Jones guessed wrong in the primary by supporting Screvane on top of an earlier mistake of offending Bobby Kennedy he was due to be dumped. His predecessor, Eddie Costikyan, understood this manifest duty in his capacity as Beame's campaign manager. On September 21 he invited all sixty-six male and female district leaders to a "social gathering" at Beame's campaign headquarters. Everybody came except Jones and a few of his friends.

Costikyan, whose small size and immensely agile mind always make me think of a chipmunk, opened the meeting by announcing that Beame would "run to a great extent on the Wagner record rather than away from it." After the meeting Costikyan settled down to private talks about a possible new county boss. His candidate was Edward I. Koch, a reformer with whom he had previously been on intimate terms. Two years ago Costikyan financed a private poll which helped Koch to repel DeSapio's attempt to regain district leadership in Greenwich Village. Moreover, Koch quarreled publicly some months ago with Jones over redistricting plans which would have had the effect, he said, of "putting all the Italians in my district" and thereby encouraging DeSapio to try another comeback. Jones retaliated by rebuking Koch for a "racist remark."

Costikyan made considerable progress in lining up a reform-regular coalition for Koch before he consulted the man he proposed to make boss. To his surprise, Koch was not interested. "I'd be running the Hall at the front door and you'd be making deals at the back door," Koch told Costikyan.

How do I know Koch said this to Costikyan? Because Koch told me so privately and I have no reason to question his word. The rest is not so clear. Apparently Costikyan was so confounded by Koch's quixotic attitude that he retreated in confusion from his effort to rule the county machine by proxy. He announced publicly that, as Beame's campaign manager, he was taking a "hands-off attitude." Opposition to Jones dwindled. Today all the regulars and some of the reformers voted for Jones. The rest of the reformers, including Koch, voted for Charles M. Kinsolving, the choice of the reform district leader caucus.

What Costikyan may have failed to take into account is that Koch's club, the Village Independent Democrats, overwhelmingly favors Lindsay for mayor. Koch, Carol Greitzer, Martin Berger, and other VID leaders may endorse Lindsay before the election. In any case, that's the never-to-be-officially disclosed backroom story of how the Chipmunk failed to unseat the Fox!

☆ ☆ ★   *October*

Friday, October 1 — The Newspaper Guild and the Publishers Association are supposed to have been negotiating for weeks. Actually they have not been in contact with each other for at least ten days. This discovery today appalled me. It underlined my inadequacy as part-time, unpaid, and largely disregarded president of the New York local of the Guild. I had not been sitting in on negotiations. Squeezing time from the crowded Lindsay schedule for an occasional turn on the picket line seemed difficult enough. Nevertheless, I had felt increasingly uneasy. By mail, phone, and in person, members of the union kept asking for assurances of progress in the negotiations, which I could not give. Since Tuesday night's executive committee meeting did not clarify the situation, I made a phone call last night to Tom Murphy, who runs the Guild. He invited me to come at noon today to Room 102 in the Hotel Commodore, where the Guild negotiators are quartered.

An unexpected hole in the campaign schedule developed around 11 A.M. On impulse I walked hurriedly through Grand Central Terminal from the Roosevelt to the Commodore where I encountered a corridor-haunting group of newspaper, radio and TV reporters.

"What's up?" one of them said.

"I'm trying to find out," I replied.

Inside Room 102 Murphy was playing double solitaire with Eddie Egan, the paid organizer at the *Times*. Joe Eisenberg, the unpaid *Times* unit president, and two other *Times* unit leaders, Farnsworth Fowle and Barney Stein, watched, read, or rested. The publishers, I learned, were playing bridge in a nearby room. Both groups had been playing cards for a long while. Having persuaded the Guild and the publishers to agree on secrecy as to progress—or lack of progress—in the negotiations, Ted Kheel, the veteran mediator, had largely switched his attention to the mailers' union and other craft unions involved in the blackout.

Kheel has a justified reputation for using time, among other devices, to wear down one side or another in a stubborn labor dispute. Since the card-playing began, of course, the *Herald Tribune* has dropped out of the Publishers Association, thereby increasing pressure on the publishers. By noon today the Guild and the publishers were supposed to produce package offers. Kheel came to the Guild room first. He was handed a bellicose and empty statement prepared last night by the *Times* unit executive committee. Smoothly, Kheel said he was afraid the publishers might take a similarly obdurate stand. He expressed my opinion, particularly since I knew that a petition for a membership meeting of the entire *Times* unit to consider compromise proposals had been rejected by the paid leadership of the Guild, but the anger rising within me focused on Kheel.

"I've a good mind to go out of this room and tell the reporters what's going on in here," I told him.

Kheel reminded me that I was bound by the Guild promise of secrecy. "I don't know about that," I said. Murphy agreed with Kheel. Morris Tarshis, Wagner's chief labor expert, had strolled in during the discussion. Unexpectedly, he winked at me. Making up my mind, I walked out of the room into a waiting semicircle of TV cameras.

"Those bums in there are still playing poker," I began. Was I criticizing the Guild?

No, I said, the bums on the publishers' side also were playing poker. I was criticizing both sides for failure to negotiate. The prolongation of the blackout affected newspapermen worse than the publishers, I argued, since newspapermen are traditionally broke and they receive small strike benefits, whereas the publishers have strike insurance and large private resources. I blamed Kheel especially for his tactic of enforced secrecy.

The resulting interviews ranged widely over strike issues from automation to the Guild shop but somehow always swung around in the end to bums playing cards in separate rooms. Back at the Roosevelt I hurried to the *Standard College Dictionary*, Funk & Wagnalls, 1963, to gauge the enormity of my statement. A bum was defined as a loafer, a dawdler. There were secondary meanings; living as a vagrant or living idly and in dissipation. What I object to, obviously, was dawdling.

A phone call came from Jack Deegan, the Guild secretary-treasurer, an old friend who often bridges differences between me and Murphy. When reporters asked Murphy how he felt about being called a poker-playing bum, his only comment, said Deegan, was that the publishers deserved some criticism for stalling. Murphy and Kheel, continued Deegan, were just following standard procedure. The mediator had been holding occasional separate meetings with the Guild negotiators— sometimes Murphy, but more often Egan and Eisenberg—and the representatives of the publishers, under a promise not to repeat to one side what the other side said. This shuttling process was designed to narrow the gap between the parties so direct negotiations could begin.

Unfortunately, I said, there had been too much dawdling and too little progress. The time had come to say so. How, for example, did Morris Tarshis feel about the stalemate? As the Mayor's man, said Deegan, Tarshis was annoyed at Kheel for grabbing all the publicity and keeping negotiations in his own hands. That was enough for me: I stood with Tarshis against Kheel.

The reaction to my outburst seems mixed. Tom Dunn of CBS-TV told me this afternoon that he considered my interview "one of the funniest in years." Unfortunately, I was serious.

When I arrived home this evening, my wife Avice criticized me for crudeness. "I heard it on TV," she said, "and it did not sound like you at all."

Saturday–Sunday, October 2–3 — Late Friday, Wagner gave negotiators in the the newspaper strike-lockout until midnight Saturday to reach agreement. The city's economy was being damaged, he said, and newspaper employes were suffering. Furthermore, he thought all the newspapers should cover "the great historic event Monday"—the visit of Pope Paul VI to the United Nations. If his deadline were ignored, Wagner threatened, he would present his own contract recommendations. Such recommendations would not be binding, but both sides wanted desperately to avoid them. Direct negotiations got under way late Saturday. The clock was stopped at midnight. Wagner himself sat in on the talks until 7 A.M. Sunday. On the advice of Morris Tarshis that some progress is being made, the Mayor has not issued his statement.

Bill Buckley is not suffering from the absence of most of the newspapers. Last Sunday's TV debate made him the darling of the McLuhan media. Even reporters from what's left of the press compete for nuggets of his wit and wisdom. As a word-fondler myself I can hardly blame them. What he says is ear-catching even when it is not apt. On Lindsay: "He is about as serious about politics as a flagpole sitter is about a flagpole." On Beame: "He has been around the present administration for exactly as many years as crime has risen." He hits Lindsay more often than Beame, he explains, "because John Lindsay is an imposter. Mr. Beame does not pretend to be anything but what he is, a very ordinary politician."

Buckley's hopes have risen as a result of a rally earlier this week at the Concourse Plaza Hotel at which 1,500 Bronx residents paid two dollars each for the privilege of cheering him wildly. Larger and wilder rallies are planned. Since Goldwater drew 801,000 votes in New York City last year, Buckley is beginning to wonder out loud whether he may not win after all. He exhibits verbal as well as political delusions of grandeur.

"There is a modern fallacy that government can save New York," he declared in an interview appearing in today's *Herald Tribune*. "Vogelin points out that the principal heresy of the age is the attempt to take eschaton (the religious concept of man's final state) and secularize it. Attempts to immunize it have failed. A politician cannot endow a Negro with a fine education. It has to be done by the individual."

Imagine a New York City politician talking eschatology— with a faint anti-Negro flavor! That should intrigue the Pope! While Buckley muses on heaven in relation to modern politics, his helots give us hell on earth. We had two extremely rough encounters yesterday with Conservative party pickets: the first at Parkchester, the huge New York Life Insurance Company housing project in the Bronx; the second in Ridgewood, a German-Irish community in Queens which was one of two areas in the entire city carried last year by Goldwater.

At Parkchester, in the late afternoon, a Buckley car preempted space for which our flatbed truck had a permit. The Buckley car was removed. Next a Buckley sound truck drove alongside our sound truck and tried to drown it out. A Raider cut off the Buckley sound. Police had to be summoned to stop the pushing and shoving. In addition to customary signs such as "Lefty Lindsay" and "Support Your Local Police," I saw a new one: "Flimsy Lindsay Say Something." Lindsay tried to say something but the bawling of the pickets covered his voice.

Since we had no press along in the evening, I was able to ride to Ridgewood in the lead car. Our advance man reported by radio-telephone that seventy-five Buckleyites were waiting at the Knights of Columbus fund-rasing affair which was on our schedule. "Are they inside or outside?" Lindsay asked. The answer was "Outside."

There were plenty of Buckleyites outside including the

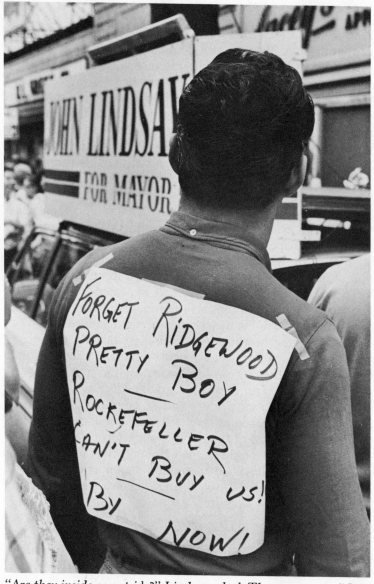

"Are they inside or outside?" Lindsay asked. The answer was "Outside."

man who had the street quarrel with David Lindsay a couple of months ago, but they also dominated a crowd of two hundred inside a large ramshackle structure lined with booths offering amusement park games of chance, various kinds of food, soft drinks, and beer. Hard liquor was being sold in an adjoining building. Perhaps this explained the ugly mood of some of the men. Catcalls and hoots followed Lindsay as he went around the room shaking hands. From the far end of the room where he was introduced, he made a few cautious remarks which could not be booed including a reference to the visit of the Pope. On the way out a scrawny youngster approached Lindsay with an outstretched hand and then unexpectedly slashed at the candidate's midriff. I was close enough to grab the nape of the boy's neck. I let go as I caught the stare of a cop who had missed the earlier surreptitious blow. Out of nowhere at the door materialized a short, plump, shiny-faced and smiling Catholic priest. It appeared to me that he deliberately detained Lindsay in friendly discourse in an effort to calm the crowd. He was a welcome sight indeed.

Even so, the howling in the dimness outside was nerve-wracking. No police were visible. Lindsay walked slowly toward his car, the rest of us following. By the time everybody got settled in the two campaign cars Buckleyites were massed around them shouting "bum" and "Communist," grimacing and spitting and shaking their fists like a bunch of Maoist demonstrators. Most of them were youngsters.

As our lead car began to inch through the crowd Lindsay reached back to boyhood memories for an effective retort. "Fairies," he shouted through the glass at his tormentors. "Fairies!"

Monday, October 4 — Can a poll reporting on the progress of a campaign affect the outcome of that campaign? Certainly it can. A sampling of voters' preferences by the *Herald Tribune* is already exerting considerable influence. Last Friday, Lindsay told an audience he had heard about a newspaper poll which would show him 15 percent behind Beame. An issue of *Newsweek* appearing over the weekend said "the first poll taken since the Democratic primary" gave Beame an 11 percent edge. Today James A. Wechsler, in his New York *Post* column, reveals that the straws so far divide as follows: Beame, 45 percent; Lindsay, 35 percent; Buckley, 10 percent; and the rest undecided. An impression has been created that Lindsay is surging forward from a trailing position. This is deceptive. The first installment in the *Herald Tribune* poll will not be published until Thursday.

Lindsay takes every opportunity nowadays to point out that LaGuardia failed of election the first time he ran as a fusion candidate for mayor in 1929 and won the second time in 1933 only because the Democratic party split and fielded two candidates in the general election. If he loses, Lindsay warns, there may not be another chance in a quarter of a century to "clean up the mess" in New York City government. This warning is not new. During the September 28 TV debate, he exclaimed that another chance to clean up the town might never come if he were defeated. Buckley promptly chided him for "megalomania."

The post-primary trend predicted by Price seems to be developing, with some exaggeration as a result of the press dimout which gives Buckley extra exposure on the air and facilitates the quiet regrouping of Democrats behind Beame. Nevertheless I see no reason to believe that Lindsay's summer lead has been erased.

Unlike the *Daily News*, which has been taking the public's political pulse for years and which was planning another poll when it was silenced by lockout, the *Herald Tribune* has no particular experience in this field. Since the paper resumed publication only recently its canvassing must have been hurriedly planned and executed. It reportedly talked to fewer than 15,000 persons out of the 3,598,784 who are eligible to vote November 2. That's about two-fifths of one percent. With such a small sampling slight errors in distribution or interpre-

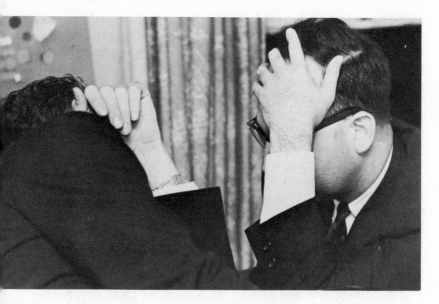

. . . these elaborately meshed personalities . . .

tation could produce a misleading verdict. The leakage of alleged results is not reassuring.

A small straw of my own runs counter to the preliminary conclusion of the *Herald Tribune*. Two weeks ago WMCA asked a young radio reporter named Gene Simpson to poll Harlem on the mayoralty. When Gene's first report showed Lindsay carrying an area where Republicans are normally swamped the station executives decided there must be something wrong with the poll and scrapped it. I know Gene quite well. When he insists that he was cautious and impartial in his interviews, I believe him. Can a Lindsay who pulls strongly in Harlem be in danger in the city as a whole? I do not believe so.

At this point in the campaign—four weeks before election day—being an underdog is supposedly advantageous. Lindsay-Price—and these elaborately meshed personalities seem increasingly to me to operate as one—would not pretend to be behind unless they thought the pretense improved their chances. The effect of Lindsay-Price's calculated pessimism on the general public is hard to gauge, but at headquarters everybody does seem to be working a little harder—if that is possible—and perhaps more harmoniously.

Tuesday, October 5 — Our White Papers, designed to be blockbusters in the post-primary campaign, were postponed because of the press blackout. They could be withheld only so long, however, and they are now exploding in irregular procession. Our first one, on law enforcement, appeared last Thursday in a Madison Avenue package as Operation Safe City. Its fifteen points included some new ideas, such as two-way walkie-talkies for cops on the beat, a radio system for policemen to dictate reports, a facsimile network to transmit fingerprints from one police station to another, and the integration of police and fire call-boxes in a single emergency system. It proposed one-man instead of two-man radio patrol cars, special lighting in the parks, and an increase in the force by 2,500 men.

Costikyan commented audaciously that Lindsay's crime program, like his programs on off-track betting and neighborhood city halls, was "a carbon copy" of what Beame has been saying. Price retorted that Lindsay produced "a sixteen-page, legal-sized, single-spaced discussion about ways to make the streets safe" whereas Beame's package was "eight pages and merely skimmed the surface." Price was right, but as our White Papers continue to appear—on housing, parks, expanding the city economy, etc.—Costikyan continues to shout copycat.

Beame would "rather switch than fight," jeers Price, trying a lighter approach. More and more impudent all the time, Costikyan offers to send copies of Beame's press releases to stimulate Lindsay's thinking on city problems.

"The best-kept secret in City Hall for the last twenty

years," commented Price today, "is any new idea Mr. Beame has ever had."

The running debate over who is plagiarizing whom amuses the public but in the process it seems to be taking the edge off many laboriously conceived constructive proposals by Lindsay task forces. For once, I guess, the campaign honors go to Costikyan.

Wednesday, October 6 — Price has again found "the" issue of the campaign. This time it's Bronx boss Buckley's refusal to permit the direct election of district leaders. From day to day, in releases, press conference statements, campaign literature, and perhaps even radio-TV spots, Price will stress the obduracy and backwardness of the seventy-five-year old boss until he feels that the issue has lost texture. Then he will turn to a new issue.

The first hint of a hidden struggle in the Bronx reached me more than a week ago. During a Lindsay walking tour in the Morrisania section of that borough, I encountered Dennis Coleman, a member of the Democratic reform movement who had won an unexpected victory in the primary over the machine choice for the state senatorial seat vacated by Ivan Warner. Coleman, bright young Negro, former Bronx head of the NAACP, mentioned rumors of a possible resignation by Buckley. Apparently the boss broke into one of his famous rages and threatened to step down rather than yield to private pressure to abandon the old system of electing district leaders by county committee groups. If he resigned he might be succeeded by Victor Campione, his representative at Beame headquarters; Henry McDonough, his factotum in the Bronx; or Bronx District Attorney Isidore Dollinger. That was the gossip. It sounded exciting enough to relay to Price, who had already heard it from Rose. I tipped off a couple of reporters to a possible story but they were unable to confirm it.

The veil of secrecy was broken by Herman Badillo, who beat Senator Warner, Buckley's choice for the Borough Presidency, in the primary. Badillo called publicly on Beame to press for the direct election of district leaders in the Bronx as a symbol of his liberalism. Francis W. H. Adams, chairman of an advisory committee of the Committee for Democratic Voters, added that the reform movement would work actively for Beame if he did as Badillo asked.

Beame was obliged to comply. He issued a statement that he favored democratic electoral procedures and that the direct election of district leaders was already practiced in Brooklyn.

"That's meaningless," snapped Badillo, when reporters relayed the statement to him. "Beame misses the point. We are all for the direct election of district leaders. The answer should be here and now."

Unless Beame joined him in an ultimatum to Buckley for a meeting by October 15 of the 4,000-member Bronx Democratic county committee to change the rules, Badillo warned, he will not campaign for the city Democratic slate.

Giving way further, Beame sent a telegram to Buckley asking for a county committee meeting to modernize the rules. Procaccino, Buckley's man on the city ticket, also pushed for the change on district leaders, which cannot take effect until next year since the present district leaders were chosen last year for two-year terms. Jay Fischer, Bronx head of the CDV, talked to Joseph Cohen, head of Buckley's law committee, on the possible wording of this and other proposed electoral changes. For a day or two it looked as if the Bronx were about to move into the twentieth century.

Buckley has now called an executive committee meeting for tomorrow. Despite heavy losses to the reformers in the primary on nominations for public office, he still controls all but one of the seventeen executive committee votes. Since the executive committee consists of district leaders he will in effect be telling them how he wishes them to be picked in the future. Asked today by a reporter what will happen Buckley said: "It's up to the leaders." Nonsense. It's up to Buckley alone.

The word by political grapevine which has aroused Price to feverish preparations is that Buckley will tell his satraps he would rather resign than pay any attention to a bunch of pinkos and fakers. He will not resign. The leaders will then cheer him and the meeting will be over. In anticipation of this result Beame is promising that he will ask the state legislature next year to make the direct election of district leaders mandatory instead of optional as at present. In reward for his futile efforts, Beame will gain the official support of Badillo and the CDV. Badillo on his part may win some promises of compaign help from Beame, including money. Price cannot attack Badillo or CDV. He can exploit their suppressed resentment of Buckley and that he will do as persistently and vehemently as possible.

Thursday, October 7 — The *Herald Tribune* today gave Beame 45 per cent of its 13,642 straws, Lindsay 35 percent, Bill Buckley 10 percent and the rest undecided. That's precisely what the clairvoyant Jimmy Wechsler foresaw several days ago. "It shows we're probably closing in," commented Lindsay, "but the odds are still very serious." Costikyan said the figures "reflect the results of the primary and show we have come up since the early days of the campaign. My own personal feeling is that Lindsay and Beame are about even-Stephen." Price, unruffled, said: "I am undaunted by claims that the machine is in the lead. It merely confirms that we're underdogs and we have to keep on working as hard as we can to win. In a comparable period before the Democratic primary in September, Screvane was leading Beame in the polls by some 15 percent." The word around headquarters is that Lindsay will gain two or three percent in the second wave of *Herald Tribune* canvassing, to be publicized next Tuesday. How could it be otherwise?

There was another non-surprise today: a unamimous vote by the Bronx Democratic executive committee rejecting Beame's request for a special meeting of the full county committee to consider direct elections. Buckley did not resign. "Mr. Beame now faces the moment of truth!" said Lindsay. "Will he split with the rascals or climb back in bed with them?" Beame answered that there was no split between him and Buckley—"just a difference of opinion." Badillo grumbled mildly for publication but he is clearly headed for Beame's bed—and maybe board.

In contrast with this slow-motion posturing was a meeting this evening of the Village Independent Democrats, the reform club which drove DeSapio out of public life. Lindsay and Beame made appearances. Lindsay argued that the city needs nonpartisan government. Beame charged that the Republicans are using Lindsay to "rejuvenate the party" locally and nationally.

The VID stalwarts questioned the candidates closely and argued with each other at considerable length. Ed Koch declined to reveal his preference between Lindsay and Beame. "I intend to vote my conscience," he said. A resulting secret ballot diluted conscience with political caution. Beame received 6 votes, Lindsay, 47, and no-endorsement, 64. The failure-to-endorse leaves club members free to work politically as they choose. Since many of the no-endorsements came from Lindsay supporters who do not wish to read the club out of the Democratic party, it's a doubly damaging repudiation of Beame.

Lindsay said he was grateful for "this vote to reject the machine and the twenty-year crowd at City Hall." Beame noted that VID has 1,200 members, most of whom did not attend the meeting. He expressed confidence that "the overwhelming majority of this Democratic club will support the Democratic ticket that has been endorsed by party leaders in the city, state, and nation."

Friday, October 8 — From day to day, here is how the 23-day newspaper strike-lockout came to an end. On Tuesday, Senators Javits and Kennedy requested the Mayor to make his delayed recommendations for a settlement. Wagner said he would do so at 9 P.M. Wednesday if no agreement had been reached by then. On Wednesday, Murphy accused the Mayor of "trying to compromise the Guild's collective bargaining program" and indicated he would balk at any proposals from City Hall. That same day, Guild units at the World-Telegram, Journal-American and Daily News undercut Murphy by asking Wagner to use his good offices promptly as promised. Meanwhile Wagner was out in Minneapolis watching a World Series baseball game. Late Thursday, Wagner returned to town and presented to both sides compromises worked out by Kheel on automation, union security, the union shop, and pensions. Today these compromises were accepted, reluctantly by Murphy and less reluctantly by the publishers. The papers will resume publication Sunday.

A baffling relationship between Vice-President Humphrey and Beame can also be traced by the chronological method. A week ago, Humphrey promised Beame to spend "all available time" campaigning for him. Later that day, liberal friends of Humphrey urged him to keep hands off the local political situation. Last weekend, the Vice-President came to New York for the opening of the Metropolitan Opera. He had no available time for campaigning. He stayed in town Monday to welcome the Pope. Tuesday he addressed the NATO Parliamentarians Conference in New York. He had no available time for Beame on either of those days. Wednesday he did other things in New York which did not include campaigning. Thursday he returned to Washington. Today, Beame was asked at his news conference when Humphrey would actually campaign. "His people and mine have been meeting to set a date," he replied, "but so far as I know no date has been decided on yet."

Saturday, October 9 — Puerto Rican affairs run late, so we were still being buffeted by cha-cha music at 12:30 A.M. today. This was a fund-raising dance of the Spanish division of the

Liberal party at the Broadway Casino, which was like most of the middle-class Negro and Puerto Rican dances we have attended. The men were dressed in their best. The women wore low-cut party dresses. Some couples had children, teenaged or older, with them and baskets of food and drink to be consumed at their tables after 1 A.M. Lindsay made a speech in Spanish and presented an award to a man named Marcellino Castro for "distinguished service to the community." After a final round of handshaking, he and Mary Lindsay started to leave. An aide mentioned another Spanish affair nearby: "More than 1,000 people and it will take only a few minutes."

"You can't see 1,000 people in a few minutes," objected Mary Lindsay. The Saturday schedule, she pointed out, began with an 8:30 A.M. arrival at some rat-and-refuse-infested lots in the Erie Basin section of Brooklyn which were to be cleaned up with the help of volunteers from a storefront. "It's too late!" she said. "Nobody else will say no, so I will. You want him for mayor; I want him for a husband." Lindsay nodded and they got into the lead car for a drive back to the Roosevelt and a day's-end conference with Price, O'Donnell, and a couple of others. I went home by subway.

Earlier Friday evening, Lindsay delivered a talk before the New Era Club of the Educational Alliance on the lower East Side of Manhattan and participated in a stormy political forum at Queens College. Douglas Yates of the *Yale Daily News* and John Twohey of the *Notre Dame Scholastic*, who were in our press contingent, got a chance at Queens College to glimpse the usually hidden savagery of politics, since the Buckleyites had contrived to purchase three-quarters of the seats in advance and they were clearly spoiling for a fight.

Buckley had spoken and left before we arrived. His still-jubilant partisans, most of whom seemed to be high-school students or adults well past college age, roared at Lindsay when he was introduced. Buckley signs jiggled all over the auditorium.

"I remember waiting an hour for politeness to set in at the

Cow Palace," said Lindsay, recalling his anti-Goldwater speech at the National Republican Convention in San Francisco in 1964. "I'm prepared to wait just as long as I have to wait. . . ."

The Buckleyites howled like tormented dogs. A white girl fought her way down the center aisle with a placard: "Lindsay, I'm a member of a minority group. What will you promise me?" Some Lindsay supporters and some neutrals in the audience began to call for silence.

When Lindsay found a relatively quiet moment he scoffed at the "extremists of the far right who would set race against race and create tension among us." Two fights broke out in the audience. Ushers separated the battlers. Talking again, Lindsay won applause by advocating mandated free tuition in city colleges. The double padlock, he said, has become a symbol of a city in crisis. He closed with the statement: "You may never have another opportunity to choose in favor of a fresh start again."

Down a long, winding, poorly lighted path to the street went John and Mary Lindsay, Lindsay aides, Raiders, and supporters, surrounded on all sides by Buckleyites. The massive exodus from the auditorium including former neutrals who had become Lindsay converts out of a sense of fair play left only a handful of persons to listen to District Attorney O'Connor, substituting for Beame. A man lunged at Lindsay with a Buckley lapel sticker. David Love, one of the Raiders, intercepted the man and rushed him against a picket fence. Love was about to slug the man when Lindsay shook his head perceptibly and Love let the fellow go.

As the swirling crowd neared the Lindsay campaign cars, the shouting of the Buckleyites increased. A short heavy man in a wrinkled tan overcoat who had been passing out Buckley literature from the top of a car parked at the curb said calmly through an electric microphone: "If you really want to help conservatism and William Buckley, please do NOT make a scene. Let's see how quiet we can be." We got away in an unnatural silence.

Sunday, October 10 — Another debate, this time over WNEW-TV. Nothing particularly new about it: Lindsay a little bolder, Beame a little glummer, Buckley a shade less scintillating.

Barry Goldwater had brunch with Bill Buckley before the debate. They may have discussed Lindsay's newly won endorsement from Americans for Democratic Action, a small, loosely organized and largely ineffectual group of liberal-leaning intellectuals which Goldwater tried to build up into a leftist ogre during his presidential campaign. However, Goldwater did not comment publicly on ADA or any other aspect of the mayoral campaign.

During the debate, Buckley said Lindsay and Beame seem to be quarreling chiefly over "who wrote which position paper first." Beame picked it up saying: "I'm glad to see Mr. Lindsay is adopting some of my ideas," but Lindsay let it go. The most vivid remark of the debate was probably Lindsay's description of Beame as a "Rip Van Winkle just waking from twenty years of civic sleep."

After the debate, Costikyan threatened a suit by Beame against Lindsay over his recently aired TV spot declaring that "the money man in this do-nothing administration that let New York become the heroin capital of the world was Abe Beame. Until Beame and his bosses leave City Hall nothing will be done." Beame says this is "vicious" because it blames him for the city's dope addiction. Lindsay replies that New York has indeed become the "narcotics capital of the world" and that Beame as a bureaucrat did nothing to stop it. Nevertheless, the spot is being withdrawn.

Monday, October 11 — Suddenly Beame seems to be on the defensive. Lindsay and Buckley have accepted offers of free time from WABC-TV, WNBC-TV, and WNDT-TV for additional debates, but Beame has been "ducking," Price declared today. Costikyan replied for Beame. "We just don't want a debate every other day," he said.

Tomorrow Costikyan will bring Franklin D. Roosevelt, Jr.,

in from Washington to denounce Lindsay for a TV remark
that "Beame could not wait for the death of Mrs. Roosevelt
and Senator Lehman, those two great leaders of the Democratic reform movement, before becoming the candidate of
organization Democrats." The remark was tasteless to be sure,
but FDR, Jr., will not be able to deny that Beame is aligned
with the bosses against whom Lehman and Mrs. Roosevelt
struggled. On Wednesday Vice-President Humphrey comes to
town again, this time to speak at the nonpartisan Alfred E.
Smith Memorial Dinner. It is expected that he will campaign
for Beame and that he will bring an endorsement from the
White House.

Tuesday, October 12 — Kitty Genovese, who became a symbol of the selfish insulation of big-city residents, was a sturdy
woman of twenty-eight accustomed to working late because
she managed a bar. Around 2:30 A.M. March 31, 1964, a chilly
night for that time of year, she parked her red Fiat in the Kew
Gardens parking lot of the Long Island Railroad and started
on foot toward her nearby apartment. A man armed with a
knife tried to rape her. She resisted. During the next thirty-five
minutes Winston Mosely, later convicted of the murder,
stabbed Miss Genovese repeatedly, retreated twice, and returned each time to the attack.

Lights flashed on in apartments all along Austin Street as
the young woman shouted for help and screamed in terror and
pain. People peered from their windows, but not one of them
did so much as phone the police. Two or three days later Police Commissioner Murphy, lunching with A. M. Rosenthal,
then metropolitan editor of the *New York Times*, complained:
"People don't help us," and mentioned a Queens murder
where thirty-eight witnesses did nothing. Reporter Martin
Gansberg was assigned to interview the thirty-eight. Their attitude ranged from "What's the use?" and "Why get involved?"
to "It was none of my business."

On the site of the murder, facing Miss Genovese's former

". . . something has gone out of the heart and soul of New York City."

apartment, with the same neighbors looking down from their windows and an additional crowd of three hundred in the street and the parking lot, Lindsay delivered a campaign talk this evening.

"What the Kitty Genovese story tells us," he said, "is that something has gone out of the heart and soul of New York City. That something is hope, morale, spirit, pride, people-to-people responsibility. The tragedy demonstrated that indifference to one's neighbors is a conditioned reflex of life in this city. What the Kitty Genovese story tells us is that as long as we permit the political machines to perpetuate the myth that the job of governing New York is hopeless, then apathy will increase."

Lindsay urged the slightly awed audience to "join ranks shoulder to shoulder to smash crime in this town." If elected mayor, he pledged, picking up an inspiration from Rose via Price, "the lights in City Hall will be on twenty-four hours a day. We will light up this street, all our streets, all our parks, everywhere in this town. We will not rest until decency in the streets and in politics prevails again!"

A few Kew Gardens residents, particularly the overpublicized witnesses of the murder, were restive over revival of the case, but the general public reaction to this ministerial amalgam was good. As in the case of last night's mass invasion of Prospect Park, the appeal was largely symbolic. After a rally at the southwest entrance to the park, all that happened last night was a half-mile surge into the park by John and Mary Lindsay, dozens of Raiders carrying torches, and a crowd of several thousand, then a half-mile surge out again, but it was an eerie and somewhat effective demonstration.

"Citizens are fearful of their lives if they walk alone or even in pairs in this park after sunset," Lindsay said in his preliminary talk. "There have been holdups, muggings, rapes, and murders right here."

As in Kew Gardens tonight, Lindsay urged the use of new electronic devices to shorten the police response to a crime, the doubling of patrol cars, the tripling of motorcycles, and the adding of 2,500 cops to the force "to provide a continuous police presence in every block." These were aspects of his anti-crime White Paper which were largely lost to public sight during the quibbling with Beame as to who said what first. In publicizing them two night in a row—and undoubtedly during the next few days, since crime is now Price's Number 1 issue in the campaign—Lindsay should be able to neturalize the damaging effect of his police review board stand on timid white middle-class residents in unsafe neighborhoods.

Wednesday, October 13 — Conservative party toughs slugged several straggling Raiders during our noisy Monday night safari into Prospect Park. No complaints were filed with the police. Identification of those who tried to commit mayhem on the edges of the flickering light cast by torches would have been difficult. Besides, any publicity on the scuffling would have marred the happy picture of future security in the parks being drawn by Lindsay. I hear that Mark Schlachtman, a Raider who was held on the grass and pummeled by several pickets, is still in hospital, with possible internal injuries.

Today, Conservative pickets egged our campaign cars as they left Featherbed Lane in the Bronx after a rally. One egg smeared the glass alongside the front seat where Lindsay sat. To judge by their placards and their disciplined rowdiness the egg-throwers today and the sluggers Monday belong to or are guided by the Birch Society. Barry Goldwater has an article in the current *National Review* suggesting that unless Robert Welch resigns as head of the Birch Society the membership should resign from the society. This is not the first anti-Welch item carried by Bill Buckley as editor of that magazine. Why then should Birch Society members continue to work for Buckley? Are they slow in understanding that they are unwanted or are the anti-Birch Society references in *National Review* just diplomatic disavowals?

Buckley is moving up in the polls. The *Herald Tribune*, which started him at 10 percent, says he now pulls 13 percent of its straws. Samuel Lubell, in a new poll for the Scripps-Howard newspapers, gives him 12 percent. As a result of Buckley's growing strength, concludes Lubell today, "Lindsay is sliding toward threatened defeat." Despite Lubell's national reputation, his tendency to contradict himself over a period of weeks induces skepticism in me. Before I worry, I'll wait to see what the *Daily News* poll reports next week.

Whether it's the polls, the Schlachtman incident in the park, or something else, Lindsay is definitely more waspish about Buckley. He commented casually today that Buckley's book, *God and Man at Yale*, was "badly written." A reporter

carried this literary criticism to Buckley. He replied grandiloquently: "I ask Mr. Lindsay: 'How can you tell?' "

At the annual dinner of the Liberal party this evening,
Lindsay said Buckley "entered this race with the single purpose of engineering my defeat and thereby wiping out that
heresy known as Lindsay liberalism. I view his attack as proof
that there will be no place for the ugly politics of reaction and
know-nothingness in my administration." New York, continued Lindsay, has become "a city divided—torn between the
desperate aspirations of the have-nots and the deepening anx-
ieties of the haves."

"The better-off," he said, "must finally learn that there
are no islands any more; that their security can be protected
and preserved only if those less fortunate are rescued from the
long night of misery and deprivation. As long as thousands of
citizens view themselves as outcasts, as long as their children
are forced to shiver in heatless slums and consigned to inferior
schools, as long as efforts to combat drug-addiction are meager
and minimal, as long as fashionable streets are fastidiously
cleaned while the lower depths are given a quick once-over, as
long as hospital care means solicitude for the rich and neglect
for the poor, as long as recreation facilities are limited and inadequate, as long as relocation is planless, as long as inequity
remains a dominant fact of life for millions, New York will be
a powder keg of unrest."

Lindsay wound up with a reference to a recent Buckley
proposal for the establishment of "rehabilitation" centers outside the city where certain welfare recipients and their children would be "relocated." "The agony of New York," he
said, "will not be relieved by cruelly driving some relief clients
beyond the city lines and trying to build a wall around our
city."

Thursday, October 14 — Lindsay's morning news conference
was converted into a testimonial meeting for Democrats. By
order of Barnie Patterson I was in charge. With help from

Wyn Kramarsky in getting biographical data I prepared a news release and a stack of three-by-five cards for Lindsay's use in introductions. As each recruit arrived I asked him to be ready to say a few words when introduced as to his reasons for supporting Lindsay.

Those baptized in this fashion included Eugene Victor, forty-five, a labor lawyer who has run unsuccessfully as a reform Democrat in Brooklyn for Borough President and for Congress; Robert Persky, thirty-five, and Terence Benbow, thirty-six, two of Ryan's lieutenants; Seymour Feller, thirty-six, and Robert Rubinstein, thirty-three, reform leaders in the Bronx; some reform and some irregular Democrats from Queens; several independent Negroes from Harlem and Bedford-Stuyvesant; and the leader of a Puerto Rican group in the Tremont Avenue section of the Bronx.

Everything went fine except that the procession of penitents to the microphone began to bore the reporters. Jane Kalmus, a former radio-TV adviser to Wagner who has joined Mollen's staff, rushed across the room to point out that the TV cameras had gone dark.

"You've offended them," she said, pointing to the idle cameramen. "If Lindsay loses on election day you will be responsible!"

If that was the risk, it had to be taken. In some CDV clubs, like the Village Independent Democrats, a simple majority vote is enough to prevent automatic endorsement of the Democratic candidate. Others, including those in the Bronx, require a two-thirds vote to prevent automatic Democratic endorsement. The struggle over these clubs is already in progress. Lindsay appeals to any club which will give him a hearing and last evening Beame visited four CDV clubs on the upper West Side of Manhattan to unveil a seventeen-point program resembling a reform manifesto.

Under the circumstances, I told Jane, one well-indoctrinated Lindsay missionary to the reform movement is worth a dozen alienated TV crews.

This is the season for testimonials . . .

This is the season for testimonials of all kinds. Vice-President Humphrey, interviewed last evening at LaGuardia Airport on his way to the nonpolitical Alfred E. Smith Memorial Dinner, draped his arm around Beame and said: "There's no news in the fact that I'm a good Democrat and that I'm supporting a good Democrat." He did not campaign for Beame beyond introducing him to Mrs. Humphrey as "Mayor Beame" and he did not bring the endorsement from President Johnson which every newspaper in town has been predicting for a week.

"The President of the United States," said the Vice-President of the United States, "is a big man, a great man, and he speaks for himself."

When reproached privately by a Beame official for failing

to bring a presidential endorsement, Humphrey asked why LBJ should endorse Beame when Mayor Wagner has not seen fit to do so. That stopped the conversation on that subject.

Meanwhile former President Eisenhower has declared that Lindsay's election "would be a shot in the arm" for the Republican party nationally and would help many Republican candidates in many states and cities. The remark hurts Lindsay's chances by emphasizing his Republicanism at an awkward moment. Did the General intend to be injurious or was he just clumsy in phrasing an endorsement? Who can tell? Four years ago, Eisenhower visited New York a few days before the city election. Pressed to say something about Lefkowitz, the former President said he really didn't know much about Lefkowitz but if Lefkowitz was the Republican candidate for mayor he would be a good man to vote for. At least Lindsay has been spared that kind of a wilted bouquet.

Lindsay won the endorsement today of the *New York Times* as "the only candidate who offers a convincing prospect of change for the better in city administration." The *Post* and the *Herald Tribune* previously endorsed Lindsay and the *World Telegram* is expected to do so soon. The *Journal American* has already come out for Beame. The *Jewish Daily Forward* is for Lindsay and the three Newhouse papers—the *Staten Island Advance*, the *Long Island Press*, and the *Long Island Star-Journal*—are for Beame. That leaves only the *Daily News*, the largest and most conservative of them all, which is torn between Beame and Buckley for mayor.

Friday, October 15 — The persistent tension and shrillness of the campaign nowadays are nerve-wracking at close range. I wonder how much of what is actually happening percolates through the excitement and the noise to the public. If an election can be considered a man-to-man struggle, then Lindsay is carrying the fight to Buckley after forcing Beame temporarily to step aside. Last night Lindsay appeared before an almost totally hostile audience of 800 at a Parents and Taxpayers

Association meeting in Queens. According to PAT officials, Beame accepted an invitation to address this group but he did not appear and when asked by reporters about it over the telephone he asserted blandly that the invitation never reached him.

As Lindsay and a half dozen others of us moved into the Richmond Hill High School auditorium, keeping close together in instinctive self-protection, the heat could be felt immediately. "Here's the gang that supports John JUDAS Lindsay," roared one fellow wearing an orange Buckley button who readily gave his name and address to reporters. The whole audience seemed to be wearing orange buttons. When Lindsay began to speak his words could scarcely be heard over the heckling. "If you'll stop being rude," he said at one point, in his faintly English manner, "we'll get to it."

Lindsay had the nerve to broach his plan for a civilian review board in the police department. Booing began immediately. "I'll tell you this: it will do more to reduce tension in this city than anything else." More booing. "It will help the police." The booing became so loud and continuous that his remarks were blanketed for a while. The metamorphosis of audience into mob was occurring before our eyes. "Down with Lindsay—shoot him in the back" shouted one fat man as we started to leave the auditorium.

A question popped into my mind which I could not answer then or now: Was Lindsay being inflammatory accidentally, instinctively, or deliberately, to reveal the rabid quality of the Buckley opposition? From two advance men left behind to report by radio-telephone we learned that Buckley entered the school auditorium to hysterical applause with a personal escort of six policemen headed by Captain John Peterson of the 102d precinct. The pandemonium did not subside as Buckley deftly plucked at alarmist strings in his harpsichord. Unlike the members of his own all Irish-Catholic slate, he said without any particular emphasis, Lindsay is a "white Protestant." Lindsay and Beame do not dare to attack Powell, he added, because Powell is a Negro. So it went.

Today our headquarters released a 22-page booklet on the restoration of fiscal stability in New York. Lindsay tried to expand on this at his morning news conference but the reporters were bent on headier things. They wanted comment on Buckley's white-Protestant and Negro references and they were determined to get it, one way or another. Lindsay responded with a comparison between Barry Goldwater and Buckley.

"I was never quite sure Senator Goldwater knew the consequences of his acts," he said. "Buckley does. That makes him doubly dangerous. In the streets, the Buckley campaign becomes a racist campaign, but let me emphasize that I am not saying Buckley is personally a racist. This kind of campaign plays on public apprehension. The next mayor will have to face the fear which now grips the city. Fear, as you know, can be as dangerous and epidemic as any disease."

Under persistent questioning, he gave them what they wanted. "The city," he said, "is a powder keg, and Buckley is doing his best to light the fuse."

Saturday–Sunday, October 16–17 — One way of exploiting religious prejudice in a campaign is to accuse the opposition of raising the issue. This is particularly effective if it is true. Getting outsiders to make the accusation has obvious tactical advantages. Accordingly, a citywide group of four Rabbis and five Protestant ministers, most of whose names are quite familiar at headquarters, have protested the "incident" at Richmond Hill High School. Their statement, prepared by a minister very favorable to Lindsay, was issued outside headquarters on unidentifiable sheets of paper.

"As clergymen," they said, "we deeply regret that Mr. Buckley resorted to racial and religious slurs. Elections are to increase the vigor and efficiency of community administration —not to create divisions and rasp past frictions. The incident is especially shocking inasmuch as eyewitnesses suggest that Mr. Buckley was 'playing' to already unruly bigots in the audience. Mr. Buckley should, we believe, apologize for his unruly remarks."

Somewhat later and perhaps more spontaneously the Flatbush Ministers Council, representing fifteen churches in that central area of Brooklyn, called Buckley "cheap and underhanded" for citing Lindsay's WASPishness at the PAT meeting. The leader of this group cited Buckley's expressed hope of exercising "a form of cultural leadership in a nation of moral imagination," and added: "We suggest to the candidate that his unethical attitude on Mr. Lindsay's religious affiliation makes him a poor choice for such leadership."

Buckley had hardly finished explaining that nothing was farther from his intention than bias of any kind when Costello attacked him on religious grounds. Costello's remarks were not cleared in advance at headquarters. They were not expected. The effect of them was to reverse our favorable position in the religious controversy at the worst possible time.

Costello's deeply engrained liberal Catholicism was one of his qualifications for inclusion on the fusion slate. He may have blundered in this instance but I do not intend to join in the susurrus of unfriendly comment at headquarters among the GOP stalwarts who are always ready to criticise the Liberal party. I am sure Professor Costello spoke carefully after considerable thought.

What he said was sweeping enough: that Buckley's "negative, divisive preachings are a threat to peace on earth, progress in the nation, the uplifting of our city, and the propagation of social doctrine of the Catholic Church."

In a Fordham University talk during which he mentioned favorably the names of the late Cardinal Hayes, Cardinal Spellman, Monsignor Harry Byrne, Father Henry Brown, Father Ahearn, Father Fitzpatrick, the Dominican Sisters, the Nursing Sisters of the Sick Poor (whom he serves as a consultant), the Carmelites, and various others, ranging from Mother Seton to Mother Cabrini, Costello added: "All of us, as New Yorkers, as Americans, and as Catholics, were inspired by Pope Paul's peace mission to the United Nations, yet the radical right, including spokesmen like Bill Buckley, can only mock that world organization for peace.

"Our Church is no new combatant in the war on poverty, injustice, and man's inhumanity to man and in the war against war itself, yet Mr. Buckley could smirk at the magnificent encyclical of the beloved Pope John, 'Pacem in Terris,' as a mere 'venture in triviality.'

"And on Pope John's other great encyclical, Mr. Buckley could only parrot: 'Mater, si, Magister, no.' This is no longer corrosive wit. This is corrosion. . . ."

Costikyan, the Protestant campaign manager of a Jewish candidate for mayor, issued a statement begging the two Catholic candidates to halt their "reckless and headlong flight into the gutter." He indicated his preference between them by characterizing Costello's attack on Buckley as "the lowest tactic of the campaign."

"When you speak of convictions," replied Costello, "you have to let such matters as tactics take care of themselves."

He soon discovered how primitive the reaction to a religious issue can be at the street level. During a walking tour Saturday afternoon in the Astoria and Sunnyside sections of Queens he was jeered in unruly unison by the Birchite pickets who normally hound Lindsay. One shopkeeper called him a Communist while a nearby woman shopper praised him for "guts." Some passersby scowled and walked away from him, others shook his hand with unusual warmth.

In response to a panicky phone call in the late afternoon, Costello and his entourage hurried to Queens Liberal party headquarters in Jamaica. While everybody was out taking part in the walking tours, the place had been entered, apparently by means of a skeleton key. Vandals had smashed desks and chairs, pulled telephones from the wall, overturned filing cabinets, torn up files, and spread a layer of garbage over the debris.

Buckley himself took a sophisticated approach to the controversy. "If I am a bad Catholic," he said in one of a series of Sunday TV appearances, "I shall be punished by Someone I fear far more than the New York Catholic voters. To whom I say this: I don't want your vote for me because I am a Catholic. I want your vote for me because of the positions I take."

Having made this claim, Buckley went on to defend his right to take positions. He would always "listen respectfully" to the views of Pope Paul or Pope John on the UN, civil rights, or other matters, he said, but he was not required to share their views. "A Pope can direct me to love Mr. Khrushchev in the abstract but he cannot direct me to love the United Nations or the World's Fair. To imply that I am anti-Catholic is as convincing as to imply that Mr. Beame is anti-Semitic which, at this rate, Mr. Lindsay will be doing next week."

Monday, October 18 — During the last few weeks various national political experts have taken soundings in New York and concluded that Lindsay's message is not getting across and that he is likely to lose because of public apathy. I do not understand how they reach such a conclusion. Maybe they are unconsciously affected by the registration figures and the polls. Our carefree summer romping is over, but Lindsay's occasional street tours, meetings, and rallies seem to be going well. He has learned to dramatize rather than merely expound his views.

The mass invasion of Prospect Park, for example, was staged the same day we issued a White Paper on parks and recreation. A White Paper on crime was advertised through one speech on the site of the Kitty Genovese murder in Queens and another on a street corner in Manhattan where Leonard Simpson, an elderly lawyer, was killed by a drug addict attempting robbery in an apartment house self-service elevator.

Only Lindsay accepted.

Last Friday a tour of Fordham Hospital focused attention on White Paper charges of neglect in all the city hospitals.

McAllister Brothers, owners of a fleet of tugboats, offered Beame, Buckley, and Lindsay free rides around the harbor to view the deterioration of port facilities. Only Lindsay accepted. This morning he took a large press-radio-TV contingent, including a reporter from *Time*, a reporter from the *Cleveland Plain Dealer* and a reporter and photographer from *Paris Match* on a two-and-a-half-hour tour by tug. The weather was fine. From the water the crumbling piers looked like decayed teeth in a shark's mouth. Quoting from a hastily assembled White Paper, Lindsay noted that New York, which a decade ago handled one-third of all U.S. shipping, has now lost half of it, but the reporters seemed more interested in the cheering of Lindsay by a group of longshoremen standing on a pier.

. . . Beame continues to campaign in a low key . . .

The thought occurred to me that we might be defeating our own purposes by too much drama. Several weeks ago, Price asked Hope Ritchie, Harry O'Donnell's former assistant, to handle the distribution of White Papers—the substantive part of the fusion campaign—to the trade press, business groups, and unions. A visit today to Hope's new office established the fact that fragmentary publicity on the White Papers has been tantalizing the experts. Hope and her assistant, Rose Bratton, can barely keep up with requests.

Meanwhile Beame continues to campaign in a low key, either because he believes that boredom benefits the party in power or, more likely, because it suits his style. This morning he made a walking tour on the lower East Side of Manhattan, behind a man on a bullhorn who shouted: "Here comes *Little*

Abe Beame, your candidate for mayor, *Little Abe* . . ." If the affectionate diminutive were actually to convert any substantial number of undersized voters to the Beame team it might be a valuable pitch.

Beame seems to rely increasingly on incantations and endorsements. Today James A. Farley, the Roman Catholic elder statesman who holds brevet rank of some kind in the Beame headquarters, called Lindsay's campaign "a sinking ship" and predicted a Beame victory by 300,000 to 400,000 votes. Once upon a time, when he was Democratic National Chairman during the New Deal days, Farley held a reputation for prophecy second only to the Delphic Oracle. I wonder if today's prediction was cleared with Costikyan. It sounds careless and it thoroughly scrambles Costikyan's vague and not always consistent effort to portray Beame as an underdog.

Beame received endorsements of dubious value today from Wagner and Powell. The Mayor, who is in bed with influenza, issued a statement noting that all the candidates for his job have been making "ungenerous, untrue, and unfair" remarks about his administration. The "calumny is regrettable," he said, but it is to be expected "in a political dogfight" and Beame has not thrown any more brickbats than the others. "On the basis of Abe Beame's political statements," the Mayor concluded, "I now feel satisfied that he will actively pursue the further democratization of the Democratic party and I shall vote for him and his running mates."

Dressed in street clothes Powell spoke this afternoon from the pulpit of his Abyssinian Baptist Church in Harlem to an audience of 300 including Baptist ministers. "It's time we proved we can elect a Jew in New York as mayor," he said blithely. "If I don't get these Southerners, these Jews, these Catholics into office, how can I ever expect to be President of the United States?"

"I just love religion," continued Powell. "I don't care what kind it is, so long as it's good religion." Noticing a TV crew setting up in an aisle of the church, he said: "I'll just kill time while these men get ready." Voices called out: "Preach, Adam, preach!" so he obliged with a small sermon on David Beame and Goliath Lindsay.

Somewhat later, Powell and Beame went handshaking along 125th Street. Hecklers gathered, shouting: "There goes the Big Devil and the Little Devil, two of the whitest men in Harlem today." The campaigners fled to the office of the *Amsterdam News*, from which they refused to budge until police arrived. Then they called off the rest of the walking tour.

Powell says the hecklers are members of the Black Arts Repertory School who are annoyed over the curtailment of Haryou Act funds for the production of plays by LeRoi Jones. That may well be so, but I am interested chiefly in the revelation that some Harlem citizens do not find Beame's humility and shortness of stature particularly endearing.

Tuesday, October 19 — The *Daily News* poll has begun. The first installment of straws shows Beame reasonably ahead in the Bronx Park and Highbridge areas of the Bronx, Buckley scoring as expected in Ridgewood and Bath Beach, and Lindsay (surprise, surprise!) carrying Flatbush, the heavily Democratic Jewish heart of Brooklyn. Citywide, Beame and Lindsay seem to be running neck and neck with Buckley closer to them than anybody anticipated. The percentages are Lindsay, 42; Beame, 41.8; Buckley 16.2.

The bulldog edition of the *News*, out last evening, came to Lindsay's attention as our campaign group left the FDR Democratic Club, the oldest and largest reform organization in the Bronx, which had voted overwhelmingly to withdraw endorsement of Beame after he failed to appear to defend himself. Noting buoyantly that the *Herald Tribune* poll still puts Beame ahead by 7 percent, Lindsay said: "Let's split it and say I'm 3½ percent behind. I'm closing the gap."

George T. Holmes, who helps to direct the *News* poll, is a member of the Guild executive committee. From week to week at Guild meetings he has been telling me about the poll's precision and secrecy. Apparently it named the winner in six previous mayoral contests, including the puzzling Impellitteri–Pecora–Corsi contest of 1950. It erred in picking Al Smith over Herbert Hoover in the 1928 presidential race and Tom Dewey over Herbert Lehman in the 1938 gubernatorial race, but it came within 1 percent of Bobby Kennedy's city vote last year.

Unlike the *Herald Tribune*, which grabs passersby at random on the sidewalk, the *Daily News* makes home calls according to a careful pattern, working from early morning to night so the men will have an equal chance with the women. Independently operating crews check their straws against previous voting records and if there is any question of the results they do the polling over again.

There is one large secret about the *Daily News* poll, according to other friends of mine at the paper. The results published on the third day are identical with the conclusions released at the end of the poll. George Holmes is too discreet to confirm this, but he concedes it might be a good idea to look at Thursday's paper. I'll look.

Wednesday, October 20 — Beame has been in bed with a virus infection for two days. He may have acquired the ailment from Wagner who left the Carlyle today for the first time in ten days on a ten-minute stroll along Madison Avenue with his wife Barbara. This kind of illness often reflects strain. During a campaign every candidate operates on the edge of exhaustion. In addition Beame has been torn between conflicting advice from Bert Podell, with whom he has a long-standing personal and political relationship; Stephen Smith, who represents the State Democratic boss, Bobby Kennedy; and Costikyan, the ostensible campaign manager for the Beame–O'Connor–Procaccino ticket.

Costikyan recently went so far in his conciliatory policy toward Bill Buckley as to chide Lindsay for attacking the Conservative candidate. I hear that Podell jumped up and down in fury over this. Podell argues that Buckley will pull more Roman Catholic Democrats than Roman Catholic Republicans if only because there are more Democrats than Republicans and that Beame must therefore hit Buckley head on. Smith meanwhile has been urging Podell and Costikyan to schedule Beame more heavily in the Negro ghettoes. They are reluctant to do this in view of Beame's recent unhappy experience with Powell in Harlem. The differences between these three strong-minded fellows could be tolerated if Beame headquarters harbored the illusion of inevitable victory. That illusion has been destroyed by the *News* poll. There may now be a showdown between the three advisers, since each will presumably contend that his program is crucial.

Though trouble starts at the top at the Summit Hotel it does not end there. The day after the primary Beame headquarters was overrun by a horde of Neanderthal characters, racetrack figures, backroom boys from the old-line political clubs, fixers, and thugs.

Members of the Democratic reform movement who dropped by have told me they were offended by the atmosphere at Beame headquarters. Respectable former followers of Screvane, Ryan, and O'Dwyer were often greeted with suspicion. When Benjamin Browdy, a wealthy Flatbush businessman, made his first visit to the Summit, somebody snarled at him: "What are you doing here? I thought you were for Screvane." He had been for Screvane, but if he had been decently received Browdy might have contributed substantially to the Beame campaign.

Beame's chief fund-raisers appear to be Martin Tannenbaum, who controls the Yonkers Raceway and more taxicabs in New York than anybody else and Abraham Lindenbaum, a Court Street (Brooklyn) lawyer representing speculative real estate interests. Lindenbaum was forced to resign as a member of the City Planning Commission in 1961 when he used his position to solicit money openly for Wagner's campaign at a Sakeles Restaurant luncheon. Despite the extensive connections of these worthies Beame has recently been obliged, I hear, to cancel important campaign appearances in order to talk privately with small groups of angels.

Since politics is as merciless as a cockfight Price has been exploiting the perceptible confusion and weakness in the Beame camp. In addition to avoiding invitations from WNBC-TV and WABC-TV to use any of several alternative periods of free time for additional triangular debates, Beame has been turning down invitations for joint appearances with the other two mayoral candidates before neighborhood groups. One of these I know about is an October 24 meeting of the Harlem Forum. To emphasize Beame's growing distaste for confrontation, Price is multiplying Lindsay acceptances of such invitations.

"Beame has decided to hide behind the machines—political and mimeograph—and a flood of taped TV commercials for the rest of the campaign," Lindsay declared in a carefully framed release today.

"The debates have helped bring the issues before the voters, but now Mr. Beame is backing out. He has twenty years of accounting for the sorry plight of the city to explain. He has the cynical deals made by the machine to explain. I won't let him hide. *We are buying a half hour of TV time and we will gladly share this time with him in debate.* I demand that he show up for this debate, that he not cancel out again . . ."

Thursday, October 21 — In an effort to understand Buckley's continuing climb in apparent popularity, I've been collecting information on his comings and goings during the last couple of days. The *Daily News* now gives him an amazing 20.4 percent of its straws to 37.2 percent for Beame and 42.4 for Lindsay. If these statistics portend what I think they portend, Lindsay will win by a comfortable margin. Naturally I would not make this dire prediction to Price or anybody else in

. . . *a super-patriot* . . .

authority at headquarters lest I be accused again of subversive optimism. It's safer to concentrate on William Frank Buckley, Jr.

An old House committee study on how to recognize an ultra-rightist remains in my mind. Representative Patman (D–Texas) had it printed at least twenty years ago. Although I have no copy at hand, I remember a few signs: a rightist hates liberals, he opposes minority groups and labor unions, he relegates women and artists to subordinate roles in society. He whittles away constantly at the bourgeois press. He is a super-patriot and a conservative in religion, he favors unrestrained police activity at home and imperialism abroad, he creates a domestic atmosphere of impending change. Quite a few of these criteria apply to Buckley.

Taking the least important item first, Buckley laces the press so lightly that it is forced to enjoy its own discomfiture. At the Overseas Press Club yesterday, for example, he said he sometimes wishes all the reporters were overseas. Everybody laughed appreciatively. At a Bankers Club luncheon before 300 members of the Investment Association of New York, he asked himself questions and then answered them, the first being:

Q.—Did Barry Goldwater give you any advice when you conferred with him recently?

A.—Yes. He told me to watch out for prying reporters.

The next question was: "Why didn't you run in the Republican primary for Mayor?"

A.—Why didn't Martin Luther King run for Governor of Arkansas?

At the Overseas Press Club Buckley said he would welcome a white backlash against "irresponsible Negro leaders" like Powell. He added that he did not want a single vote on the basis that he would cut back programs for the Negro. Asked about a recent cartoon in the *National Review* to which Puerto Rican groups object, he replied as editor of the magazine: "I did not see the cartoon before it ran. Although it was not meant to be offensive, I do apologize for it." He denied he was directing his campaign more against Lindsay than Beame. "Beame is just a routine catastrophe," he explained, "whereas Lindsay is a poseur who seems to be saying that rejecting him would be like rejecting Pericles."

Having managed at the Bankers Club by his original form of political ventriloquism to call Lindsay a Republican deserter, a double-crosser, a charlatan, and an ally of Socialism, Buckley went uptown to announce that he intended to complain against Lindsay to the Fair Campaign Practices Committee. He was upset, he said, by Costello's charge that he was "anti-Catholic"—since he is a Catholic—and by Javits' characterization of him as "a political assassin." Since I was also upset over Javits' remark, I know precisely what the Senator said in his initial appearance with Lindsay in the Washington Heights section of Manhattan. I took notes. It went as follows:

"Mr. Buckley's sole purpose in this campaign is to politically assassinate John Lindsay. His idea is to attract enough votes to give the radical right a veto over which candidates will run in this town. If we let this kind of campaign prevail, then I fear for freedom in New York City."

I objected to references to assassination which might put ideas in the disturbed minds of some of the Birchite pickets who were then howling at us. If Javits received my message to one of his aides, it did not deter him from repeating the incendiary phrase during subsequent street appearances with Lindsay in Brooklyn and Queens.

What Javits said was true, Buckley said, "to the extent that I am attempting to shoot down the empty hypocritical things Mr. Lindsay is saying." He felt uneasy, however, over "the implication that a vote for the Conservative party is a vote for bloody revolution." Since Javits has a "cool head," Buckley continued, he must have been panicked by "Lindsay's desperation." Buckley added: "If a vote for me is a vote for Beame and a vote for me is a vote to ignite the powderkeg, then a vote for Mr. Beame is a vote for the devastation of the city. You figure it out."

In an interview with the Associated Press today, Buckley clarified his views on the white backlash. If he were Mayor, he said, the best thing he could do for Negroes would be to "help purge their own bad set of leaders." He pledged he would help Harlem by "personally ostracizing Adam Clayton Powell, Jr." He authorized the following statement to the Negro community: "I guarantee you justice. I guarantee you order. I guarantee you moral cooperation in replacing your bad leadership. Beyond that, I don't guarantee you a single thing."

During the day, Buckley exposed new portions of his program. He wants to break "the labor monopoly" of the unions, impose a one-year residency rule for relief, phase out rent control over a five-year period and end urban renewal. All these changes would adversely affect the minority groups which bulk large among the city's poor.

In the evening the candidate who originally said he did not intend to campaign went to Manhattan Center for a rally of 4,000 of his supporters. Pretty girls ran through the aisles throwing confetti as he entered the hall and strode on to the stage. For five minutes the crowd roared and sang. When he finally got a chance to talk, Buckley said the purpose of his candidacy is to prevent somebody—meaning Lindsay—from being elected mayor "who would hold sacred every left-Democratic dogma."

After ridiculing Lindsay for various "liberal" views, Buckley shifted abruptly to the "young slobs" who paraded last week in New York against the war in Vietnam. "I wonder how those selfconscious boulevardiers of protest would have fared if a platoon of American soldiers who have seen the gore in South Vietnam had parachuted down into their mincing ranks. 'Will not die for Vietnam' indeed! What would those young slobs die for? Why do they demand that the U.S. withdraw, but fail to demand that the Communists withdraw?"

Having roiled everybody's viscera, Buckley asserted that

The frenetic laughing of the audience merged into solid applause . . .

Lindsay expressed opposition last winter "to the use of laughing gas—or something—against the Viet Cong."

"Lindsay, as a moderate," he shouted, "would not permit us to use any stronger weapons against the Viet Cong than poison *ivy!*"

The frenetic laughing of the audience merged into solid applause as Buckley finished his speech. He could hardly escape from his admirers. "I touched him," murmured one adult as Buckley sped off in a red station wagon. "I got his autograph."

Friday, October 22 — There are two kinds of issues: the official ones and the sleepers. In this campaign those of the first category include bossism, crime in the streets, the need for political change, improving the quality of city life, traffic, and transit, the sales tax, job opportunities, housing, and education. Among the sleepers are race and religion, the effect of this election on the Republican party nationally, and whether "Little Abe" Beame dares to debate.

Beame contributed today to the nondiscussion of religion by pouncing upon a statement of the Presbytery of New York, governing body for the city's 117 Presbyterian churches, that a "lack of imagination and vigor has crippled City Hall" and that a political change is therefore necessary. "I have not sought and do not want any vote because of my Jewish faith," Beame declared at a news conference called to demand a repudiation by Lindsay of the implied endorsement.

"I practice my Jewish faith privately according to the dictates of my conscience," continued the Democratic candidate. "Official religious appeals from pulpits is repugnant to everything I have been taught this country stands for. . . . I believe in the American principle of separation of church and state. . . . I would deeply resent any edict from my temple telling me how to exercise my American right to a secret ballot. . . ."

Lindsay replied that he had not sought backing from the Presbyterians (he is an Episcopalian), that the statement did not name him, and that he was flattered by Beame's assumption that he fitted the Presbyterian prescription for a sick city. The incident then took an unexpected turn. The Reverend Graydon McClellan, the General Presbyter in New York, revealed during an interview that Lindsay had actually been endorsed by name in a first draft of the church statement.

The reason for the endorsement had nothing to do with Beame and a great deal to do with the ultra-conservative forces aligned behind Bill Buckley. The churchmen had eliminated Lindsay's name after an hour of private discussion, the General

Presbyter explained. "In extraordinary circumstances—for example, the candidacy of a John Birch member whose policies and actions would subvert the church's teachings about the dignity and brotherhood of man—Presbyterians reserve the right to oppose or endorse specific candidates. Of course, such circumstances do not obtain in this election. . . ."

In our news conference today, Lindsay dragged Barry Goldwater and the radical right into a discussion of our new White Paper on civil rights. "William Buckley has opposed every piece of civil rights legislation presented in the last five years," he said. "Perhaps the reason why I have not found him as amusing as some of my friends is that I know the record behind his clever jokes. Controller Beame is an honorable man with none of William Buckley's views but anybody who truly believes that Mr. Beame is going to make New York City into a place of equality for all has not got one shred of evidence for his enthusiasm."

Mentioning a not-unexpected endorsement of Beame by Bronx boss Charley Buckley, Lindsay continued: "I'm running against Buckley, Buckley, and Beame. I mean Buckley's boy Beame and Barry's boy Buckley. All three are anxious for my defeat."

Asked if Buckley, Buckley, and Beame were anything like Beethoven, Brahms, and Bach, Lindsay grinned. "No," he said. "Buckley, Buckley, and Beame is a cacophony of misgovernment."

The row over Beame's growing reluctance to meet his opponents in public discussion really began yesterday afternoon when he and Lindsay appeared before the Community Council of Greater New York to answer questions.

Beame, still shaky from his recent illness, became agitated when Lindsay remarked in passing that "Beame is afraid to debate." Speaking in his turn, Beame called for "an end to personal attacks" in the campaign. "If Lindsay were a man, he'd do it," he said plaintively.

Since a campaign is not particularly chivalrous, we issued a news release later in the day accusing Beame flatly of "running out" on additional debates and joint appearances. His reaction was odd: as a result of Lindsay's "irresponsible personal charges," he old reporters, he found it "distasteful" to appear on the same platform with him. This position seems untenable to me. All candidates find their opponents distasteful to some degree, but that does not usually preclude debate.

Today I learn that Beame has already modified his position. In a WINS news conference taped for Sunday airing he reportedly says he will debate if Lindsay apologizes for his "despicable attacks" and explains why he wants additional public argument. I can imagine Lindsay making the explanation, but not the apology.

Saturday, October 23 — The incident which haunts me tonight occurred during the morning. We were trying to squeeze another installment of drama out of our White Paper on hospitals. The superintendent of Harlem Hospital had agreed on a visit to his old, under-staffed, under-equipped and over-crowded institution on condition that patients not be unduly disturbed. When four or five newspaper reporters and three photographers appeared for the tour, I asked them to choose pool representatives. Objections were raised, particularly by Paul Weissman of the *Herald Tribune,* a journalistic lone wolf in the old tradition. The best I could do, with Lindsay's approval, was to drain off excess campaign personnel. These disgruntled exiles and I remained outside the hospital, while Lindsay and the press went inside with the superintendent.

A few minutes later John Reilly of CBS-TV arrived: a tall, handsome fellow who avoids the truculent bluster practiced by some of his colleagues. Reilly wanted to set up in a reception room for an interview with Lindsay on the way out. A guard said he needed permission. Reilly and I went to the superintendent's office. Nobody there would give permission but a thin, elderly official offered to lead us to the superintendent who must now, he said, be visiting the emergency room.

We were hurrying along a corridor when our guide began to slow up. He was shaking all over. From his throat came odd rattling noises which I had heard only once before in my life. The man's body fell forward in slow motion, twitching and perceptibly stiffening. Reilly and I were close enough to catch him, but we were frozen with consternation. The man's temple hit the corner of a white table on the way down. His body slammed face down to the floor, he twitched and gurgled a few seconds and then was still.

Nearby a woman screamed. White-coated men hurried in with a stretcher. A doctor said: "Who are you? What happened?" We told him. He hurried after the stretcher. We were alone. "I did it," I told Reilly. "I could have caught him but I couldn't move." Reilly shook his head. "I was closer than you," he said.

The next I remember, Reilly and I were walking along a corridor on the main floor. Lindsay and his party spilled out of elevators in front of us. There was a brief conference during which the superintendent suggested a last-minute visit to a children's ward. "No press this time," said Lindsay sharply. He and the superintendent entered an elevator. The doors were closing when Weissman darted inside. I reached in, holding back the doors with my body, took Paul by the hips, and heaved him into the corridor. As the elevator doors closed I turned to face Paul, who was still standing. I expected a punch but Paul had himself under control. "I don't have to stand treatment like that," he said, with dignity. "I'm leaving!" To my surprise the other reporters supported Weissman. "You shouldn't have done that, Ollie," said the gentleman from the *Times*, with entire seriousness. Others chimed in. Not wanting to say that I was upset because I had just killed a man, I stood in silence with them until Lindsay and the superintendent returned. Lindsay agreed to be interviewed by Reilly in the reception room and the interview turned into a general press conference.

Weissman was waiting on the sidewalk. I could not bring myself to apologize, but I gave him my seat in the first press car so he could get a fill-in on the press conference. Back at headquarters I began to brood about the hospital incident. I was sure the man was dead because the noises he made were the same as those of a feature editor of the *Post* who died almost instantly from a heart attack in my presence about a year ago.

A phone call to the hospital brought incredible relief: the man was not dead after all! He was an epileptic. What we had witnessed was an epileptic fit. Except for a gash in his forehead where he struck the table in falling, he was in good condition. I phoned John Reilly, who had just called the hospital himself. We rejoiced over our joint stupidity. I was almost light-headed when Price came into my room. He did not seem greatly interested in my story of the epileptic official. I told how I had manhandled Paul Weissman, a reporter with whom he was on close terms. "You shouldn't have done that, Ollie," he said, parroting the *Times* reporter without knowing he was doing so.

On impulse, I told Price that according to inside information on the *News* poll Lindsay would win by a comfortable margin. He wanted to know the plurality. I guessed 100,000 votes. He did not give any opinion of his own. Instead he noted that Lindsay was now 3 percent ahead in the *News*, two percent behind in the *World Telegram* and seven or eight percent behind in the *Herald Tribune*. Averaging these polls Lindsay was perhaps two points behind and still closing the gap. The closeness of the election, Price said, might help the fusion ticket. Many Republicans were tempted to throw their votes to Buckley in protest over one thing or another. In a tight election, they might still vote for Lindsay in preference to

Beame. They would certainly not do so, Price added with no expression on his face, if they got the notion that a Lindsay victory was assured.

Sunday, October 24 — Ever since I first heard the Beame team theme song sung, I've been trying to get the words. Today I found the text in a letter which had been lying around my apartment unopened for weeks. "To the Freshest Guy in Town"—which is sung to the tune of "The Wearing of the Green"—really says more about Lindsay than about Beame. Some of the verses, with italics and caps by Joe Rogers, the author, go as follows:

> Oh, John's the best at DOUBLE-TALK
>   New York will ever meet.
> He flits the BOW'RY cha-cha-cha,
>   SILK STOCKINGS on his feet.
>
> In a beauty contest, there's no doubt,
>   Don John would lead the pack,
> But a PRETTY FACE will not replace
>   The SKILLS a man may LACK.
>
> So, Johnny dear, you may be fresh,
>   But you're not *both* THIS and THAT;
> For a donkey ain't an elephant
>   And you're NO REPUBLOCRAT.
>
> Oh Lindsay dear, your ads are clear;
>   You're the freshest guy in town;
> You've tried to TRICK old Father Knick
>   And play him for a clown.
>
> You've got plenty bucks and money talks
>   But by November three
> You'll find the rank and file have led
>   Our Abe to victory.

My ostensible purpose in staying home today was to visit

the hospital official who became ill in my presence yesterday, but I neglected to get dressed. I compromised on a phone call to the hospital which revealed that the man is still in good shape. While lounging around the house in pajamas, bathrobe, and slippers, I caught up on my mail and then did some concentrated reading of the *Daily News* and the *Journal American*, the two newspapers which consistently sing the Beame team theme song.

Buckley is the only real Republican in the race but he needs something approaching a miracle to win, the *Daily News* declares editorially. The *News* therefore endorses Beame as something of a conservative and as the only practical alternative to the major menace of Lindsay. Meanwhile today's installment of straws in the *News* poll divides as follows: Lindsay, 42.6 percent; Beame, 39.6; Buckley, 17.8. In other words, the paper's heart belongs to Buckley, its head to Beame, and its statistical stomach to Lindsay.

In a featured front-page article in the Sunday *Journal American*, Harold Harris, the paper's ranking political authority, issues the first flat local journalistic prediction about the election which has come to my attention. Under the headline: EXPERT SIZE-UP: ABE BEAME BY 150,000 VOTES, Harris writes: "The rosiest prediction of the Lindsay forces is that they will be able to pull an upset victory by a hairline plurality of 90,000 to 120,000, whereas the Beame managers say privately he (Beame) should come home a winner by a 250,000 plurality." Harris concludes: "I believe the spunky city Controller will win the battle for City Hall by a 150,000 plurality."

The mathematics justifies the prediction. Harris is too good a reporter to write a story like that without consulting Price and Costikyan. Reading between the lines, Price must have told him Lindsay is still an underdog who is gaining and who may conceivably win, whereas Costikyan must have boldly pictured Beame as an upperdog in an effort to gain additional votes from those who like to be identified with a winner.

Monday, October 25 — By a coincidence which is not conspiratorial, Lindsay and Beame are giving a wider national slant to their contest for mayor. This began yesterday on radio-TV shows which I missed but which I was able to review today in transcript form.

Beame (on the taped WINS News Conference): "One of the chief issues in the campaign is whether we are going to allow City Hall to be captured for the purpose of reviving the Republican party nationally. Lindsay has been receiving campaign contributions from people in forty states who have absolutely no interest in New York City except that they want a Republican in City Hall here as a shot in the arm for the national Republican party."

This is a reasonable point. Beame might have gone farther by listing some of the remote GOP tycoons—Leonard K. Firestone of California and H. J. Heinz, II, of Pittsburgh, for example—who have unloosened their pursestrings. The only part of Beame's comment which bothers me is a racist-sounding suggestion that Mississippi Republicans are especially interested in the fusion campaign.

Meanwhile Lindsay (on the taped WOR-TV show, "Ladies of the Press"): "Bill Buckley's candidacy is an act of vengeance by the ultra-right for my refusal last year to support Goldwater. In the streets it's translated into a very, very extremist business. It brings out the worst in people, that I've been able to see . . . people carrying Buckley banners and calling me 'Judas,' 'nigger-lover,' 'Commie,' and 'pinko' . . . I didn't go into this business for safety or security but I do think this is a radical right thing that you've seen in Southern California and other parts of this country and it's now penetrated quite deeply in New York."

In a news release, Lindsay made Beame an accessory to Buckley's act of vengeance. He said: "Beame and Buckley have a coincidental and common purpose—to defeat me. They are allies of convenience. If Beame wins, it will be a major victory for Goldwater and the radical invaders of the right and it will have been engineered from outside New York. I warn New Yorkers not to allow themselves to be used as a political vehicle by right-wing forces from Connecticut and Arizona for the comeback of Goldwater and the radical right wing groups which cluster about him."

Buckley, who on Sunday radio and TV shows took seriously for the first time his chance of being elected mayor, was traced to his Greenwich home later in the day for comment on Lindsay's charges. "Goldwater had nothing to do with it," he said indignantly. "As a matter of courtesy, I called him and told him I was going to run before I announced it publicly, but I did not consult him."

Beame also was asked to comment. "Lindsay is trying to paint me with a Buckley brush," he complained. "I'm getting sick and tired of his irresponsible charges. They are insulting me and the public."

An exclusive story in the *Times* today strengthened the right-wing issue. It disclosed that Kent Courtney, chairman of the Conservative Society of America, has mailed at least 1,000 letters from New Orleans to New Yorkers denouncing Lindsay as "pro-Communist" and urging them to vote for Buckley. Courtney, a forty-nine-year-old former airline pilot who belongs to the John Birch Society and who lists several other Birch Society members on his letterhead, told a reporter by telephone that each letter to a New Yorker was accompanied by two copies of a pamphlet entitled "Beware of Lindsay."

Lindsay is being built up as an "ultra-liberal" prospect for President in 1968, the pamphlet declares, and must be defeated to show that the country will repudiate "candidates who consistently support legislation which is detrimental to the welfare of our constitutional republic." Citing this in a news conference this morning, Lindsay charged that sixteen Texans—otherwise unidentified—have been brought to New York "to work on the streets for Buckley." No doubt I will recognize them by their cowboy hats and boots.

Buckley has been reacting in an amateurish way to the

Courtney story. Some years ago, he volunteers, he addressed a group in Chicago which included Courtney. Later when the Conservative Society was formed he criticized it in his magazine, the *National Review*. Calling Lindsay pro-Communist is preposterous and irresponsible, says Buckley. "That's straight Birchite vocabulary," he adds. "Courtney is a kook."

Beame is again complaining about unfair criticism. "Mr. Lindsay knows down deep in his heart that I violently oppose Mr. Buckley's political philosophy," he says, as if he has been saying so right along—which he has not. His own charge about Lindsay rejuvenating the elephant is being ignored in the furore over the radical right.

Tuesday, October 26 — In every headquarters at this late stage in the campaign, false optimism struggles with accumulated weariness. The Lindsay camp is no exception. This afternoon, for example, we were elated by the heckling of Eugene L. Sugarman at the West Bronx Y.M.H.A. and Y.W.H.A. Sugarman, a trusted lawyer in Boss Buckley's Bronx machine, was representing Beame in a joint appearance with Lindsay. After Lindsay noted that he kept encountering Sugarman instead of Beame in the Bronx and other substitutes for Beame in other boroughs, a housewife interrupted Sugarman to ask: "Where is Beame?" Another woman who should, I suppose, have been wearing a Lindsay button, yelled repeatedly: "Beame is a coward!" and others took up the cry.

During the noon hour Lindsay appeared at an anti-air pollution rally on the steps of the Sub-Treasury building in the financial district. A group of young Birchites who have been distributing literature daily at the corner of Wall and Broad Streets hooted at him. This delighted our trend-watchers. What greater boon could a Republican candidate for mayor have, they said, than to be hooted at in Wall Street less than a week before election day? They had a point but I was chiefly concerned over how far these violent youngsters might go. The winds blow so strongly from so many directions these days that I often feel mindlessly apprehensive, like a Key West resident battening down for an approaching hurricane, awaiting only the event.

Lindsay is probably the best-equipped candidate. Beame seems vulnerable as a man and Buckley seems vulnerable as a politician. Sometimes I feel sorry for them. Beame has found no adequate reply to the continuing challenge to debate or be convicted of pusillanimity and Buckley apparently cannot struggle out of the net thrown around him and "the raiders of the radical right."

According to a friend of mine, a reporter who cherishes Buckley quotes as if they were the sayings of Sam Johnson, the Conservative candidate had a fey look at his news conference yesterday over the Lindsay and *New York Times* revelations about the Conservative Society. "If I were born in a cave and I had never come out," he said at one point, "I'd still be anti-Lindsay." Asked what he would do "if he awoke November 3 as mayor," Buckley smiled ferociously. "I'd spread a net under the *New York Times*' window," he said.

Today Buckley held another news conference to unveil his solution of the city traffic problem: an overhead highway down Second Avenue for cyclists. "You could get from 125th Street to 1st Street, if anyone wanted to get there, in twenty minutes," he pointed out. Murray Kempton hailed the project as "the Buckley bikeway." "Yes," murmured the candidate, "this is my finest hour." He confessed: "I did have trouble getting the idea through the Conservative party hierarchy." How can anyone underestimate a man like that?

In the elevator on the way down to our own news conference at the Roosevelt today, Lindsay told somebody in my presence that the volunteers in our 120 storefronts around town have already canvassed 70 percent of the voters. Though I appreciate that no participant in the campaign can now be a sure judge I am strongly tempted to seize upon this at least as a good omen. I do not believe that any party or combination of parties ever canvassed that high a proportion of the voters in any previous corresponding election.

At the news conference, which was attended by more than the usual number of local reporters and an out-of-town contingent ranging from a Stockholm reporter to one from Columbus, Ohio, Lindsay issued a White paper on education, asserting that schools, teachers, parents, and students have been "shortchanged for years by the Beame administration."

"Beame says he is being unfairly attacked by you," said Ted Knap of the Scripps-Howard newspapers. "What is your comment, sir?"

"Beame apparently feels the energy of my campaign," replied Lindsay. "The city is on its knees because of the refusal of the Beame administration to make decisions—and people are crying out about it." Mentioning a previously released comparison of Wagner and Beame voting records in the Board of Estimate over the past four years, Lindsay added: "The odds are 15,316 to 4 that Beame will be just another Wagner."

Q.—Beame keeps saying you will not serve out your four-year term as mayor if elected, because you have your mind on higher office. Is that so?

A.—No. I intend to serve out my term and I hope to do well enough to be reelected to a second term.

On TV two days ago, Lindsay said that so long as there was a struggle "for control of the country" between his moderate philosophy and that of the radical right, he would hold himself in readiness to take part. I waited for somebody to remind him of this enduring excuse to move into national politics, but nobody did. Lindsay continued to field questions with the practiced smoothness of a big-league infielder until he was asked about three Brooklyn Congressmen who met publicly the other day to announce that Beame as mayor could indeed count on greater cooperation in Washington than Lindsay.

"All out on parole, were they?" flashed Lindsay, with a

". . . Beame will be just another Wagner."

grin. The reporters laughed but I was furious with Lindsay. With everything going in his favor the man cannot refrain from a Buckley-type wisecrack. Is it possible that Lindsay will blow this election after all with some last-minute irrelevancy?

Wednesday, October 27 — Whether the public cares much one way or the other is debatable, but the politicians are still gasping and gossiping over President Johnson's failure to endorse the Beame–O'Connor–Procaccino ticket. Eddie Costikyan, who as Beame's campaign manager was more upset last night than anybody else, is regaining his confidence. In fact he uses the word four times in a brief statement issued this morning. He is confident, he says, that Vice-President Humphrey's campaign appearance in New York was "not against the wishes of the President." He is confident that an endorsement will come "in due time" from the banks of the Pedernales where the President is resting after an operation. "I am confident," adds Costikyan, "that the President of the United States is supporting Mr. Beame and we are confident that the President has the right and duty to do what he wants to do when he wants to do it."

Costikyan could not conceal his dismay last night when Humphrey, addressing 2,200 of the faithful at a $100-a-plate fund-raising Democratic dinner at the Waldorf-Astoria, said merely that the President had asked him to "convey to each and every one of you and to Abe Beame and the whole ticket his warm regards, good fellowship, and hearty greeting on this evening." To the ordinary citizen that might sound like lavish praise but the politicians understood immediately that it did not commit the President.

In his own name, Humphrey eulogized Beame and his running mates. When he finished his speech, workers at Lindsay headquarters deserted the TV sets around which they had gathered and poured into the campaign corridor, exclaiming to each other: "The President did not endorse Beame!"

After a conference with his advisers, Lindsay decided to make no statement. When reporters cornered him he said: "Out of respect for the President, I should not make any statement. What the President says or does only he can decide."

Costikyan implies now that the President postponed his endorsement out of annoyance over newspaper stories. "About five of them wrote that there would be an endorsement," he says, "and the President decided there wouldn't be one. The President feels he shouldn't be second-guessed." The word from reporters is that the leak about impending Presidential action came from Costikyan but Costikyan denies this.

The *Daily News*, Beame's most recent and most belligerent journalistic supporter, reports editorially today that "there was a stunned silence" after Humphrey sat down. "Then the noise of guests' chins falling to their chests became as thunder and many a faithful Democrat walked out. ... ." The *News* wonders "whether LBJ may have made some sort of a deal with John V. Lindsay . . . Is it possible that he wants the Lindsay slate elected for reasons best known to LBJ?"

Without being in the President's confidence, I question this paranoiac notion. President Johnson may wish to avoid entanglement in a possible Democratic defeat in New York. He may not want to set a precedent for taking a role in other mayoral contests. On the other hand, he may still endorse Beame. If so, it is not likely to be of much benefit now to the Democratic slate.

According to Mark Finston, a reporter on the *Newark Star-Ledger* who covered Beame yesterday and Lindsay today, Beame's humiliation was most perceptible at three outdoor rallies before the big dinner.

Both Humphrey and Bobby Kennedy praised Beame at these rallies but the Vice-President said he was appearing at the Senator's request and Kennedy shared what applause there was with Humphrey. Beame did not seem disturbed that his own remarks aroused virtually no enthusiasm. According to Finston he took no part in the chattering between Humphrey and Kennedy and a horde of lesser Democratic politicians during this brief campaign tour. When the others spoke, he listened impassively, staring at a point above the crowd and applauding when applause was indicated. At the final rally, at Broadway and 73d Street in Manhattan, Bobby Kennedy instructed the crowd to clap loudly for "Abe Beame" and the crowd did as it was told. Then Beame spoke and the audience, lacking further instructions from Kennedy, gave him scant applause.

Thursday, October 28 — Bobby Kennedy is taking over the direction of Beame's campaign in an effort, I suppose, to eliminate Lindsay as a possible national opponent. On the Senator's recommendation, the formerly meek Democratic candidate for mayor turned melodramatic today in accepting Lindsay's long-standing offer of an additional TV debate. By calling Lindsay various kinds of a liar and daring him to meet face to face—which is, after all, how they would normally meet in debate—Beame is actually suggesting to the public that he will be the host. He will not, however, pay any portion of the approximately $2,000 cost for a half-hour of prime air time.

It must be conceded that Lindsay provoked Beame. He told a news conference that whenever he goes up in the Bronx to debate Beame he encounters Eugene Sugarman. When he sets forth in Manhattan on a similar mission he meets Paul O'Dwyer. "In Queens I run into Representative Benjamin Rosenthal and in Brooklyn, Deputy Commissioner of Public Events James J. O'Brien. They are all debating for Beame. When will Beame debate for himself?" Lindsay then sent a telegram to Beame: "Your consistent refusal to debate leads me to conclude that you are seeking to avoid many questions. If I don't receive an acceptance by noon Friday of my challenge to you to debate on TV Saturday evening, I will be forced to cancel the time or use it in another manner."

When Beame agreed to take a fighting stance on Kennedy's insistence that the race is too close for complacency, Costikyan tried to make the change seem plausible. "We made a mistake," he told one reporter, "and it's a big one. Beame has been boiling right along, but we attempted to curb his desire to take on Lindsay on his level—in the gutter. As a result, Abe has been painted as innocuous. We should have said: 'Abe, if you feel like punching, go ahead and punch.'"

Abe started punching at a news conference in the Summit Hotel. "Mr. Lindsay has been running a dirty, no-holds-barred campaign," he said. "From the growing cesspool of his false charges has sprung a need for prompt and forthright action. Mr. Lindsay's lies must be exposed. . . . I dare him to let the people see his face on television when I ask him to explain his vicious lies. I will hold him up to the electorate as a liar unfit for public office. I challenge Mr. Lindsay to cease hiding behind moderators and other outsiders. I dare him to meet me face to face. I dare him to answer my questions and I dare him to put questions to me. . . ."

This evening . . . a triangular CBS *radio debate . . .*

This evening Beame, Buckley, and Lindsay took part in a triangular CBS radio debate which had been scheduled long before Beame decided to avoid triangular debates. Habit being an insidious thing, Beame did not consistently live up to his new role of bookkeeper-turned-tiger. In his opening statement he deplored Lindsay's "vicious lies" and went through his routine of challenging Lindsay to take part in a debate already arranged for Saturday. Then he felt obliged to apologize to Buckley for relegating him to the sidelines. "I'm sorry I can't offer this debate to you," he said. "It's Mr. Lindsay's time. He paid for it."

The chief flare-up came over Lindsay's criticism of Buckley proposals to put narcotics addicts and people on relief into rehabilitation centers outside the city.

"You've been calling them concentration camps," said Buckley. "That phrase conjures up Nazi visions of horror specifically aimed at the Jewish people."

It was Javits who made the concentration camp references during a joint walking tour with Lindsay in Washington Heights and at a later garment center rally but apparently Lindsay saw no point in apologizing for the Senator.

"Your remark," he told Buckley, "is offensive and irresponsible and I'll ask you not to make it again."

"I don't have to take instructions from you on what to say and what not to say!" flashed Buckley. "You are trying to do to Jewish voters what the Ku Klux Klan has been trying to do to the white people in the South—keep them scared. You are in there saying in effect to the Jewish voters: 'Vote for me, vote for me, because over here is an ultra-rightist who is trying to bring bloodshed to the city.' "

Beame intervened with every indication of genuine passion. "There's no one more guilty of prejudice than you," he told Buckley, "and you know it!"

Up to this point Buckley had been getting satisfaction out of his analysis of political tactics but he must have realized that he was exposing himself politically.

"All right," he said abruptly, ignoring Beame. "Cut it out, Mr. Lindsay, and I'll cut it out."

The rest of the debate was dull. Lindsay called for change.

"I'm the only Democrat," said Beame. "Both of my opponents are Republicans."

"If Mr. Lindsay is still a Republican," commented Buckley in one of his familiar indirect appeals for Roman Catholic votes, "it's the best-kept secret since Mother Fatima's."

Mother Fatima's secret, which is not particularly secret in religious circles, involves the apparition in 1917 of the Virgin Mary to three shepherd children in Portugal. The place where this occurred is revered particularly by Catholics who are traditional in church practice and conservative in politics.

Friday, October 29 — Various inside explanations have been advanced for President Johnson's recent failure to embrace Beame in public. One is that somebody annoyed him by a premature leak to the press. Another is that he did not wish to alienate his old ally, the Liberal party. A third is that he did not dare to use Vice-President Humphrey as a transmission belt for an endorsement lest that offend supporters of Bobby Kennedy who expect a Humphrey-Kennedy struggle for post-Johnson control of the Democratic party.

Without settling the issue, White House Press Secretary Bill Moyers let it be known today that the President "believes Mr. Beame would make a fine mayor of New York City." He volunteered this during a press briefing in Austin, Texas, far from the LBJ ranch. Was it an endorsement? reporters asked.

"I want to make it very clear that the President over the years has never tried to dictate to others how to vote," replied Moyers. "Now in this particular situation the President does not believe that his unwillingness to dictate to others how to vote should be misinterpreted as an abdication of his responsibility as the leader of his party or misconstrued as a lack of support for Mr. Beame.

"The President believes the Democratic party consistently, most effectively, and most strongly serves the interest of the people. . . . He is always pleased, satisfied and proud when qualified Democrats are elected to office. He supports them in their efforts. That includes New York, Louisville, Akron, New Jersey, and anywhere Democrats are running for office. . . ."

When some of the reporters professed to be still puzzled, Moyers summed up as follows: "The President believes very simply that the average New York family is going to be better off with a Democratic mayor."

These words, said Beame, gave him "a tremendous lift." Costikyan was also pleased though he grumbled that the President's delay had been "a bit of a setback." Lindsay said the action at Austin was "to be expected" and Buckley scored his usual verbal point. Asked if he would lose sleep over the President's "endorsement" the Conservative candidate declared: "No, I'd lose sleep if he endorsed me."

Ryan, the most conspicuous local holdout, announced today that he will vote for the Democratic city slate. He did not praise Beame and he will not campaign for Beame. Pressed for a recommendation to his followers including stalwarts in his own Riverside Democratic Club who are openly for Lindsay, Ryan gave a statesmanlike answer: "I think every voter should vote the dictates of his conscience."

Saturday, October 30 — The campaign is virtually over, but nobody can afford yet to relax. By now Lindsay's voice is harsh and cracked from too much talking and his eyes are hollow from too many four-hour nights of sleep. He keeps his outer control but I suspect he is seething inside. After our morning news conference he agreed to give a short special interview to a young and comely TV reporter. He and she chatted idly while her crew set up in one corner of the grill room of the Roosevelt. Something was wrong with the TV camera. The delay was intolerable.

Grasping the dead microphone, Lindsay said: "All right, I'll interview you! Who'd you sleep with last night?"

"With my pillow, darn it," she replied. "How about you?"

Lindsay had to choose between alternatives. "Mary wouldn't like it," he said.

"Oh, I don't know," mused the reporter, looking mischievous. "Maybe I should speak to her about it."

Except for one man from the *Herald Tribune*, the other reporters and photographers had left. The *Tribune* reporter was writing furiously on his pad. Noticing him for the first time Lindsay and the TV gal broke off their light dialogue. After the formal interview the *Tribune* man carried the joke a step farther by suggesting to Miss TV that she might care to sleep with him to keep the earlier conversation out of the paper.

"It isn't worth it," she snapped, and left.

The *Tribune* guy is a good guy, but a little unpredictable. He surely wouldn't write about a kidding exchange between a handsome candidate and an attractive young TV reporter! Would he?

Suppose by some incredible mischance the *Trib* man did write about it and it got into the paper, what then? The effect on the election might be negligible or it might be catastrophic. Who could tell in advance? I had been careful not to ask him to keep out of the paper something he was not likely to put in. Yet the temptation to slide an explosive account through the city desk might be difficult for him to resist.

On an impulse of which I shall always be ashamed—after all, I am still president of the New York Newspaper Guild and the *Trib* reporter is a member of that union—I went to Walter Thayer's daughter Ann, one of Price's secretaries, and suggested that she tell her father, the president of the *Herald Tribune*, to have somebody look carefully at the man's copy before putting it into type.

Sunday, October 31 — For several hours yesterday afternoon at the Waldorf Towers, Bobby Kennedy drilled Beame in the projection of "honest outrage." Taking the role of Lindsay, the Senator hurled at Beame the roughest questions he could devise and insisted on rougher answers and an entirely truculent attitude. Beame seems to have benefited from the training. During the half-hour WPIX-TV debate last evening which he accepted so tardily he shook visibly with anger over everything from Lindsay's opening remark that Democrats-for-Lindsay were paying for the telecast to Lindsay's description of him as a tool of the machine. As Beame tried to swarm over him Lindsay's smile vanished but he kept his tongue moving and his forefinger wagging.

No new issues were raised at the debate. Each candidate seemed more interested in making points than rebutting them. After a while I got lost in the welter of words and that may have been the general reaction of the viewers. When the debate ended George Lindsay, the coolest of the Lindsay brothers, rushed across the studio to exclaim: "If you were a

"that zoo back there."

girl, John, I'd kiss you," so our side must have done fairly well.

Beame again displayed his Kennedy tactic of fact-filled irateness during a TV show today in which Clifford DeBerry of the Socialist Workers party, Eric Hass of the Socialist Labor party and Vito Battista of the United Taxpayers party joined the three better-known mayoral candidates. Events took an unexpected turn this time partly because the NBC show, known as "Direct Line," was not set up as a debate. The format called merely for the six candidates to say in turn how they felt about things like taxes, the selection of judges, and the long-range goals of the parties supporting them.

Beame endured the restrictions until Lindsay said his program envisaged no new taxes. Then he snorted that a sixth-grade school class would not accept an answer like that. Soon everybody was interrupting everybody else under an NBC rule that any candidate could reply briefly to a personal attack. Buckley, who sat with Beame and Lindsay in the front row, infuriated DeBerry, Hass, and Battista, who sat in a second row, by referring to "that zoo back there." Long after the other two subsided Battista was still yelling: "Let me talk. Am I a backdrop here?"

You never know where you will find a chink in a politician's armor. Buckley seemed upset over a conspicuous new button which I wore into the studio. Next to the IF I WERE 21 I'D VOTE FOR LINDSAY button worn by so many of our teenagers (and matrons) this button is probably my campaign favorite but I stuck it in my pocket lest it gave the man apoplexy at such an important moment. The button merely read: BUCKLEY FOR HALLOWEEN.

When the debate ended Buckley glided away before reporters could catch him. Beame strode over to Lindsay. "You're a faker," he said. "I challenge you to a press conference." That sounded like a duel with peppermint sticks. Lindsay looked down at his smaller rival with distaste. Price tapped him on the arm. "Go ahead, John," he said.

Battista decided to take part. The three contenders and their handlers surged out into the hall. Reporters surrounded them. "Now tell me what federal funds I didn't use," said Beame to Lindsay. "You're a faker."

Battista, who is as small as Beame, tumbled some words in edgewise. Lindsay began citing failures of the Wagner-Beame regime to apply adequately and in time for available federal grants.

"You're making a speech," said Beame. "If you're going on like that, I'm getting out of here."

He got out. Since the reporters were not interested in a Lindsay-Battista argument, that wound up the last campaign debate. It was exciting for a few seconds but I doubt that Beame won many friends by his belligerence.

"You're making a speech," said Beame.

☆☆★ *November*

Monday, November 1 — Price always did intend to end the Lindsay mayoral campaign as it began, with a heavy concentration of attention on the town's poorest and least white citizens. Now our Republican strategist is really blitzing Negro and Puerto Rican neighborhoods on the theory that some "slippage" may have resulted from President Johnson's endorsement of Beame. The big drive began Friday evening outside the Hotel Theresa on 125th Street. Dick Gregory, Sugar Ray Robinson, Sammy Davis, Jr., Josephine Premice, Diana Sands, Lionel Hampton, the Reverend George Lawrence, and a score of other Negro notables drew a record crowd of 7,500 to our final Harlem rally.

This morning's newspapers, as a result of carefully selected walking tours yesterday afternoon in Brooklyn and Queens, are full of pictures of Lindsay joking with Negro and Puerto Rican children and talking seriously with Negro and Puerto Rican adults. These pictures contrast sharply with group photographs of Beame and his running mates taken last night at dinner in the luxurious Top-of-the-Fair restaurant which are simultaneously appearing in the press.

Today Lindsay made twelve more walking tours, three in Harlem and the rest in the Bronx. Everywhere he went he said: "I was asked earlier in the campaign if I would come back. I said yes and I am here. I'll be here always. I promised I wouldn't let you down and I won't." The emotional response to this assurance was moving, particularly in minority-group areas. Lindsay felt it, I am sure, and was himself committed by it.

During forty years of newspaper work I have never before witnessed such a continuing voracious appetite for information about a political campaign. In addition to local radio, TV

"I promised I wouldn't let you down and I won't."

and newspaper reporters and cameramen, our campaign cars today carried Stephen Shapiro and Richard Rogan from *Life* magazine, Paul Hope of the *Washington Star*, Mary Mc-Grory of the *Washington Post*, John Driescke of the *Chicago Sun-Times* and James Doyle of the *Boston Globe*.

A Nigerian journalist named Edun Akenzna has been observing us, as well as Vanderbilt Ziever, Washington correspondent of a German newspaper called the *Esslinger Zeitung*; Jacques Salibert of French television; and a woman publisher of a Parisian newspaper whose card I have mislaid but who seemed particularly amused by a rash of NO STEAM? NO BEAME! signs in Harlem. The weather having turned cold, our alert partisans up there are trying to focus in our favor the resentment of tenants against landlords who have been slow to supply heat.

The closeness of the contest may be increasing our news coverage. Most political experts now avoid flat predictions of the outcome. Jimmy Breslin slides farther out on a limb than anybody else today with a column in the *Herald Tribune* tracing the shift in betting odds from pro-Beame to pro-Lindsay.

The results of the newspaper polls are contradictory and only whispers apart. They wind up as follows:

Daily News: Lindsay, 42 percent; Beame, 40; Buckley, 18.

Herald Tribune: Lindsay, 41.5 percent; Beame, 42.3; Buckley, 16.2.

Samuel Lubell in the *World Telegram:* Lindsay, 37.9 percent; Beame, 36.6; Buckley, 18.8; and the rest undecided.

"We've been behind pretty steadily but we're coming up fast," commented Lindsay. "Even today could make a difference."

What of Beame and Buckley on the last day of the campaign?

Well except for the publicizing by his headquarters of a telephone number which if dialed gives citizens an incendiary version of his creed, Buckley has dropped out of sight during the past 24 hours.

Beame seems at last to have alienated Bobby Kennedy. Several things contributed to this. One was an address yesterday afternoon to 750 of Boss Buckley's followers in the Bronx. Beame began with a thundering announcement that "Buckley's philosophy is repugnant to me" and he continued in this vein without realizing the audience was sitting on its hands because it thought he was referring to its own Charley Buckley, not Bill Buckley. Beame's relative incompetence at truculence in debate despite desperate schooling and his failure to focus on minority group areas as recommended by the Senator have also reportedly disturbed Kennedy.

Today Beame scheduled eight windup street-corner rallies in the Bronx with Bobby Kennedy. When he failed to show up at one after another of his own rallies at this climax of the campaign, the Senator's mood shifted from annoyance to amusement.

"Did you hear about Bill Buckley?" Kennedy asked one crowd consisting chiefly of teenagers and parochial school students. "If he gets in he'll make you go to school on Saturdays and he'll make the nuns hit you with a ruler. Let's hear some real loud boos for Bill Buckley!" He thanked the nuns for letting the children out of school on All Saints Day. "If the Republicans get in," he warned, "who knows what they'll do with All Saints Day."

Kennedy instructed one mixed crowd of adults and children to cheer every mention of Beame and to boo every mention of Buckley and Lindsay. At the next rally he burlesqued conventional campaign rhetoric. "The Democratic party," he shouted, with running advice to the audience on the required responses, "produced Roosevelt (cheers), Truman (cheers), Kennedy (cheers), Johnson (cheers), and Huey Long (no cheers). To a quizzical reporter who later joined our caravan the Senator explained he was "just having a little fun" but the reporter got the impression that Bobby was spoofing his own mayoral candidate.

Tuesday–Wednesday, November 2–3 — When did the campaign end? It might have been as early as last Saturday night when Mary Lindsay celebrated her birthday by staying up until 3 A.M. at headquarters to work on a large final mailing with other members of the Lindsay family and such Raiders as Squirt, Wheezy, and the Weasel.

It might have been the following night when Harry O'Donnell retired at 1 A.M. only to be awakened an hour later by the city desk of an afternoon newspaper which had mislaid Lindsay's overnight release on the revitalization of small business. Harry revitalized himself and as his last personal sacrifice for the press took a substitute release to the waterfront plant of the newspaper.

Clearly the campaign was over Monday night when I climbed into bed at home to watch an 11 P.M.-to-1 A.M. Lindsay telethon in pursuit of voters whose minds by this time were presumably fixed. I had no idea until next morning that the candidate drove out on impulse to Queens at 1 A.M.—five hours before the polls opened—to pay $350 for a half-hour of question-answering over Negro radio station WWRL. Other terminal gestures during the day Tuesday included a five-county Lindsay tour of polling places.

Approaching midnight Tuesday, a hint by a telecaster that Beame, already ahead in early returns, would win drove down my spirits to the point of numbness. Later, when the trend changed, I had no emotional response left. My job was to handle the fourth-floor press office while Harry O'Donnell coped with the horde of reporters, cameramen, staff members, volunteers, campaign contributors, and others who had overwhelmed the grand ballroom downstairs. Occasionally I went down with some journalist or broadcaster who had been denied entrance by the distracted cops despite impeccable credentials.

During one such visit I heard a college cheer from the balcony where Raiders perched precariously above their outflung banner: BREAK A LEG, JOHN. They were cheering me loud enough to be heard over the yammering of a calypso band, so I waved back, wondering what sustained their enthusiasm. During this same visit, a Liberal party official mentioned that Bobby Kennedy conferred with Alex Rose in the Oak Room at the Plaza for a half-hour in the afternoon. Apparently the Senator realized what was happening in the morning when he had to stand in a long line at his east-side polling place. "I don't like the looks of this heavy vote," he muttered. Soon afterward, without awaiting the returns, he called Rose for a meeting to build bridges into the future.

At 1:45 A.M., with most of the districts reported, Lindsay had 46 percent, Beame 41 percent and Buckley 13 percent of the vote. Lindsay's running mates were losing to O'Connor and Procaccino, and Badillo was winning in the Bronx. Unlike LaGuardia, Lindsay would not even have control of the city's major legislative body, the Board of Estimates.

Around 2 A.M. a weeping female campaign worker broke into my office to exhibit a hot-off-the-press *Herald Tribune* with a headline: "Lindsay by a Squeaker." She was weeping in relief. I shooed her away. Beame had not yet conceded but I was already getting out the Lindsay victory statement. To be more precise, I was watching anxiously as my secretary Mable (correct), an invariably good-natured Negro girl who practiced faith-healing on the side, tried to do the stencil. She was so obviously faltering from exhaustion and emotion that *Times* reporter Pat Spiegel finally took her hand, pulled her out of her chair, and finished the stencil himself.

It must have been close to 3 A.M. when the deafening chant of "We Want Lindsay" subsided in the grand ballroom. John and Mary Lindsay and their three daughters were entering in a shower of confetti from shredded newspapers.

Johnny, awakened and dressed after half a night of sleep, rode in on a polceman's back making a V-for-victory sign with his chubby fingers. Price, Costello, Mollen, Connie, Harvey, and all the rest were somewhere in the milling crowd. It took

. . . five hours before the polls opened . . .

"... *We will work together to make our great city once again the empire city of the world.*"

almost ten minutes to quiet everybody down and to remove the photographers from in front of the platform so the mayor-elect could be seen and heard as he said:

"I've always been proud to be a New Yorker, but never as proud as I am tonight. . . . I plan to give New York the most exciting and successful administration this city has ever seen. . . . We will work together to make our great city once again the empire city of the world."

Back upstairs again I could not find energy enough to go home. I dozed at my littered desk until Sid Davidoff came by to offer half of his double bed in the hotel. Since in another three hours we were to start on a five-county Lindsay tour to thank the voters, I accepted the offer with gratitude. In bed I lay on my back looking at the ceiling and listening to the snoring of the Raider General. The past six months had been the most turbulent period in my life but I could now turn to quieter things. For Lindsay an impossible campaign was already merging into an impossible administration which would break him or make him a national leader.

John Lindsay would rule an almost bankrupt metropolis facing almost incurable problems, yet New York was still full of money and of people with great vitality and creative talent. I remembered Harry O'Donnell approaching the winner several hours ago to say: "Congratulations, John. You have only yourself to blame." With the reassuring thought that however difficult the task, this was what Lindsay wanted to do, I fell asleep.

☆☆★ *Index*